Preface

The economy of a country is controlled by several factors, namely, population size, industrial activities, agriculture, policies of the government, culture of the people, educational system, infrastructure facilities, etc. The policies and guidelines of both the central and state governments facilitate the integration, coordination and control of all the activities of the nation with the objective of maximising the growth of the nation. Hence, it is clear that each entity of the nation is forced to have a competitive role to maximise its productivity for its survival. The productivity of different organisations can be improved through several research studies.

As a professional economist, you would be required to carry out the task of analysing many specific economic situations and indicate their impact on economic policy framework. In order to perform these tasks, you need to be equipped with the various constituents of Research Methods and the different techniques applied in data collection/analysis. This book **"Research Methods in Economics (MEC-009)"** aims to cater to this need. The theoretical perspectives that guides research, tools and techniques of data collection and methods of data analysis together constitute the research methodology. The present book deals with all these aspects.

This book is written specially in question & answer format to provide students the instant gratification of a correct answer. In this book, we have tried to solve all possible questions from the exams' point of view. Solutions of previous years questions papers have also been included to help students to understand the unique examination structure. We hope that this book would not only be a favourite study material for the students but also can be a nice resource for teaching.

An attempt has been carefully made to present this book more useful and meet the requirement and challenges of the course prescribed by IGNOU University.

We wish you a successful and rewarding career ahead. Feedback in this regard is solicited.

– GPH Panel of Expert

Acknowledgement

Our compliments go to the **GullyBaba Publishing House (P) Ltd.,** and its meticulous team who have been enthusiastically working towards the perfection of the book.

Their teamwork, initiative and research have been very encouraging. Had it not been for their unflagging support, this work wouldn't have been possible. The creative freedom provided by them along with their aim of presenting the best to the reader has been a major source of inspiration in this work. Hope that this book would be successful.

– GPH Panel of Expert

Publisher's Note

The present book of the MEC series is targeted for examination purpose as well as enrichment. With the advent of technology and the Internet, there has been no dearth of information available to all; however, finding the relevant and qualitative information, which is focused, is an uphill task.

We at **GullyBaba Publishing House (P) Ltd.,** have taken this step to provide quality material which can accentuate in-depth knowledge about the subject. GPH books are a pioneer in the effort of providing unique and quality material to its readers. With our books, you are sure to attain success by making use of this powerful study material. Provided book is just a reference book based on the syllabus of particular University/Board. For a profound information, see the textbooks recommended by the University/Board.

Our site **gullybaba.com** is a vital resource for your examination. The publisher wishes to acknowledge the significant contribution of the Team Members and our experts in bringing out this publication and highly thankful to Almighty God, without His blessings, this endeavor wouldn't have been successful.

– Publisher

Research Methods in Economics

MEC-09

For

Master of Arts [Economics]

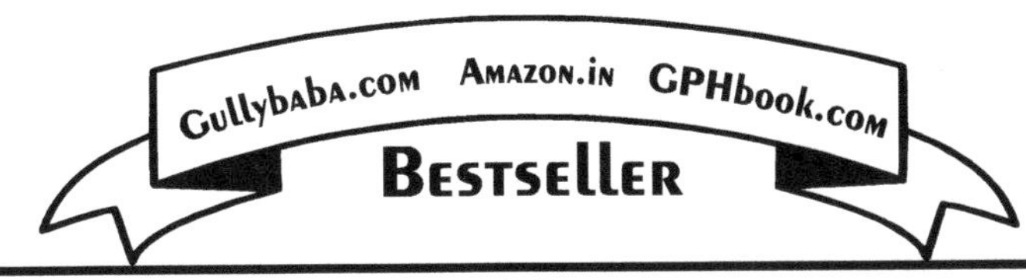

Useful For

IGNOU, KSOU (Karnataka), Bihar University (Muzaffarpur), Nalanda University, Jamia Millia Islamia, Vardhman Mahaveer Open University (Kota), Uttarakhand Open University, Kurukshetra University, Himachal Pradesh University, Seva Sadan's College of Education (Maharashtra), Lalit Narayan Mithila University, Andhra University, Pt. Sunderlal Sharma (Open) University (Bilaspur), Annamalai University, Bangalore University, Bharathiar University, Bharathidasan University, Centre for distance and open learning, Kakatiya University (Andhra Pradesh), KOU (Rajasthan), MPBOU (MP), MDU (Haryana), Punjab University, Tamilnadu Open University, Sri Padmavati Mahila Visvavidyalayam (Andhra Pradesh), Sri Venkateswara University (Andhra Pradesh), UCSDE (Kerala), University of Jammu, YCMOU, Rajasthan University, UPRTOU, Kalyani University, Banaras Hindu University (BHU) and all other Indian Universities.

Closer to Nature  We use Recycled Paper

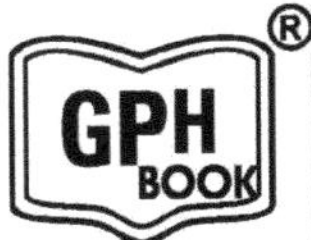

GULLYBABA PUBLISHING HOUSE (P) LTD.

ISO 9001 & ISO 14001 CERTIFIED CO.

Published by:

GullyBaba Publishing House Pvt. Ltd.

Regd. Office:
2525/193, 1st Floor, Onkar Nagar-A,
Tri Nagar, Delhi-110035
(From Kanhaiya Nagar Metro Station Towards Old Bus Stand)
Call: 9991112299, 9312235086
WhatsApp: 9350849407

Branch Office:
1A/2A, 20, Hari Sadan,
Ansari Road, Daryaganj,
New Delhi-110002
Ph.011-45794768
Call & WhatsApp:
8130521616,8130511234

E-mail: hello@gullybaba.com, **Website**:GullyBaba.com

New Edition

ISBN: 978-93-81066-67-6

Author: Gullybaba.com Panel

Topics Covered

Block-6 Data Base of Indian Economy

Contents

Question Papers

Research Methodology: Issues and Perspectives

An Overview

Research methods are core to scientific activity. They constitute an important part of scientific curricula and provide a means through which intellectual development and understanding of phenomena are enhanced. The status as a 'science' is justified by alluding to the technical aspects of research methods, while the very term carries with it ideas of areas study that are accessible only to those who have undergone lengthy training processes in order to understand the inner workings of disciplines.

The aims of science are definition and demonstration, and methods are induction and deduction.

Regarding aims and methodology two views have been dominant, 'Inductivism' by Fransic Bacon and 'Hypothesism" by Rene Decartes. Positivism has been a movement in the philosophy of the first half of the 20th century. Of these two, the developments in the latter one significantly attributed to principal contributors viz. Karl Popper and Kuhn Thomas.

Q1. Why has science occupied a central place in intellectual world?

Or

What is aim of science?

Ans. Science as a collective institution aims to produce more and more accurate natural explanations of how the natural world works, what its components are, and how the world got to be the way it is now. Science has not only shaped our mode of living in the world but also our ways of thinking about the world. It is for this reason it has acquired a central place in the intellectual life of our times. Because of its central place in the modern culture, three disciplines have emerged which have made science itself their object of inquiry. These three disciplines are History of Science, Sociology of Science and Philosophy of Science. Whereas science studies the world natural, social, or psychological, these three disciplines study science itself. History of Science and Sociology of Science are essentially twentieth century disciplines. No doubt, Philosophy of Science has a great past built by the contributions of individual philosophies in different centuries. However, as a widespread and coordinated discipline, it is also an essentially twentieth century phenomenon. Philosophy of Science is a study of Science as a cognitive enterprise, that is, as a knowledge-seeking activity. Though the word "Science" came to be used as late as the beginning of the 19th century, the inquiry, which we call "Science" today, is very old. The aim of science is to arrive at laws i.e. established generalisation.

Q2. What is the distinction between inductivism and hypothesisism?

Or

State the historical background of method of science evolved since 17th century.

Ans. In the whole period of three centuries – from the seventeenth to nineteenth – two views stand out prominently as answers to the question, what is the method of science? The first view is called inductivism according to which the method of science is the method of induction. The second view is called hypothesisism according to which the method of science is called the method of hypothesis.

Inductivism is pioneered by Francis Bacon and hypothesisism by Rene Descartes. The two views sought to provide two models of scientific method. Hence, one can speak of the Baconian model and the Cartesian model of scientific method. Inductivism is rooted in empiricism according to which only those ideas, which are traceable to sense experience, are legitimate. Hypothesisism is grounded in rationalism according to which a significant portion of human knowledge cannot be traced to, and therefore is independent of sense experience.

Inductivism looked upon certainty and breadth as the hallmarks of scientific knowledge. That means science must aim at knowledge, which is definite, on the one hand, and on the other, broad in the sense that it must encompass more and more of the world we seek to know. The search for certain or definite knowledge led inductivists to legislate that science must confine itself to observations since it is only our observations that we can be certain. In other words, science, according to inductivists, must not make any reference to anything unobservable. The means of realising knowledge that is broad Bacon found in the principle of induction, which allows us to go from particular observations to generalisations. Thus, according to inductivists, science must aim at arriving at, with the help of the principle of induction, generalisations, which cryptically contain knowledge of indefinite number of as yet unmade observations. We first collect observational data without recourse to any theory. We then put forward a tentative generalisation, which we verify. Once verified, the tentative generalisation becomes a law enabling us to go from a limited number of already made observations. The aim of science is to arrive at laws, i.e. established inductive generalisations that are only cryptic statements regarding as yet unmade observations. By accumulating such established inductive generalisations, inductivists claimed, we will have at our disposal an enormous amount of observations the totality of which constitutes reality. Science, according to the inductivist theory, thus begins with observations, remains at the level of observations and ends with observations. If according to inductivism, the hallmarks of scientific knowledge are certainty and breadth, according to hypothesisism, they are novelty and depth. That is to say, science must aim at knowledge, which is new in the sense of being trans-observational and deep in the sense of referring to entities underlying the phenomena given to us in observations. In other words, whereas inductivists insist that science must remain from beginning to end at the level of observations, hypothesists maintain that science begins only when it goes beyond observations. According to hypothesisism, genuine science must not remain content with generalisations based on observations but must seek to explain observations in terms of the unobservable or deeper entities and processes.

The term, "hypothesis" in seventeenth century meant a statement regarding unobservable entities and processes though today by hypothesis we only mean a tentative solution to a problem or hunch. Whereas there is no place for hypotheses in the inductive scheme, the hypothesists maintain that the aim of science is to generate hypotheses to explain what we observe. The term, "theory" means a statement of a set of statements involving at least one theoretical term. A theoretical term (for example, "electron", "proton", etc.), unlike an observational term, does not designate observable or measurable. Inductivists are empiricists, and empiricists maintain that anything, which exists, must be observable. Hence, inductivists do not admit that theoretical term designates real entities. They contend that theoretical entities are fictitious entities conjured up by us for the purposes of either economic description of observations or prediction. Hence, according to inductivists, theories are not descriptions of a real world of unobservable. As against this, the hypothesists maintain that the theoretical terms designate real entities not given to us in observations and theories, are descriptions of a real world of unobservable entities. Therefore, while hypothesists are called realists, inductivists are called anti-realists.

Inductivism and hypothesisism were thus rival methodologies advocating antagonistic views regarding the method of science. The two methodologies competed with each other for acceptance. Both had strong followers among scientists and philosophers. Hypothesisism had an upper hand in the beginning. It had among its champions not only Descartes, but also Boyle, Hooke, Huygens and other eminent scientists. But inductivism emerged as the dominant theory of scientific method in the early eighteenth century. The setback suffered by hypothesisism and the consequent domination of the scene by inductivism are to be traded to the fact that the method of induction had had its adherent Issac Newton whose eminence as a scientist lent inductivism a remarkable scientific respectability.

However, inductivism very soon began to face serious challenges. As early, as 1740s and 1750s, there began to dawn the realisation that many areas of scientific inquiry could not be forced into the inductivist framework. Franklin's Fluid Theory of Electricity, the Vibratory Theory of Heat, the Buffonian Theory of Organic Molecules and Phlogiston Chemistry, etc. that developed in the middle of the nineteenth century went against the spirit of the inductivist cult of observations as they involved reference to entities and processes. The scientific grounds against the inductivist position were cleared with the appearance of chemical and gravitational theories of George Le Sage, the Neurophysiological theories of David Hartley and the General Matter Theory of Roger Boscovich. These scientists accurately realized that their theories would face stiff opposition not so much on scientific considerations but due to the methodological implications considered absolutely undesirable by the prevailing methodological orthodoxy, namely, inductivism. Hence, they felt the need for methodological legitimisation in terms of an alternative model. It is this need, which motivated them to resurrect the method of hypothesis.

Apart from the above mentioned challenge from the protagonists of the method of hypothesis, the method of induction faced an internal crisis. David Hume, an eminent eighteenth century inductivist, undermined it from within. He showed that the very principle of induction, which allowed us to proceed from observed to as yet unobserved phenomena itself stood unjustified. Any attempt to justify the principle of induction, Hume conclusively shows, results in circularity or infinite regress. Hume was himself an inductivist. He did not accept the method of hypothesis because of his commitment to empiricism. He concludes that since we have no alternative to the principle of induction, our belief is irrational; we have to boldly accept that the whole of our knowledge including science, the paragon of knowledge, rests on an irrational belief, an animal faith.

After Hume, every inductivist attempted to show that Hume was wrong in his contention that the principle of induction could not be justified. The most significant attempt in this connection was made by John Stuart Mill who realised that the main plant of the attack on induction was its inability to lend the claims based on it the degree of certainty comparable to deductive inferences. For example, in a deductive inference such as „All men are mortal, X is a man with certainty. That is to say, given the truth of the premises, the truth of the conclusion necessarily follows. But, in an inductive inference where the premises are about particular observations and the conclusion is a generalisation, the generalisation does not necessarily follow. That is to say, given the truth of the statements about certain particular observations, the truth of the generalisation is not guaranteed. The generalisation is at best a probable one. That is why logicians like Aristotle could develop a system of rules for deductive inferences. By knowing those rules, we could find which of our conclusions necessarily follow and which do not. Mill took the cudgels in favour of the method of induction, which he attempted to demonstrate to be on equal footing with the rules of deduction, whose capacity to lend certainty to the claims based on them was unproblematic. In other words, he set out to construct an inductive logic, which was supposed to be almost on par with deductive logic.

Every inductivist after Hume tried to ward off the ghost of Hume by solving the problem of Induction, i.e. by showing that our belief in the principle of Inductivist was a rationale one. However, no one succeeded. The problem has remained in the words of C.D. Broad "a skeleton in the cupboard of philosophy".

Q3. 'Experience is the source of knowledge' – in the light of this statement, critically examine the central tenets of Positivist Philosophy. [Dec-2011, Q.No-1]

Ans. The twentieth century begins with the emergence of a school of thought called positivism. Positivism is an extremely well-known and till recently very influential theory of science and its method. The acknowledged founder of positivism or "the positive philosophy" was the French philosopher and social scientist Auguste Comte (1798-1857). Comte also invented the term "sociology" to describe his proposed positive science of society. Positivism is, above all, a philosophy of science. As such, it stands squarely within the empiricist tradition.

Positivists maintained that Metaphysics was a spurious discipline because metaphysical statements are meaningless since they are not verifiable in experience. "A statement" they claimed "is meaningful if and only if it is verifiable". Apart from being anti-metaphysical, they were empiricist, i.e. according to them, experience is the source of knowledge. They called themselves "Neo-Empiricist" to distinguish themselves from the Traditional Empiricists of 17th and 18th centuries like Locke, Berkeley and Hume.

The methods of science can give us knowledge of the laws of coexistence and succession of phenomena, but can never penetrate to the inner essences or natures of things. It is a closely-knit set of tenets formulated with an admirable amount of clarity and consistency. Some of these tenets are:

- Science is qualitatively distinct from, superior to and ideal for all other areas of human endeavor (Scientism).
- Science is distinct from other areas of human creativity because it possesses a method which is unique to it (methodological).
- There is only one method common to all sciences irrespective of their subject matter (methodological monism).
- The method of science is the method of induction (inductivism).
- The hallmark of science consists in the fact that its statements are systematically verifiable.
- Scientific observations are or can be shown to be "pure" in the sense that they are theory-independent.
- Theories are winnowed from facts or observations such that a theory is nothing more than a condensed version of and

therefore reducible to a set of statements describing observations.

- The relation between theory and observation is unilateral in the sense that theories are dependent on observations whereas observations are theory-independent.
- To a given set of observation-statements, there corresponds uniquely a theory such that we can deduce the latter from the former.
- Our factual judgments are value-neutral and our value judgments have no factual content (fact-value) dichotomy). Science, being the paradigmatic instance of actual inquiry, does not have any value commitments.
- All scientific explanation must have the following pattern.

  L_1....................L_n

  I_1....................I_n

  Therefore, E.

  Where L_1....................L_n is a set of laws, I_2....................I_n is a set of statements describing initial conditions and E is the statement describing phenomenon to be explained. That is to say, to explain a phenomenon scientifically is to deduce its description from a set of laws (which are called "Covering Laws") via a set of statements describing initial conditions. In sum, all explanation worthy to be called 'scientific' must contain laws and involve deduction (Hence, this is called Deductive-Nomologism where 'nomological' means 'concerning laws').
- The aim of science is either economical description of phenomena or precise prediction of facts and not providing an account of observations in terms of unobservables. Hence, scientific theories are not putative descriptions of the unobservable world. The aim of science has nothing to do with alleged reality of such a world (Anti-Realism).
- Unlike other areas of activity, science is progressive in the sense that scientific change is always change for better, whereas other areas exhibit just change: the progress of science consists in the accumulation of observations, on the one hand, and, cumulative growth of theories, on the other hand. The latter means that any new theory includes the old theory (plus something). Thus, the growth of science essentially exhibits continuity.

- Science is objective in the sense that its theories are based on 'pure' observations or facts, which are theory free. Interpretations may be subjective but observations/facts are objective because they are free from interpretation/theory.
- Science is rational because the principle of Induction, which is central to the method of science is Rationally defensible, inspite of Hume's skepticism regarding its defensibility.

Positivists tried to justify the Principle of Induction by invoking the concept of pure observation. According to them, theories are arrived at on the basis of the Principle of Induction.

Q4. Give counter arguments against the positivist thesis of pure observation.

Ans. The various arguments against the positivist thesis of pure observation are as follows:

First, observations presuppose some principle of selection. We cannot go on observing anything we come across. We need "relevant" observations. In science, it is the problem that decides what is relevant and thus provides the principle of selection. Hence, there cannot be observations without a prior problem. To quote Karl Popper, "Before we can collect data, our interest in data of a certain kind must be aroused; the problem always comes first". It may be objected that the problem itself is due to the observations we make, and hence, observations come first. But this objection does not hold. Two persons might make similar observations though only one might come out with a problem. This shows that mere observations will not generate a problem. How, then, are scientific problems generated? It is usually when there is a clash between what we observe and what we expect. Of the two persons making similar observations one may come out with a problem whereas the other may not because the former has expectations which conflict with the observations s/he makes, whereas the latter does not have any expectations. The expectations are generated due to our belief in a theory. Thus, problem generation presupposes a prior theoretical commitment. In other words, a prior belief in a theory is necessary for a problem to be generated and a prior awareness of the problem is necessary for making relevant observations.

Secondly, in science, observations are taken into account only if they are desirable in a language that is currently used in a particular science. An observation, which howsoever genuine, cannot be expressed in the recognised idiom for all scientific purposes is no observation at all. It is the theory, which provides the language or the idiom to be used in describing observations. It is tempting to quote in this connection words of the physicist and philosopher Pierre Duhem:

"Enter a laboratory: approach the table crowded with an assortment of apparatus, an electric cell, silk-covered copper wire, small cups of Mercury, spools, a mirror mounted on an iron bar; the experimentor is inserting into small openings, the metal ends of ebony-headed pins; the iron bar oscillates, and the mirror attached to it throws a luminous band upon a celluloid scale; the forward-backward motion of this spot enables the physicist to observe the minute oscillations of the iron bar. But ask him what he is doing. Will he answer "I am studying the oscillations of an iron bar which carries a mirror?" No, he will say that he is measuring the electrical resistance of the spools. If you are astonished, if you ask him what his words mean, what relation they have with the phenomenon he has been observing and which you have noted at the same time as he will answer that your question requires a long explanation and that you should take a course in electricity."

Thirdly, most of the observations in science made with the help of instruments are constructed or designed in accordance with the specifications provided by some theories. These theories, one may say, constitute the software of these instruments. Belief in the reliability of these instruments implies the acceptance of these theories, which have gone into the making of these instruments. Thus, observations presuppose prior theoretical commitments.

Fourthly, observations in science need to be legitimised or ratified by a theory. We all know that Galileo used some telescopic observations to support his theory. His opponents did not consider telescopic observations accurate. It is not that they did not believe in the reliability of telescope. They had no problem in using telescope for terrestrial (of the earth) purposes. They opposed its extension to celestial (of heavenly) sphere where things like background, neighbourhood, possibility of verification which are usually found in normal instances of perception are absent. They rightly demanded from Galileo a theory of optics, which would justify the extension of the use of telescope from terrestrial to celestial sphere. Galileo had no such theory. But he rightly believed that in future such a theory could be formulated.

Thus, Galileo believed that it was possible to justify the type of observations on which he was dependent. This instance brings out how observations need ratification or justification in terms of either an actual or possible theory. In this sense too, our observations are theory-laden. All this does not imply that observations are theory-dependent whereas theories are observation-independent. Theories and observations depend on each other. All this only implies that positivists were wrong in claiming that observations are theory-independent. Thus, no observation is pre-suppositionless as positivists thought. An observation is not a passive reception constitution the beginning of knowledge, but involves the active participation of our cognitive faculties characterised by purposiveness, prior knowledge and expectations. After all, observations are not "given" but are "made".

Q5. On what basis according to proper, a line can be demarked between science and rest of knowledge.

Ans. According to Popper, the central task of philosophy is not to solve Hume's problem or problem of Induction as thought by Positivists. This is because (1) the problem of Induction cannot be solved, and (2) it need not be solved because the method of science is not the method of Induction. The central task of philosophy of science, Popper maintains, is to solve what he calls the problem of demarcation or Kant's problem, i.e. the problem of identifying the line of demarcation between science and non-science. Popper maintains that **what distinguishes science from the rest of our knowledge is the systematic falsifiability of scientific theories.** Thus, falsifiability is the line of demarcation between science and non-science. Falsifiability is the criterion of scientificity. A statement is scientific if and only it is falsifiable.

Scientific theories are falsifiable in the sense that they transparently state under what conditions they would be rejected as false. Whenever scientific theories are advanced. It is also apparent under what conditions they turn out to be false so that we try to bring about those conditions in order to reduce the possibility of the theory being falsified. In other words, a model scientific theory or statement should readily yield testable implications and thus lend itself to falsification. It should not seek to survive by not yielding testable implication, i.e. not stating under what conditions it becomes false. It is in this connection, Popper attacks Marxism as a pseudo-scientific theory. When Marx propounded his theory of the dynamics of the Capitalist society, his theory was scientific because it was falsifiable since it yielded testable implications such as disappearance of middle classes, revolution in industrially advanced societies, reduction in the value of the wages, etc. However, the test implications were not borne out, i.e., the predictions failed. Hence, the theory, which was scientific, proved to be a false theory. But the followers of Marx tried to explain away the failure of Marx's predictions by taking recourse to adhoc explanations and thus insisted that there was nothing wrong with the theory. In the process they went on building safety valves for the theory with the result the theory became unfalsifiable. A religious theory about the world is, of course, also unfalsifiable. But the prepounders of religious theories about the world never claim scientificity for their views whereas Marxist do so very vehemently. Hence, Marxist theory is not unfalsifiable and therefore non-scientific, but also pseudo-scientific. It is this pretension to be scientific while being unfalsifiable that makes the theory pseudo-scientific.

Q6. Identify the main difference between Inductive Model and Hypothetico-Deduction Model.

Or

Explain how Hypothetico-Deductive Model of scientific method is superior to Inductivist Model.

Or

Discuss the fundamental differences between Popper's and positivists' views about the theory of scientific method.

Ans. Popper puts forward what he considers to be an adequate model of scientific method characterises his model of scientific method as Hypothetico-Deductive model positivists tried to work out a sophisticated version of inductivism. According to Popper, the method of science is not method of induction but the method of Hypothetico-Deduction. The differences between these two models are as follows:

The inductivist model maintains that our observations are theory-independent and therefore are indubitable. That is to say, since observations are theory-independent, they have probability value 1. It also says that our theories are only winnowed from observations and therefore our scientific theories have the initial probability value 1 in principle. Of course, inductivists admitted that in actual practice, the theories may contain something more than what observation based statements say, with the result that our actual theories may not have been winnowed from observation.

Hence, the need for verification arises popper rejects the inductivist view that our observations are theory-free and hence rejects the idea that our observation statements have probability equal to 1.

We can bring out the fundamental difference between verificationism (inductivism) and falsificationism (Hypothetico-Deductivism) by drawing on the analogy between two systems of criminal law. According to one system, the judge has to start with the assumption that the accused is innocent and consequently unless one finds evidence against him, he should be declared innocent. According to the other, the judge has to start with the assumption that the accused is a culprit and consequently, unless evidence goes in his favour, he should be declared to be a culprit. Obviously, the latter system of criminal law is harsher than the former. The inductivist scheme is analogous to the former kind of criminal law, where as the Hypothetico-Deductive scheme is akin to the latter one.

Popper claims that the Hypothetico-Deductive model of scientific method is superior to inductivist model for the following reasons:

Firstly, it does justice to the critical spirit of science by maintaining that the aim of scientific testing is to falsify our theories and by maintaining that our scientific theories are, however corroborated, going to permanently remain tentative. In other words, the hypothetico-Deductivist view presents scientific theories as permanently vulnerable with the sword of possible falsification always hanging on their head. The inductivist view of scientific method makes science a safe and defensive activity by portraying scientific testing as a search for confirming instances and by characterising scientific theories as established truths. According to Popper, the special status accorded to science is due to the fact that science embodies an attitude which is essentially open-minded and anti-dogmatic. Hypothetico-Deductivism is an adequate model of scientific practice because it gives central place to such an attitude.

Secondly, Popper thinks that if science had followed the inductivist path; it would not have made the progress it has. Suppose a scientist has arrived at a generalisation. If he follows the inductivist message, he will go in search of instances, which establish it as a truth. If he finds an instance, which conflicts, with his generalisation, what he does is to qualify his generalisation saying that the generalisation is true except in the cases where it has to be held unsupported. Such qualifications impose heavy restrictions on the scope of the generalisation. This results in scientific theories becoming extremely narrow in their range of applicability. But if a scientist follows the Hypothetico-Deductivist view, he will throw away his theory once he comes across a negative instance instead of pruning it and fritting it with the known positive facts. Instead of being satisfied with a theory, tailored to suit the supporting observations, he will look for an alternative, which will encompass not only the observations, which supported the old theory but also the observations, which went against the old theory and more importantly which will yield fresh test implications. The theoretical progress science has made can be explained only by the fact that science seeks to come out with bolder and bolder explanations rather than taking recourse to the defensive method of reducing the scope of the theories to make them consistent with fact. Hence, Popper claims that the

Hypothetico-Deductive model gives an adequate account of scientific progress. According to him, if one accepts the inductivists account of science one fails to give any explanation of scientific progress.

Thirdly, the **Hypothetico-Deductive** view according to Popper avoids the predicament encountered by inductivist theory in the face of **Hume's** challenge. Hume conclusively showed that the principal of induction could not be justified on logical grounds. If Hume is right, than science is based upon an irrational faith. According to Hypothetico-Deductivist view, science does not use the principle of induction at all. Hence, even though Hume is right, it does not matter since follows the Hypothetico-Deductivist lines of procedure. Also, Popper seeks to establish that inductivism and Hypothetico-Deductivism are so radically different that the latter in no way face any threat akin to the one faced by the former. In this connection, he draws our attention to the logical asymmetry between verification, the central component of the inductivist scheme, and falsification, the central component of the Hypothetico-Deductivist scheme. They are logically asymmetrical in the sense that one negative instance is sufficient for conclusively falsifying a theory, whereas no amount of positive instances are sufficient to conclusively verify a theory. It may be recalled that Hume was able to come out with the problem of induction precisely because a generalisation (all theories according to Inductivism are generalisations) cannot be conclusively verified.

Q7. Explain why Popper drops the concept of truth and replaces it by the concept of verisimilitude.

Or

How does Popper characterises scientific progress?

Ans. According to Popper, one finds in the history of science invariable transitions from theories to better theories. Further, he said that no scientific theory however corroborated can be said to be 'true'. Hence, Popper drops the very concept of truth and replaces it by the concept of **Verisimilitude** (truth-likeness or truth-nearness) in his characterisation of the goal of science. In other words, though science cannot attain truth, i.e. though our theories can never be said to be true, science can set for itself the goal of achieving higher and higher degrees of Verisimilitude, i.e. successive scientific theories can progressively approximate to truth. So, in science we go from theory to better theory and the criterion for betterness is Verisimilitude.

The criterion of the Verisimilitude of a theory is nothing but truth content minus the falsity content of a theory. In the actual history of science, we always find, according to Popper, theories being replaced by better theories, that is, theories with higher degree of Verisimilitude. In other words, of the two successive theories, at any time in the History of Science, we find the successor theory possessing greater Verisimilitude and is therefore better than its predecessor. In fact, according to him, a theory is rejected as false only if we have an alternative, which is better than the one at hand in the sense that it has more testable implications and a greater number of its testable implications are already borne out. The growth of science is convergent in the sense that the successful part of the old theory is retained in the successor theory with the result the old theory becomes a limiting case of the new one. The growth of science thus shows continuity. In other words, it is the convergence of the old theory into the new one that provides continuity in the growth of science. It must also be noted in this connection that unlike the Inductivists or Positivists, Popper is a Realist in the sense, according to him, scientific theories are about an unobservable world. This means that the real world of the unobservable thought can never be captured entirely by our theories. Popper contends that, with greater and greater the Verisimilitude attained by our theories, evidence that though the gap between Truth and our theories can never be completely filled, it can be progressively reduced. Consequently, the real world of unobservable will be more and more like what our theories say though not completely so.

Q8. List the main theses of Popper's philosophy of science.

Ans. We arranged the list of main theses of Popper's philosophy of science with the list of theses of positivist philosophy of science as follows:

- Science is qualitatively distinct from, superior to and ideal for all other areas of human endeavour (scientism).
- The distinction, superiority and idealhood that science that science enjoys is traceable to its possession of a method (Methodologism).
- There is only one method common to all science irrespective of their subject matter (Methodological Monism).
- That method which is common to all science, natural and human, is the method of Hypothetic-Deduction (Hypothetico-Deductivism).
- The hallmark of science (i.e. the distinguishing mark of science) consists in the fact that its statements are systematically falsifiable (falsifiability).

- Scientific observations are not and cannot be shown to be pure; that is, they are theory-dependent.
- Theories are not winnowed from observations or facts; they are pure inventions of human mind, i.e. only conjectures and not generalisations based on 'pure observations'.
- The relation between observation and theory is one of interdependence.
- To a given set of observation-statements there might correspond more than one theory.
- Our factual judgements may have value commitments and our value judgements may have cognitive content (hence, fact-value dichotomy is unacceptable); science is not value neutral but the value commitments can be critically discussed and therefore they are not subjective.
- All scientific explanation must have deductive-nomological pattern and thus the thesis of Deductive-Nomologism is acceptable.
- The aim of science is to provide an account of observable world in terms of unobservable entities and to provide accounts of those unobservable entities in terms of further unobservable entities. Unobservable entities are, therefore, real and our theories are putative descriptions of such real entities ('Realism').
- Unlike positivists, Popper rejects the idea the progress of science is characterised by cumulative growth of theories. Unlike positivists, Popper rejects the idea that progress of science is characterised by cumulative growth of theories. According to him, a new theory is entirely new and not an old theory plus an epselon as Positivists thought. Thus, in Popper's scheme, the growth of science is essentially discontinuous. Of course, Popper makes some room for continuity also when he says that old theory (atleast true part of it) is a limiting case of the new theory.
- Science in not objective in the sense scientific theories are based on pure observations as positivists thought because there are no pure observations. Science is objective in the theories are inter-subjectively testable.
- Lastly, science is not rational in the sense the principle of Induction can be rationally justified as Positivists thought. The

principle of Induction cannot be rationally justified: nor is it used by science. Science is rational in the sense it embodies critical thinking. Apart from insisting that our theories be falsifiable, science has institutional mechanisms for practicing and promoting critical thinking.

Positivists and Popper differ from each other. The theses (1), (2), (3) and (11) are common to both Positivists and Popperians. Popper rejects most of other theses of Positivists, especially their central thesis, which concerns the idea of pure observation. Finally, he agrees with the Positivists that science is uniquely progressive, objective and rational; but his nations of progressiveness. Objectivity and rationality of science are entirely different from those of Positivists.

Q9. Which two stages come in the life of every major science?

Ans. According to Kuhn (who's work The Structure of Scientific Revolutions is a milestone in the history of the 20th century of the philosophy of science), in the life of every major science there are two stages (1) Pre-paradigmatic stage, and (2) paradigmatic stage.

In the pre-paradigmatic stage, one finds more than one mode of practicing that science. That is, there was a time in the history of Astronomy when different schools of Astronomy practiced Astronomy differently. So is the case with Physics, Chemistry and Biology. In that stage their situation was similar to that which obtains today in areas like art, philosophy and even medicine wherein divergent modes of practicing these disciplines co-exist. Today, we speak of schools of Art (e.g. painting), schools of Philosophy and systems/schools of medicine. But today we do not speak of Schools of Astronomy or Physics or Chemistry or Biology.

This is, according to Kuhn, in areas like art, philosophy and medicine that did not, and cannot make a transition from pre-paradigmatic stage to paradigmatic stage, which marks the disappearance of plurality, that is, disappearance of schools. In other words, the transition means replacement of plurality by monolith.

Such a transition is made possible, Kuhn claims, by acquisition of a **paradigm.** When a science makes such a transition, we may say, it has become 'mature' or 'science' in the proper sense of the term. Astronomy was the first to make such a transition followed by Physics, Chemistry and Biology in that order. Social Sciences are still, according to him, in the pre-paradigmatic stage, though Economics is showing signs of such a transition. This is evident from the fact that in Social Sciences there is no consensus on fundamentals as we can see prevalence of distinct schools in every Social Science.

Q10. What do you understand by the term 'scientific revolution'? Explain the radical implications of Kuhn's position in this regard.

[June-2011, Q.No.-1]

Ans. Scientific practice is not exhausted in terms of day-to-day research or 'normal science'. When a paradigm fails to promote fruitful, interesting and smooth normal science, it is considered to be in a crisis. The deepening of the crisis leads to the replacement of the existing paradigm by a new one. This process of replacement is called **'scientific revolution'.** Therefore, scientific revolutions are "the tradition-shattering complements to the tradition bound activity of normal science." Thus, once a science enters the paradigmatic stage, it is characterised by (1) normal science, and (2) revolutions. In sheer temporal terms, normal science occupies much larger span than revolutionary science. That is to say, science is revolutionary once a while and mostly it is non-revolutionary or normal. Also the scientific activity engaged in by most of the practitioners can be characterised aptly in terms of normal science. On account of this temporal and numerical magnitude we can say that much of the scientific activity as we ordinarily encounter is normal though this normal course is occasionally interrupted by revolutions which change the form, content and direction of the process of the scientific activity. Which is basically normal by which we mean a non-revolutionary committed and tradition bound activity. Normal science demands a thorough going convergent thinking and hence is preceded by an education that involves 'a dogmatic initiation in a pre-established tradition that the student is not equipped to evaluate'. "Normal science is an activity that purports not to question the existing paradigm but to (1) "Increase the precision of the existing theory by attempting to adjust the existing theory or existing observation in order to bring the two into closer and closer agreement.", and (2) "to extend the existing theory to areas that it is expected to cover but in which it has never before been tried." In other words, normal science consists of solving puzzles that are encountered in forcing nature into the conceptual boxes supplied by the reigning paradigm.

It is in this way Kuhn attempts to account for the smooth, defined and directional character of day-to-day scientific research in terms of the features of what he calls "Normal Science". Normal science has no room for any radical thinking. It is limited to the enterprise of solving certain puzzles in accordance with the rules specified by the paradigm. These rules are never questioned but only accepted and followed. The aim of scientific education is to ensure that the paradigm is internalised by a student. In other words, the professional training in science consists in accepting the paradigm as given and equipping oneself to promote the cause of the paradigm by giving a greater precision and further elaboration. The day-to-day scientific research does not aim at anything fundamentally new but only at the application of what has already been given, namely the theoretical ideas and the practical guidelines for solving certain puzzles. It is in this sense that normal science is a highly tradition-bound activity.

Q11. How does Kuhn explain the growth of knowledge?

Ans. Perris makes reference to the philosopher Thomas Kuhn and his description of scientific knowledge growth. Kuhn (1970) says that knowledge grows by adding more and facts to a constantly growing body of knowledge. However, this cumulative and incremental change is not the only way for knowledge to grow: scientific revolutions must also be taken into account, which means that the existing paradigm is replaced. Such a paradigm shift takes place when the previous paradigm does not exist anymore. Existing theories are replaced by new theories, and the corresponding methods, facts, and criteria of accepted knowledge are changed. Perris says that the developed of our own collected knowledge is similar to the process of knowledge growth as Kuhn describes it; how we perceive ourselves in relation to the world we are living in, how we think and feel in different situations, how we receive and solve problems, or the growth of our structures of meaning. Our fundamental structures of meaning (i.e. paradigms) decide both how we define our world and our specific way to act upon in different situations. Nevertheless, there are periods when the cumulative knowledge growth is not working anymore and a change in the paradigm must take place. Boland and Tenkasi (1995) say that Kuhn's insights are particularly relevant for understanding how knowledge is produced in a community of knowing (such as a team of co-workers or a project team) by refining and clarifying the perspective within it.

"Development of knowledge in a community is a process of posing and solving puzzles, thereby elaborating and refining the vocabulary, instruments and theories that embody the perspective. Agreements that knowledge is progressing are agreement that the perspective is strengthening. Unexpected events or findings can only be recognised as such from within a perspective."

Q12. What is the relation between old paradigm and new paradigm?

Ans. According to Kuhn, in no obvious sense one can say that the new paradigm is better or truer than the old one. Kuhn's maintains that the two successful paradigms cut the world differently. They speak different languages. In fact, when a paradigm changes, to put it metaphorically, the world changes. With his characteristic lucidity he says, the transition from a paradigm in crisis to new one from which a new tradition of normal science can emerge is far from accumulative process, one that is achieved by an articulation or extension of the old paradigm. Rather, it is a reconstruction of the field from new fundamentals, a reconstruction that changes some of the field's most elementary theoretical generalisations as well as many of its... methods and applications." This apart Kuhn contends that the two paradigms talk different languages. Even if the same terms are used in two paradigms, the terms have different meanings. What can be said in the language of one paradigm cannot be translated into the other language. Based on these reasons, Kuhn claims that relation between two successive paradigms is incommensurable. No wonder Kuhn compares paradigm shift to gestalt shift. With this, the idea of scientific progress as a continuous process and the idea of truth as the absolute standard stand totally repudiated. Kuhn advances what might appear to be an undiluted relativism according to which truth is intra-paradigmatic and not inter-paradigmatic. That is to say, what is true is relative to a paradigm and there is no truth lying outside all paradigms.

Q13. How did Popper differ with Kuhn about essence of science?

Ans. Some of the radical implications of Kuhn's position can be brought about by juxtaposing his views with those of Popper.

Firstly, the hallmark of science according to Popper is **critical thinking.** In fact science exemplifies critical thinking at its best. Since critical thinking considers nothing to be settled and lying beyond all doubt, fundamental disagreements and divergent thinking must and in fact do characterise science, according to Kuhn, what constitutes the essence of scientific practice is normal science. Thus if Popper sees the essence of science in divergent thinking and fundamental disagreements, Kuhn sees the essence of science in convergent thinking and consensus. In other words, the hallmark of science to Kuhn is tradition-bound thinking. In fact, according to Kuhn, what distinguishes science from other areas of creative thinking is that whereas in science one finds institutional mechanisms of enforcing consensus, the other areas suffer from perpetual disagreements even on fundamentals.

Secondly, if **Popper** considers the individual to be the focus of scientific activity, Kuhn bestows that status upon the scientific community. Both positivists and Popper looked upon science as the sum total of the work of individual scientists working in accordance with a method though the Positivists and Popper fundamentally differed on the characterisation of that method. As opposed to this individualistic account of scientific enterprise, Kuhn propounds a collectivistic view of scientific activity. In Kuhn's scheme, it is the scientific community, which constitutes the pillar of stability and locomotive of change.

Thirdly, Popper and Kuhn differ fundamentally in their attitude towards the transition from one theory to another theory of science. According to Popper, we can explain every case of change of theoretical framework in terms of certain norm which science always adopts and follows meticulously. In fact, scientific rationality consists in following these norms; But Kuhn contends that an adequate explanation of change of theoretical framework must be in terms of the value judgments made by a community while making the choice. According to Kuhn, recourse to the so-called methodological norms explains nothing.

Q14. Write short note on the following:

(a) Paradigm

Ans. We all know that Ptolemy's *Almagest* Newton's *Principia* and Darwin's *Origin* of the *Species* are path-breaking works in the areas of Astronomy, Physics and Biology respectively. According to Kuhn, these works provided paradigms for these disciplines. They did so by specifying the exact manner in which these disciplines ought to proceed. They laid ground rules regarding what problems these disciplines must tackle and how to tackle them. Hence, paradigms are universally recognised achievements that for a time provide model problems and solutions to community of practitioners.

Hence, in the **first** place, a paradigm specifies what the ultimate constituents of that sphere of reality, which a particular science is inquiring into, are.

Secondly, it identifies the model problems.

Thirdly, it specifies the possible range of solutions.

Fourthly, it provides the necessary strategies and techniques for solving the problems. Lastly, it provides examples, which show how to solve certain problems. In other words, a paradigm is a disciplinary matrix of a professional group. Once a science possesses a paradigm, it develops what Kuhn calls, a 'normal science tradition'. Normal science is the day-to-day research activity purporting to force of nature into conceptual boxes provided by the paradigm. The practitioners of normal science, that is, a scientist who engages in day-to-day research, internalises the paradigm by professional education.

(b) Critics against Popper Philosophy

Ans. A serious lacuna in Popper's position concerns his idea of scientific progress.

First, according to Popper, the growth of science is essentially discontinuous in the sense that a new theory, which displaces an old theory, is not the old theory plus an epsilon because it is entirely new. Yet, he seeks to make room for continuity in the growth of science by insisting that the old theory is a limiting case of the new theory. In this connection, he cites an examples of Newtonian mechanics and Relativistic mechanics. The former is the limiting case of the latter in the sense that in a certain domain both give the same results. Thus, the former is contained in the latter. Hence, there is some continuity in the growth of science. But Popper overlooks the fact that examples of an old theory being a limiting case of the new one are rare. For example, it is absurd to say that Phlogiston theory is a limiting case of oxygen theory or that Ptolemy's theory is a limiting case of Copernican theory.

Secondly, Popper says that successive theories in any domain exhibit increasing verisimilitude, i.e. truth nearness. That is, reality constituted by unobservable entities is more like what a new theory says than what its immediate predecessor says. This means that following Popper we have to say that the ultimate constituents of matter are more like fields as the present physical theory says than like particles (atoms) as claimed by Newtonian theory. This is unintelligible. What does it mean to say that the ultimate constituents of matter are more like fields than particles called atoms? Either they are like fields of like particles.

Thirdly, when Popper says a new theory is better than the old one (in the sense, it is more true), he assumes that the two theories can be compared. This means that they have something common, which makes them comparable. But this has been ably questioned by Thomas Kuhn who sought to show that when one fundamental theory replaces another, the two theories are so radically different as to make any talk of comparison between them highly questionable.

(c) Scientific method

Ans. The scientific method is the accurate observation of facts and the determination of order among the facts. The scientific method usually has at least five steps:

- Stating the problem

- Forming the hypothesis
- Observing the experiments
- Interpreting the data
- Drawing the [tentative] conclusion

Q15. Discuss the unified rule of positivism provided by Kolakowski.

Or

What are the main characteristics of positivist?

Ans. The main characteristics (unified view) of positivism lie in a set of its four rules – phenomenalism, nouminalism, the rule of value free statements and the rule of unity of science.

Kolakowski provides such a unified view by simplifying Positivism into these set of rules:

K_1 The Rule of Phenomenalism

The Rule emphasises phenomena as the basis of knowledge. Sensory experience is the basis. The basis of knowledge is only the record of that which is actually manifested in experience. It is phenomenon not noumina. It is existence, not essence. Simply, it is facts and objective facts only that from the basis of knowledge.

K_2 The Rule of Nouminalism

Nouminalism refers to Insight representative of facts. Any insight formulated in general terms cannot have any real reference other than individual facts. Therefore, every abstract science is abridging the recording of experience and gives no extra independent knowledge.

K_3 The Rule of Value-free Statements

Knowledge is value-free. The rule refutes to call value judgments and normative statements as knowledge. There is no room for good or bad or ethical judgments in statement of science or knowledge.

K_4 The Rule of Unity of Science

There is only one method of scientific knowledge. The unity of science refers to a single fundamental form from which all other laws are ultimately derived.

Q16. Explain and state the rules of logic.

Ans. Rules of logic have become important part of the whole structure of scientific explanation under positivism.

'Categorical Syllogism'

A categorical syllogism is an argument consisting of two premises and a conclusion such that the conclusion is not entailed by either premise alone (by an immediate inference, for example).

Two categorical statements if logically formulated, taken together would lead to a conclusion. The two statements should serve as the premises. If there is no premises, then there will be a fallacy or enthymeme.

For example, the following two examples stand for categorical syllogism:

(I) All As are B	}	→	Major Premis
	} Premises		
C is an A	}	→	Minor Premis
Therefore, C is B		→	Conclusion
All Politicians are corrupt	}	→	Major Premis
	} Premises		
Blogg is politician	}	→	Minor Premis
Therefore, Blogg is corrupt		→	Conclusion

The following is an example of a fallacy of enthymeme because it leaves out the premises:

Blogg is a politician.

Therefore, he is corrupt.

Hypothetical Syllogism

Hypothetical Syllogism is referred to as **Modes Poneus,** affirming the antecedent.

The major premise has if ..... then form.

The following are two examples:

If A is true, (Antecedent)	**then B is true** (Consequent)	Therefore, B is true.
If Blogg is a politician, (Antecedent)	**then he is corrupt** (Consequent)	Therefore, Blogg is corrupt.

Hypothesis statements may have a major Hypothesis (H) and auxiliary $(A_1A_2....A_n)$ hypotheses.

'Logical Truth' and 'Material Truth' Type

All statements, which are logically true, are not necessarily "materially true". For example:

All politicians have two tongues.

Blogg is a politicians.

Therefore, Blogg has two tongues.

The above statement is "logically true" but "materially" not true.

Deductive Fallacies

Deductive fallacies are those where premises do not lead necessarily to the stated conclusions. There are three main types of deductive fallacies:

(1) Logical (formal) Fallacies (Fallacies of affirming the consequent)

Correct Reasoning or 'Modus Poneus'	**'Logical (Formal) Fallacy**
(Affirming the antecedent)	(Affirming the consequent)
If A is true, then B is true.	If A is true, B is true.
A is true.	B is true.
Therefore, B is true.	Therefore, A is true.

(2) Verbal Fallacies (Fallacy of Composition)

The verbal fallacy involves a statement where something, which is true of the part, is also made true of the whole. For example, in case of people waiting to see a procession:

If one rises on one's tip-toes, one can see better.

If people rise on their tip-toes, they can see better.

(3) Material Fallacies (All others):

Material fallacies are of several kinds.

(a) **Post hoc ergo propter hoc:** (After this, therefore because of this).

Because event B occurs after event A, then event B is necessarily caused by event A.

(b) **"Argument by Analogy":** It refers to a statement where, "A is similar to B, therefore whatever is true of A is also true of B". For example, Singapore was backward in 1950s. It developed faster because of "open economy policies". India was backward in 1950s. Therefore, India would have prospered by 'open economy policies'.

(c) **"Appeal to Authority":** It refers to a statement where the truth is sought to be asserted by referring to an authority. "A is true because (so& so) say it so." For example, "India is shining because Milton Friedman has said so."

Q17. What do you mean by the term 'Scientific explanation'? Explain the characteristics of Hypothetico-Deductive model as model of scientific explanation. [June-2012, Q.No.-2]

Or

Explain the different models of scientific explanation.

[Dec-2010, Q.No.-2]

Ans. Explanation has three meanings: One interpretation of explanation is to remove a perplexity or solve mystery i.e. 'puzzle solving'. The second meaning is to change the unknown into the known. The third interpretation of explanation is to give causes of phenomenon to be explained. The first two meanings are too relativistic and subjective. It is the third one emphasising causal explanation sub serving regularity, and law like explanations that fits the meaning of scientific explanation.

The basic modes of scientific explanation within the positivist approach are: Hypothetico-Deductive Model (HD), Deductive-Nomological (DN) Model, and Inductive Probabilistic (IP) models.

Hypothetico-Deductive Model

At a time when the Positivists were not ready to concede any role to theoretical explanation, **Carnap and Hempel,** in their writings, came out with a model-which later came to be known as **Hypothetico-Deductive (H-D) model** of explanation. The H-D model not only describes the structure of theories, but provides answers to the questions of the status and functions of theories, as well. H-D model explicitly address the problems of a theory's structure. H-D model also addresses the problem of status of theoretical terms which may not be testable directly, to gain meaningfulness indirectly by the successful confirmation of theory in which they are embedded.

In H-D model theories as a whole are tested by comparing their deduced consequences (prediction) with data. Every theoretical term need not be given empirical counterparts via correspondence rules. H-D model also turns the old realist-instrumentalist controversy into a moot debate. **Realists** claim that all theoretical terms must refer to real entities, and theories which do not, are false Instrumentalists insist that theories are only instruments for predictions. Only relevant question for them is whether theories are adequate for prediction. H-D model seems to accommodate both these concerns, and defuse the controversy.

The H-D model rejects the earlier notion that theories have no role but are only instruments. H-D model emphasises the following positive functions of theories:

- They allow generality in the specification of scientific laws.
- They possess 'a certain formal simplicity' which allows the use of 'powerful and elegant mathematical machinery'.

- They can serve the practical function of allowing the scientist to discover interdependencies observable.
- They are convenient and fruitful heuristic (intellectual) devices, often serving an explanatory function of their own.

Thus, the H-D model without minimising the importance of observable phenomena for scientific explanation, allowed far more substantial role for theories and theoretical terms than did their predecessors.

Covering-Law Models

Carl G Hempel and Paul Oppenheim developed Deductive-Nomological (D-N) Model of scientific explanation and much later, Hempel extended it to include Inductive-Probabilistic (I-P) Model. These two models together are referred to as Covering-Law Models of explanation.

Deductive-Nomological (D-N) Model

Hempel and Oppenheim advanced an account of scientific explanation, which later came to be known as deductive-nomological (D-N) model, in their paper entitled "Studies in the Logic of Explanation". They divided an explanation into two major constituents—the explanandum and the explanans. The Explanandum means the sentence describing the phenomenon to be explained (not that phenomenon itself). The Explanans means the class of those sentences, which are adduced to account for the phenomenon. The explanans falls into two sub-classes, viz., certain antecedent conditions $C_1, C_2 \ldots C_K$ and certain general laws $L_1, L_2 \ldots L_r$. If a proposed explanation is to be sound, conditions of adequacy must be satisfied. The following four conditions of logical and empirical adequacy must be satisfied:

(1) Logical Conditions of Adequacy

(R_1) The explanandum must be a logical consequence of the explanans; in other words, the explanandum must be logically deduced from the information contained in the explanans, for otherwise, the explanans would not constitute adequate grounds for the explanandum.

(R_2) The explanandum must contain general laws, and these must actually be required for the derivation of the explanandum. Though not a necessary condition, the explanans must contain at least one statement, which is not a law.

(R_3) The explanans must have empirical content, i.e. it must be capable, at least in principle, of test by experiment or observation. The point deserves special mention because certain arguments, which have been offered as explanations in the natural and in the social sciences, violate this requirement.

(2) Empirical Condition of Adequacy

(R_4) The sentences constituting the explanans (the explanatory premises) must be true.

The characteristics of explanation discussed may be summarised into the following schema:

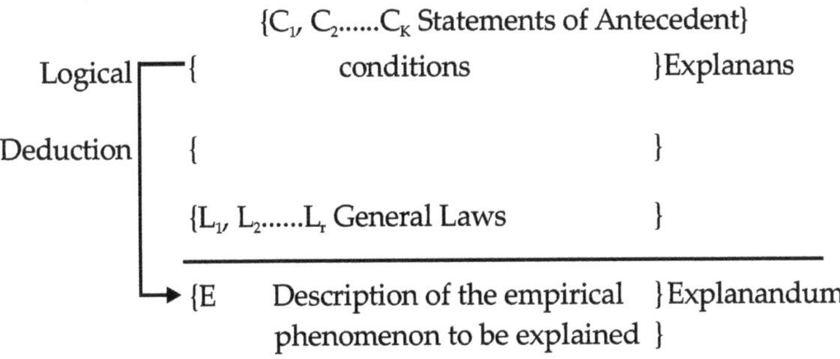

Fig. 1.1: Summarisation of characteristics of explanation

Hempel and Oppenheim argued that the same formal analysis, including the four necessary conditions, applies to scientific predictions as well as to explanation. They went on to argue that an explanation is not fully adequate unless its explanans, if taken account of in time. Could have served as a basis for predicting the phenomenon under consideration. Consequently, whatever is said about the logical characteristics of explanation or prediction will be applicable to either, even if one of them is mentioned. This resulted what is known as Covering-Law Model extended to the D-N Model of Explanation.

Extension of characteristics of explanation to prediction could formally be presented in the following schema:

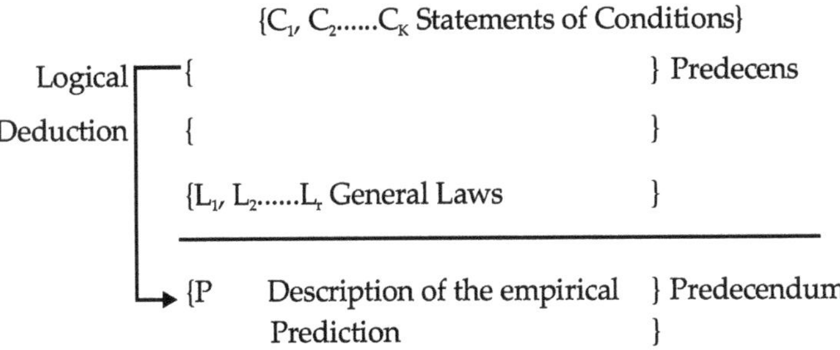

Fig. 1.2: Extension of characteristics of explanation

The symmetry visualised between explanation and prediction has often drawn criticism.

Inductive-Probabilistic (I-P) Model

In 1960s, Hempel developed Inductive-Probabilistic Model. In the I-P model, the explanans consists of sentences describing the requisite initial conditions along with statistical laws and is expected to confer upon the explanandum highly logical, or inductive probability. The characteristics are similar to D-N Model. The symmetry holds and hence another Covering-Law Explanation.

Q18. Critically examine the Covering-Law Model of explanation.

Ans. The Covering-Law Model of explanation offered by the D-N and I-P models are subject to a number of limitations. For convenience, we shall confine here to the limitations of D-N model, some of which are also applicable to I-P model.

First is about the necessity of laws and theories in the pursuit of scientific explanation. Laws are distinct from ordinary statements. Ordinary statements or statement of mere facts refer to particular statements and express "contingent truths", like "John went home and had dinner". Laws refer to universal statements and express "necessary truth". For example, "all objects are attracted to one another with a force inversely proportional to the square of the distances between them" is a universal and law like statement: However, there are many apparently universal statements which are not really universal statements,. These may be the ones that involve mere "accidental generalisations" like, "all coins in my pocket are nickels".

This distinction between laws and ordinary statements does not make laws as necessary requirement for explanation. Particularly in biology, astronomy and social sciences explanations need not be in the form of laws. Explanations may be in the form of questions and answers. The often cited example is: why do Hopi Indians continue to perform rain making ceremonies even though their ceremonies do not normally produce desired result. This explanation does not require any law like statement.

Second, to explain requires not only the factors one cites to be causally relevant but also that they be causes. D-N model is often satisfied by citing relevant causes. Causes explain effects, but effects do not explain their causes, and effects of common cause do not explain one another. Based on David Hume's famous guillotine of time, two contiguous events do not become cause and effect. Inferring event B as the effect of event A because it followed the late, amounts to the "Billiard Ball Model of Causation", where the ball reaching the pouch is seen, "as if' the player knew all the laws of time and motion of the billiard ball.

Third, much of the criticism of Covering Law model of explanation relates to the symmetry thesis, that explanation and prediction are inherently linked, and that only difference is the sequence. But critics point out that explanation need not predict. For example, Darwin's Theory of Evolution provides a great deal of explanation on the origin and evolution of species, but it does not predict anything. Similarly, prediction need not explain anything. For instance, prediction of weather does not explain anything.

Fourth, the D-N model ignores the divergence between the norms and practices and thereby eliminates much of science from the ambit of explanation. Many functional or technological explanations get eliminated because they are not through any laws or regularities. Purposive behaviour needs explanation of motivation and in motivated behaviour future affects the present. Determining motives to be classified in antecedent conditions and not in causal relation. Hempel and Oppenheim also recognise the problems in applying their model of explanation in social sciences. Human behaviour often is characterised by uniqueness and irrepeatability. It depends upon situation and previous history of individuals.

Q19. Describe the limitations of application of scientific models to social science.

Ans. Causal type of explanation is essentially inadequate in fields other than physics and chemistry. And it is more so in the case of social sciences which involve explanation of purposive behaviour. Hampel and Oppenheim point out to some limitation of applying models of scientific explanation to social sciences.

First, events involving the activities of humans singly or in groups have a peculiar uniqueness and irrepeatability, which make them inaccessible to causal explanation. Causal explanation presupposes uniformities and repeatability, which may not hold for phenomena in social sciences.

Second, the establishment of scientific generalisations and explanatory principles for human behaviour is impossible because the reactions of an individual in a given situation depend not only upon that situation, but upon the previous history of the individual.

Third, the explanation of any phenomenon involving purposive behaviour calls for reference to motivation and thus for teleological rather than causal analysis. Many of the explanations, which are offered for human actions, involve reference to goals and motives. Motivational explanations often tend to have less cognitive significance.

Attempts to extend scientific models of explanation to non-physical sciences without closer understanding of the context often lead to inappropriate explanations. One possibility is there are contexts or areas within social sciences like economics where there is room for application of scientific or to be specific, positivist models of explanations. But at the same time there are vast aspects of economics where such application may not be easily amenable.

Q20. State the efforts made by mainstream economics to adopt the model of explanation of positivism.

Or

Explain the characteristics of Ricardo's method of explanation.

Or

State the general preposition advanced by N.W. Senior in support scientific status of Ricardion system.

Or

What is methodological pluralism?

Ans. The urge to model Economics on Political Economy as a science on the lines of physical sciences dates back to the period of Classical Economics.

Ricardo's Method

Ricardo did not write on methodology of economics but his method explaining the principles of political economy is clearly discerned as positive abstract and deductive, and it has come to be called **'hypothetico-deductive model of explanation'.** It vigourously denies that facts can speak for themselves and contends that it is theory that can make sense. Ricardo died in 1823, leaving behind the claim that political economy was a science. His Principles of Political Economy, which was a set of laws based on deductive reasoning, measures up to that claim. Questions were raised soon whether a deductive body of laws without empirical content could claim the status of science. The task of defending Ricardo's method and the claim of political economy as a science was left to his followers of classical political economy. The defence came from the writings of N.W. Senior, J.S. Mill, J.E. Cairnes and J.N. Kynes.

N.W. Senior

It was N.W. Senior in his 1927 lecture, which was later elaborated as **Outline of the Science of Political Economy,** (1936), that first made a statement on the distinction between a pure and strictly positive science, and an impure and inherently normative art of economics. He went on to claim scientific status for the Ricardian system. Science of Political Economy, according to him rests essentially on "a very few general propositions, which are the result of observation, or consciousness, and which almost every man, as soon as he hears them, admits, as being familiar to his thoughts". From this conclusions are drawn which hold true only in the absence of "particular disturbing causes".

Senior reduced these "very few general propositions" of political economy into the following four:

- that every person desires to maximise wealth with as little sacrifice as possible;
- that population tends to increase faster than the means of subsistence;
- that labour working with machines is capable of producing a positive net product; and
- that agriculture is subject to diminishing returns.

J.S. MILL

It is Senior, who for the first time introduces the concept of 'economic man' or 'maximising man', as could be seen from the first proposition above. J.S. Mill, though staunch advocate of inductive method and a stout defender of methodological monism in science, was nonetheless sympathetic to Ricardo's deductive method of political economy. *Mill,* in his essay O*n the Definition of Political Economy and on the Method of investigation Proper to* It (1936), treats political economy as an "inexact science" and a "separate science", and thereby defends deductive method in economics. Elaborating on Senior's notion of 'economic man', Mill observes "political economy proceeds ...under the supposition that man is a being who is determined, by the necessity of his nature, to prefer a greater proportion of wealth to a smaller in all cases...". Mill does consider "economic man" as fictional man to facilitate the propositions of political economy. The pages on 'economic man' in Mill's essay are followed immediately by the characterisation of political economy as "essentially an abstract science" that employs "the method of priori". The "disturbing causes" and "the tendency laws" in political economy necessitate ceteris paribus clauses.

J.E. Cairnes

J.E. Cairnes in his **Character and Logical Method of Political Economy (1875),** goes on to argue that political economy is a hypothetical, deductive science. and its conclusions "will correspond with facts only in the absence of disturbing causes, which is, in other words, to say that they represent not positive but hypothetical truths". By late 19th century, there were growing doubts on the method of political economy. J.N. Keynes tried to argue that what is referred to as deductive reasoning in political economy was indeed preceded by inductive inferences based on observation of human behaviour.

J.N. Keynes

J.N. Keynes, in **The Scope and Method of Political Economy (1890),** argued that deductive reasoning was indeed preceded by concrete observations. Deductive reasoning comes at a later stage drawing upon specific individual experiences. J.N. Keynes is known for comprehensive reconciliation of the classical methodological approaches.

The following observation stands as a testimony to his comprehensive understanding of the methodological approaches underlying a complex subject like economics. He observes "...economic science deals with phenomena that are more complex and less uniform than those with which the natural sciences are concerned; and its conclusions, except in their most abstract form, lack both the certainty and the universality that pertain to physical laws. There is a corresponding difficulty in regard to the proper method of economic study; and the problem of defining preconditions and limits of the validity of economic reasonings become one of exceptional complexity. It is, moreover, impossible to establish the sight of any one method to hold the field to the exclusion of other. Different methods are appropriate, according to the material available, the stage of investigation reached, and the object in view; and hence arises the special task of assigning to each its legitimate place and relative importance".

Q21. What is logical empiricism? State the contribution made by T. Hutchison in this regard. [June-2011, Q.No.-2]

Ans. Logical positivism, also called logical empiricism, a philosophical movement that arose in Vienna in the 1920s and was characterised by the view that scientific knowledge is the only kind of factual knowledge and all traditional metaphysical doctrines are to be rejected as meaningless.

According Hutchison, science contains statements which are either conceivably falsifiable by empirical observation or are not. Those, which are not falsifiable, are tautologies and are thus devoid of empirical content. The primary reason why the propositions of pure theory have no empirical content is that they are posed in the form of deductive inferences. In Economics, widespread use of ceteris paribus clause robs empirical content. Irresponsible use of ceteris paribus clause make microeconomic theory effectively unfalsifiable.

Hutchison examines the formal structure of economic theory, which consists of a series of deductions from basic postulates. These deductions are analytical in nature. These analytical statements are logical statements without any empirical content. Therefore, pure economic theory is empty and thus there is need for more empirical content. Hutchison insisted on the need for testability, and falsification tests at that, for even the basic assumptions. The insistence of testing not only the theory, but the assumptions as well, for validity sparked-off a wider debate in economics later. But the immediate response was to describe Hutchison as an 'ultra-empiricist'.

Hutchison's attempt to establish the analyticity of fundamental generalisation of economic theory and to wean economists away from pure theory did not succeed very much. But his proposal to make proposals in economics in increasingly testable of falsifiable form; to increase empirical investigations of various aspects of economics, and the need for economists to abandon their psychological method received universal acceptance by economists.

One of the interesting aspects of Hutchison's contribution relates to the issue of testing assumptions as well as the theory or hypothesis. This provoked a debate between Hutchison and Fritz Machlup. Machlup believes that only deduced or 'lower level' hypotheses require 'verification', and he outlines how such testing could be carried out. While Hutchison does not require that every statement in a theory be tested, he does insist that each be 'testable' and one should be able to conceive of how a test could be carried out. Further, Hutchison prefers that the behavioural postulates of economics reflect the actual observed and statistically recorded behaviour of economic agents. Machlup requires no such correspondence. The crucial behavioural postulate is the assumption of rational, maximising behaviour. And machlup is more reasonable in arguing that this assumption need not be tested directly, which was insisted by Hutchison, but indirect testing of the same could be done. Much before the debate on testing of assumption sparked by Hutchison's contribution, Milton Friedman's independent contribution suggested that testing of assumptions as such was not an important issue.

Q22. What is instrumentalism? State the contribution made by Milton Friedman in this regard. [Dec-2011, Q.No.-2]

Or

Distinguish between realism and instrumentalism. Discuss the contribution made by Milton Friedman towards instrumentalism in Economics. [Dec-2012, Q.No.-2]

Or

Which criteria have laid down by Milton Friedman for acceptability of theory or hypothesis?

Ans. In the philosophy of science, instrumentalism is the view that a scientific theory is a useful instrument in understanding the world. A concept or theory should be evaluated by how effectively it explains and predicts phenomena, as opposed to how accurately it describes objective reality.

Instrumentalism avoids the debate between anti-realism and philosophical or scientific realism. It may be better characterised as non-realism. Instrumentalism shifts the basis of evaluation away from whether or not phenomena observed actually exist, and towards an analysis of whether the results and evaluation fit with observed phenomena.

Instrumentalism is particularly popular in the field of economics, where researchers postulate fictional economies and actors. Milton Friedman is a famous proponent of the instrumentalist approach.

Friedman sets out by stating that the purpose of his essay is to counter criticism of two pillars of neo-classical, economics, viz., (a) the maximisation behaviour, and (b) the model of perfect competition. He goes on to establish the methodological foundations of new-classical economics by positing his own version of positivism, which late come to be branded as "instrumentalism".

Goal of Science

According to Milton Friedman the ultimate goal of positive science "is the development of a 'theory' or 'Hypothesis' that yields valid and meaningful... predictions about the phenomenon." the criteria for acceptability of theory or hypothesis are three:

- That theory/hypothesis be logically consistent and contain categories which have meaningful empirical counterparts;
- That there are 'substantive hypotheses' which are testable; and
- That "the only relevant test of the validity of a hypothesis is comparison of its predictions with experience".

Further, when an infinite number of hypotheses generally consistent with an observed set of facts generally exist, other criteria–simplicity and fruitfulness–be invoked to chose among competing hypotheses.

Relationship between Significance of Theory and 'Realism' of Assumptions

For Friedman, disparaging a theory for having 'unrealistic assumptions' is ludicrous. He tries to show that most significant theories are actually characterised by descriptively inaccurate assumptions. He observes: "Truly important and significant hypotheses will be found to have "assumptions" that are widely inaccurate descriptive representations of reality, and, *in general, the more significant the theory, the more unrealistic the assumptions".*

Realism of assumption does not matter except when certain hypotheses are derived from assumptions, and when there is no test available, realist description is in order. With these two exceptions, realism of assumptions does not matter for the following reasons:

(1) Theory is supposed to lead to simplification of complex reality by abstraction. There is inverse relationship between realism and abstraction. The more realism one insists upon, the more abstract and the complex the explanation.

(2) The uninformativeness of knowledge of discrepancies between assumptions and facts makes one to treat realism of assumptions as of no importance. He cites the example of Galileo's Law of falling Bodies:

"*If* a body falls towards the earth in *vacuum*, its instantaneous acceleration is constant, $s=\frac{1}{2}gt^2$. The realism of vacuum need not be tested. Since the prediction is true, then the assumption be treated as *if* true. Turning to economic theory, Friedman cites the "Billiard Ball Player" example and where once the ball reaches the pouch one could assume as *if* the player knew all the laws of time and motion and extends it to profit maximisation: "under behave as *if* they were seeking rationally to maximise their expected returns...and have full knowledge of the data needed to succeed in this attempt."

(3) The presence of 'undesigned' classes of implications can be avoided by as *if* assumption.

Milton Friedman concludes his essay by asserting unity of method in all positive sciences. For him there are no methodological differences between natural and social sciences. He regards economics as "objective" as physical sciences. His main conclusions are:

- That realism of assumptions is "largely" irrelevant to validation of theories, which ought to be judged 'almost; solely in terms of heir instrumental value in generating accurate predictions.

- Standard economic theory has an excellent predictive record as judged by countless application to specific problems.
- The dynamics of competition over time accounts for this splendid track record.

Critical Appraisal of Friedman's Instrumentalism

Milton Friedman's methodological approach is criticised widely. The major criticism relates to the proposition that realism of assumption does not matter. Friedman's assertion that not only the realism of assumptions is not necessary but "in general, the more significant the theory, the more unrealistic the assumptions" is called by Samuelson as a flamboyant exaggeration, as the extreme version of "F-Twist" (meaning Friedman-Twist). It is one thing to say that proving realism of all assumptions is difficult, but altogether different to say that further the assumptions move away from realism, closer is the theory to predictions. Even Fritz Machlup, L. Osoland and Nagel, who were generally in defence of Friedman's methodology, would insist on the realism of at least second order assumptions. It is pointed out that direct evidence about assumptions is not necessarily more difficult than testing a theory. Test assumptions may yield important insights into the theory. Caldwill points out that philosophically, Friedman's insistence on prediction not explanation may result in correlation not causation, i.e., it may result in "measurement without theory". Blaug points out that accurate predictions are not the only relevant test of the validity of a theory and it would be impossible to distinguish between genuine and spurious correlations, Further, Friedman's instrumental attitude to theories, ignores 'truth value, of theories as many philosophers of science would insist upon.

Q23. Discuss the contribution of Paul Samuelson to economic methodology.

Ans. The contribution of Paul Samuelson to economic methodology could be seen in terms of two theses, which he advances. One has come to be described as 'operationalism' and the other as 'descriptivism'. The discussion on these two theses are as follows:

Operationalism

According to him, economists should seek to discover 'operationally meaningful theorems'. Theories are strategically simplified description of observable and refutable empirical regularities. He begins with the criticism of Friedman for the latter's F-Twist on realism of assumptions and emphasises the need for methodological clarity. He proposes the thesis of "logical equivalence" as the basis for methodological consistency. According to "logical equivalence", theories are merely equivalent restatements of assumptions and conclusions, i.e. $A \equiv B \equiv C$, where A is defined as 'assumptions', B is defined as theory and C as consequences or predictions.

Theory (B) consists of "a set of axioms, postulates or hypotheses that stipulate something about observable reality..." The set is either confirmable or refutable in principle by observation. A theory has a set of consequences (C) which are logically implied by theory, and a set assumptions (A) which logically implies the theory. The degree of "realism", "factual correctness", "empirical validity" or "truth" of any one of A,B,C, is shared by the other two. Referring to 'F-Twist', he observes first, it is a contradiction to maintain all consequences (C) are valid and the theory (B) and the assumptions (A) are not valid.

Second, it's absurd to maintain, in case where only some of the consequence (C) are valid, that the theory (B) and assumptions (A) are important though invalid. The part of the theory set and assumptions set corresponding to the invalid part of the consequence set should be elminated.

Descriptivism

Samuelson has certain exalted view of explanation, which he considers different from the usual notion in science. He observed, "scientists never "explain" any behaviour, by theory or any other hook. Every description that is superseded by a "deeper explanation" turns out...to have been replaced by still another description..." An explanation, as used legitimately in science, is a better kind of description and not something that goes ultimately beyond description. It is this emphasis and elaboration of 'description' that earns Samuelson's approach the title of 'descriptivism'. Why only description? First, a theory is just description of observable experience; a convenient mnemonic representation of empirical reality Second, knowledge consists essentially of observational reports. A theory expressible in observational language is superior to those which are not. Explanations are ultimate. Apriorisms must be avoided; hence, theories should be expressed in observational language. All known theories in science are expressible in terms of observational statements, i.e. basic statements.

Samuelson is criticised for not practicing what he preaches methodologically. Machlup, citing Samuelson's famous work on 'factor price equalisation', accuses him for not following his own norm of deriving "operationally meaningful theorem" and for basic on unrealistic assumptions.

Q24. Discuss the Amartya Sen's view on heterogeneity of explanation in economics.

Or

Do you agree that different methodological approaches are needed in economics?

Ans. In a broad based critique of contemporary economic methodology, Amartya Sen (1989) draws attention to the heterogeneity of the subject matter of economics. Any attempt to think of mono-method for all the diverse concerns of economics is bound to cause the kind of disquiet that we experience today. He cogently argues for heterogeneity of methodological approached in economics.

Heterogeneity of Substance and Methods of Economics

According to Sen. Economics as a subject is concerned with many different types of problems. The diversity of the discipline of economics should be kept in view to achieve an adequate grip on the methodological issues in the subject. The subject of economics includes three diverse, though interrelated, exercise:

- Predicting the future and causally explaining the past events,
- Choosing appropriate descriptions of state and events in the past and the present, and
- Providing normative evaluations of states, institutions, and policies.

These exercises are interrelated but each requires a different methodological approach. For instance, the method of scientific explanation that insists on prediction is concerned only with the first set of exercises. The 'methodology of economics' has to admit enough diversity to be able to deal with other classes of problems as well.

Testing and Verification

Testing and Verification are important for many types of economic analyses since they are concerned with causal relationships and with making predictions. But these are not suitable for all economic theories. For instance, evaluative exercises are not open to testing. Normative evaluation is a different discipline from that of making predictions on the basis of causal hypotheses. Similarly, some descriptive propositions do not have predictive content, and "testing" would be the wrong operation to seek. As far as causal theories are concerned, the need for testing them with empirical information is fairly accepted in principle by economists. Conceptual and analytical issues need to be explored very substantially to understand what types of relationships might be involved. Analyses at this stage are not meant for testing and verification. Of course, one should not end at this state and move up the next where testing is possible.

Value Judgements and Welfare Economics

Sen draws attention to the fact that following Robbins value judgments are kept out of economics. "The decision to keep economics 'value-free' would, of course, militate against the subject of welfare economics as such". Welfare economics still is accepted as important and in this domain to keep economics value-free may not be a value that would be appreciated. In evaluative exercises in welfare economics descriptive methods becomes indispensable.

Formalisation and Mathematics

Mathematics helps to an extent in formal reasoning and helped in systematisation of many economic propositions. However, there are severe limitations of formal language of mathematics. Not all economic propositions can be reduced into mathematics. Lack of balance often has resulted in certain degree of over-formalisation of economics. While recognising the positive contribution of mathematics in lending rigour to certain economic propositions, the negative contribution is through over concentration on mathematic to the exclusion of other disciplines. Such excesses of formalisation need to be corrected. The main aim of GPH Book is to provide knowledge as well as good marks in exams.

2 Methods and Design of Research

An Overview

Research is an academic activity and as such the term should be used in a technical sense. According to Clifford Woody research comprises defining and redefining problems, formulating hypothesis or suggested solutions; collecting, organising and evaluating data; making deductions and reaching conclusions; and at last carefully testing the conclusions to determine whether they fit the formulating hypothesis. After hypothesis is formulated, a researcher has to formulate a suitable research design. The important step in the formulation of research design is the selection of a suitable methodology and a guideline to proceed further. It clearly means the exact nature and character and course of the entire work in a systematic manner and includes the structure of entire research work. Research design sketches out the entire plan of sampling design, observational design, statistical design and operation design.

Q1. What do you understand by the research? Discuss its various types.

Ans. Research in common parlance refers to a search for knowledge. Once can also define research as a scientific and systematic search for pertinent information on a specific topic. In fact, research is an art of scientific investigation.

The Advanced Learner's Dictionary of Current English lays down the meaning of research as "a careful investigation or inquiry specially through search for new facts in any branch of knowledge".

Redman and Mory define research as a "systematised effort to gain new knowledge."

Some people consider research as a movement, a movement from the known to the unknown. It is actually a voyage of discovery. We all possess the vital instinct of inquisitiveness for, when the unknown confronts us, we wonder and our inquisitiveness makes us probe and attain full and fuller understanding of the unknown. This inquisitiveness is the mother of all knowledge and the method, which man employs for obtaining the knowledge of whatever the unknown, can be termed as research.

Types of Research: The basic types of research are as follows:

(1) Descriptive vs. Analytical: Descriptive research includes surveys and fact-finding enquiries of different kinds. The major purpose of descriptive research is description of the state of affairs, as it exists at present. In social science and business research, we quite often use the term Ex post facto research for descriptive research studies. The main characteristic of this method is that the researcher has no control over the variables; he can only report what has happened or what is happening. Most ex post facto research projects are used for descriptive studies in which the researcher seeks to measure such items as, for example, frequency of shopping, preferences of people, or similar data. Ex post facto studies also include attempts by researchers to discover causes even when they cannot control the variables. The methods of research utilised in descriptive research are survey methods of all kinds, including comparative and correlational methods. In analytical research, on the other hand, the researcher has to use facts or information already available, and analyse these to make a critical evaluation of the material.

(2) Applied vs. Fundamental/Theoretical: Research can either be applied (or action) research or fundamental (to basic or pure) research. Applied research aims at finding a solution for an immediate problem facing a society or an industrial/business organisation, whereas fundamental research is mainly concerned with generalisations and with the formulation of a theory. "Gathering knowledge for knowledge's sake is termed 'pure' or 'basic' research."

(3) Quantitative vs. Qualitative: Quantitative research is based on the measurement of quantity or amount. It is applicable to phenomena that can be expressed in terms of quantity. Qualitative research, on the other hand, is concerned with qualitative phenomenon, i.e. phenomena relating to or involving quality or kind. For instance, when we are interested in investigating the reasons for human behaviour (i.e. why people think or do certain things), we quite often talk of 'Motivation Research', an important type of qualitative research. This type of research aims at discovering the underlying motives and desires, using in depth interviews for the purpose. Other techniques of such research are word association tests, sentence completion tests, story completion tests and similar other projective techniques. Qualitative research is specially important in the behavioural sciences where the aim is to discover the underlying motives of human behaviour.

(4) Conceptual vs. Empirical: Conceptual research is that related to some abstract idea(s) or theory. It is generally used by philosophers and thinkers to develop new concepts or to reinterpret existing ones. On the other hand, empirical research relies on experience or observation alone, often without due regard for system and theory. It is data-based research, coming up with conclusions which are capable of being verified by observation or experiment. We can also call it as experimental type of research. In such a research, it is necessary to get at facts firsthand, at their source, and actively to go about doing certain things to stimulate the production of desired information. In such a research, the researcher must first provide himself with a working hypothesis or guess as to the probable results. He then works to get enough facts (data) to prove or disprove his hypothesis. He then sets up experimental designs, which he thinks will manipulate the persons or the materials concerned so as to bring forth the desired information. Such research is thus characterised by the experimenter's control over the variables under study and his deliberate manipulation of one of them to study its effects. Empirical research is appropriate when proof is sought that certain variables affect other variables in some way. Evidence gathered through experiments or empirical studies is today considered to be the most powerful support possible for a given hypothesis.

(5) Some Other Types of Research: All other types of research are variations of one or more of the above stated approaches, based on either the purpose of research, or the time required to accomplish research, on the environment in which research is done, or on the basis of some other similar factor. Form the point of view of time, we can think of research either as one-time research or longitudinal research. In the former case, the research is confined to a single time-period, whereas in the latter case the research is carried on over several time-periods. Research can be field-setting research or laboratory research or simulation research, depending upon the environment in which it is to be carried out. Research can as well be understood as clinical or diagnostic research. Such research follow case-study methods or in depth approaches to reach the basic causal relations. Such studies usually go deep into the causes of things or events that interest us, using very small samples and very deep probing data gathering devices. The research may be exploratory or it may be formalised. The objective of exploratory research is the development of hypotheses rather than their testing, whereas formalised research studies are those with substantial structure and with specific hypotheses to be tested. Historical research is that which utilises historical sources like documents, remains, etc. to study events or ideas of the past, including the philosophy of persons and groups at any remote point of time. Research can also be classified as conclusion-oriented and decision-oriented. While doing conclusion oriented research, a researcher is free to pick up a problem, redesign the inquiry as he proceeds and is prepared to conceptualise as he wishes. Decision-oriented research is always for the need of a decision-maker and the researcher in this case is not free to embark upon research according to his own inclination. Operations research is an example of decision-oriented research since it is a scientific method of providing executive departments with a quantitative basis for decisions regarding operations under their control. Participatory research is another type of research. It deals with real world problems aimed at finding out practical solution or answer them.

Q2. State the various types of research approaches applied in pursuing research.

Ans. There are two basic approaches to research, viz. quantitative approach and the qualitative approach. The former involves the generation of data in quantitative form, which can be subjected to rigourous quantitative analysis in a formal and rigid fashion. This approach can be further sub-classified into inferential, experimental and simulation approaches to research. The purpose of inferential approach to research is to form a database from which to infer characteristics or relationships of population. This usually means survey research where a sample of population is studied (questioned or observed) to determine its characteristics, and it is then inferred that the population has the same characteristics. Experimental approach is characterised by much greater control over the research environment and in this case, some variables are manipulated to observe their effect on other variables. Simulation approach involves the construction of an artificial environment within which relevant information and data can be generated. Qualitative approach to research is concerned with subjective assessment of attitudes, opinions and behaviour. Research in such a situation is a function of researcher's insights and impressions. Such an approach to research generates results either in non-quantitative form or in the form, which are not subjected to rigourous quantitative analysis. Generally, the techniques of focus group interviews, projective techniques and depth interviews are used.

Q3. Explain the constituents of research methodology.

Or

Distinguish between research methodology and research methods.

Ans. Research Methodology is a wider term. It consists of three important elements: (i) theoretical perspectives or orientation that guide research and logic of inquiry, (ii) tools and techniques of data collection, and (iii) methods of data analysis.

Research Methods, comprises of research techniques and tools. Research techniques refer to the practical aspects of collecting data and the way the information/data obtained/collected is organised and analysed. Tools are the instruments that are used for data collection and its analysis. It includes questionnaire/schedules, dairies, checklists, maps, photos, drawings, etc. Census and survey methods are mainly used to collect quantitative data. Data analysis involves a set of statistical techniques used in establishing relationships between the different variables and in evaluating the accuracy of the results. Thus, methodology, methods and tools/techniques are three distinct elements of the research process. Any one of these three elements by itself may not be adequate in many situations. For instance, no data can be systematically collected without adequate knowledge of techniques of data collection. Similarly, data cannot be explained without comprehending the philosophy or perspective behind the characteristics underlying the variables to which the data relates. A sound knowledge of statistical techniques is also necessary to analyse the data efficiently.

Q4. Enumerate the various steps involved in research process.

Or

State the various steps involved in carrying out research.

[Dec-2012, Q.No-5]

Ans. Research process consists of series of actions or steps necessary to effectively carry out research and the desired sequencing of these steps.

(1) Formulating the research problem: There are two types of research problems, viz., those, which relate to states of nature and those, which relate to relationships between variables. At the very outset the researcher must single out the problem he wants to study, i.e. he must decide the general area of interest or aspect of a subject-matter that he would like to inquire into. Initially the problem may be stated in a broad general way and then the ambiguities, if any, relating to the problem be resolved. Then, the feasibility of a particular solution has to be considered before a working formulation of the problem can be set up. The formulation of a general topic into a specific research problem, thus, constitutes the first step in a scientific inquiry. Essentially two steps are involved in formulating the research problem, viz. understanding the problem thoroughly, and rephrasing the same into meaningful terms from an analytical point of view.

At the same time, the researcher must examine all available literature to get himself acquainted with the selected problem. He may review two types of literature—the conceptual literature concerning the concepts and theories, and the empirical literature consisting of studies made earlier which are similar to the one proposed. The basic outcome of this review will be the knowledge as to what data and other materials are available for operational purposes, which will enable the researcher to specify his own research problem in a meaningful context. After this the researcher rephrases the problem into analytical or operational terms, i.e. to put the problem in as specific terms as possible. This task of formulating, or defining, a research problem is a step of greatest importance in the entire research process. The problem to be investigated must be defined unambiguously for that will help discriminating relevant data from irrelevant ones. Care must, however, be taken to verify the objectivity and validity of the background facts concerning the problem.

(2) Extensive literature survey: Once the problem is formulated, a brief summary of it should be written down. It is compulsory for a research worker writing a thesis for a Ph.D. degree to write a synopsis of the topic and submit it to the necessary Committee or the Research Board for approval. Now the researcher should undertake extensive literature survey connected with the problem. For this purpose, the abstracting and indexing journals and published or unpublished bibliographies are the first place to go to, Academic journals, conference proceedings, government reports, books, etc. must be tapped depending on the nature of the problem. In this process, it should be remembered that one source will lead to another. The earlier studies, if any, which are similar to the study in hand, should be carefully studied. A good library will be a great help to the researcher at this stage.

(3) Development of working hypotheses: After extensive literature survey, researcher should state in clear terms the working hypothesis or hypotheses. Working hypothesis is tentative assumption made in order to draw out and test its logical or empirical consequences. Hypothesis can be formulated as a proposition or set of propositions providing most probable explanation for occurrence of some specified phenomenon. Hypotheses when empirically tested may either be accepted or rejected. A hypothesis must, therefore, be capable of being tested. A hypothesis stated in terms of a relationship between the dependent and independent variables are suitable for econometric treatment. The manner in which hypothesis is formulated is important as it provides the required focus for research. It also helps in identifying the method of analysis to be used.

Prior thinking about the subject, examination of the available data and material related to the study, discussion with colleagues and experts help the researcher in formulation of hypothesis. Exploratory or descriptive research can be carried out even without hypothesis.

(4) Research Design: Research design is the conceptual structure within which research is conducted. It is the blueprint for the collection, measurement and analysis of data.

(5) Collection of Data: Collection of data is an essential part of the research process. Data can be primary or secondary. Data collected by the researcher, say by a survey is primary. The data already collected by some agency and available in some published form is secondary.

(6) Analysis of data: After the data have been collected, the researcher turns to the task of analysing them. The analysis of data requires a number of closely related operations such as establishment of categories, the application of these categories to raw data through coding, tabulation and then drawing statistical inferences. The unwieldy data should necessarily be condensed into a few manageable groups and tables for further analysis. Thus, researcher should classify the raw data into some purposeful and usable categories. Coding operation is usually done at this stage through which the categories of data are transformed into symbols that may be tabulated and counted. Editing is the procedure that improves the quality of the data for coding. With coding, the stage is ready for tabulation. Tabulation is a part of the technical procedure wherein the classified data are put in the form of tables. The mechanical devices can be made use of at this juncture. A great deal of data, specially in large inquiries, is tabulated by computers. Computers not only save time but also make it possible to study large number of variables affecting a problem simultaneously. Analysis work after tabulation is generally based on the computation of various percentages, coefficients, etc. by applying various well defined statistical formulae. In the process of analysis, relationships or differences supporting or conflicting with original or new hypotheses should be subjected to tests of significance to determine with what validity data can be said to indicate any conclusion(s). For instance, if there are two samples of weekly wages, each sample being drawn from factories in different parts of the same city, giving two different mean values, then our problem may be whether the two mean values are significantly different or the difference is just a matter of chance. Through the use of statistical tests we can establish whether such a difference is a real one or is the result of random fluctuations. If the difference happens to be real, the inference will be that the two samples come from different universes and if the difference is due to chance, the conclusion would be that the two samples belong to the same universe. Similarly, the technique of analysis of variance can help us in analysing whether three or more varieties of seeds grown on certain fields yield significantly different results or not. In brief, the researcher can analyse the collected data with the help of various statistical measures.

(7) Hypothesis-testing: After analysing the data as stated above, the researcher is in a position to test the hypotheses, if any, he had formulated earlier. Hypothesis-testing will result in either accepting the hypothesis or in rejecting it. If the researcher had no hypotheses to start with, generalisations established on the basis of data may be stated as hypotheses to be tested by subsequent researches in times to come.

(8) Generalisations and interpretation: If a hypothesis is tested and upheld several times, it may be possible for the researcher to arrive at generalisation, i.e. to build a theory. As a matter of fact, the real value of research lies in its ability to arrive at certain generalisations. If the researcher had no hypothesis to start with, he might seek to explain his findings on the basis of some theory. It is known as interpretation. The process of interpretation may quite often trigger off new questions, which in turn may lead to further researches.

(9) Preparation of the report or the thesis: Finally, the researcher has to prepare the report of what has been done by him. Writing of report must be done with great care keeping in view the following:

(a) The layout of the report should be as follows: (i) the preliminary pages; (ii) the main text; and (iii) the end matter. In its preliminary pages, the report should carry title and date followed by acknowledgements and foreword. Then there should be a table of contents followed by a list of tables and list of graphs and charts, if any, given in the report.

(b) Report should be written in a concise and objective style in simple language avoiding vague expressions such as 'it seems', 'there may be', and the like.

(c) Charts and illustrations in the main report should be used only if they present the information more clearly and forcibly.

(d) Calculated 'confidence limits' must be mentioned and the various constraints experienced in conducting research operations may as well be stated.

Q5. What is research design? What type of research design would you like to suggest for exploratory and descriptive research?

Ans. The formidable problem that follows the task of defining the research problem is the preparation of the design of the research project, popularly known as the "research design". Decisions regarding what, where, when, how much, by what means concerning an inquiry or a research study constitute a research design. "A research design is the arrangement of conditions for collection and analysis of data in a manner that aims to combine relevance to the research purpose with economy in procedure." In fact, the research design is the conceptual structure within which research is conducted; it constitutes the blueprint for the collection, measurement and analysis of data. As such the design includes an outline of what the researcher will do from writing the hypothesis and its operational implications to the final analysis of data.

We can state the important features of a research design as under:

- It is a plan that specifies the sources and types of information relevant to the research problem.
- It is a strategy specifying which approach will be used for gathering and analysing the data.

- It also includes the time and cost budgets since most studies are done under these two constraints.

Different Research Designs

Different research designs can be conveniently described if we categorise them as: (1) research design in case of exploratory research studies; (2) research design in case of descriptive and diagnostic research studies.

(1) Research design in case of exploratory research studies: Exploratory research studies are also termed as formulative research studies. The main purpose of such studies is that of formulating a problem for more precise investigation or of developing the working hypotheses from an operational point of view. The major emphasis in such studies is on the discovery of ideas and insights. As such the research design appropriate for such studies must be flexible enough to provide opportunity for considering different aspects of a problem under study. Inbuilt flexibility in research design is needed because the research problem, broadly defined initially, is transformed into one with more precise meaning in exploratory studies, which fact may necessitate changes in the research procedure for gathering relevant data. Generally, the following three methods in the context of research design for such studies are talked about: (a) the survey of concerning literature; (b) the experience survey; and (c) the analysis of 'insight–stimulating' examples.

In an exploratory of formulative research study, which merely leads to insights or hypotheses, whatever method or research design outlined above is adopted, the only thing essential is that it must continue to remain flexible so that many different facets of a problem may be considered as and when they arise and come to the notice of the researcher.

(2) Research design in case of descriptive and diagnostic research studies: From the point of view of the research design, the descriptive as well as diagnostic studies share common requirements and as such we may group together these two types of research studies. In descriptive as well as in diagnostic studies, the researcher must be able to define clearly, what he wants to measure and must find adequate methods for measuring it along with a clear cut definition of 'population' he wants to study. Since the aim is to obtain complete and accurate information in the said studies, the procedure to be used must be carefully planned. The research design must make enough provision for protection against bias and must maximise reliability, with due concern for the economical completion of the research study.

The design in such studies must be rigid and not flexible and must focus attention on the following:

(a) Formulating the objective of the study (what the study is about and why is it being made?)
(b) Designing the methods of data collection (what techniques of gathering data will be adopted?)
(c) Selecting the sample (how much material will be needed?)
(d) Collecting the data (where can the required data be found and with what time period should the data be related?)
(e) Processing and analysing the data.
(f) Reporting the findings.

In a descriptive/diagnostic study, the first step is to specify the objectives with sufficient precision to ensure that the data collected are relevant. If this is not done carefully, the study may not provide the desired information.

Then comes the question of selecting the methods by which the data are to be obtained. In other words, techniques for collecting the information must be devised.

While designing data–collection procedure, adequate safeguards against bias and unreliability must be ensured. It is always desirable to pretest the data collection instruments before they are finally used for the study purposes. In other words, we can say that "structured instruments" are used in such studies.

In most of the descriptive/diagnostic studies the research takes out sample(s) and then wishes to make statements about the population on the basis of the sample analysis or analyses. More often than not, sample has to be designed.

To obtain data free from errors introduced by those responsible for collecting them, it is necessary to supervise closely the staff of field workers as they collect and record information.

The data collected must be processed and analysed. This includes steps like coding the interview replies, observations, tabulating the data, and performing several statistical computations. To the extent possible, the processing and analysing procedure should be planned in detail before actual work is started. Finally, statistical computations are needed and as such averages, percentages and various coefficients must be worked out. Probability and sampling analysis may as well be used. The appropriate statistical operations, along with the use of appropriate tests of significance should be carried out to safeguard the drawing of conclusions concerning the study.

Last of all comes the question of reporting the findings. This is the task of communicating the findings to others and the research must do it in an efficient manner. The layout of the report needs to be will planned so that all things relating to the research study may be well presented in simple and effective style.

Thus, the research design in case of descriptive/diagnostic studies is a comparative design throwing light on all points narrated above and must be prepared keeping in view the objective(s) of the study and the resources available. However, it must ensure the minimisation of bias and maximisation of reliability of the evidence collected. The said design can be appropriately referred to as a survey design since it takes into account all the steps involved in a survey.

Q6. Discuss the census and sampling methods of collection statistical data with their merits and demerits.

Ans. The two methods of collecting statistical data are as follows:

(1) Census Method

Census method is that method in which information or data is collected from each and every unit of the population relating to the problem under investigation and conclusions are drawn on their basis. This method is also called as Complete Enumeration Method. For example, suppose some information (like Monthly Expenditure, Average Height, Average Weight, etc.) is to be collected regarding 2000 students of college. For that purpose if we collect data by inquiring each and every student of the college then this method will be called as Census method. In this example, the whole college, i.e. all 2000 students will be considered as a population and every student as an individual will be called the unit of the population. Population census in India is conducted after every ten years by using census method.

Merits of Census Method

- **Reliable and Accurate Data:** Data obtained by census method have more reliability and accuracy because in this method data are collected by contacting each and every unit of the universe.
- **Extensive Information:** This method gives detailed information about each unit of the universe. For example, Indian population census does not only provide the knowledge about the number

of persons but information about their age, occupation, income, education, marital status, etc.

- **Suitability:** This method is more suitable for the population with limited scope and diverse characteristics. Use of this method is also appropriate where intensive study is desired.

Demerits of Census Method

- **More Expensive:** Census method is an expensive one. More money is needed for it, as information is collected from each unit of the population. This is why this method is used by Government mostly for very important issues like Census, etc.
- **More Time:** This method involves much time for data collection because data are collected from each and every unit of the population. This results in delay in making statistical inferences.
- **Not Suitable for Specific Problems:** This method is not suitable relating to certain specific problems and infinite population. For example, if the population in infinite or items of the population are perishable or very complex type, then the census method is not suitable.

(2) Sampling Method

Sampling method is that method in which data is collected from the sample of items selected from population and conclusion are drawn from them. For example, if a study is to be made regarding the monthly expenditure of 2000 students of a college, then instead of collecting information from each student of the college, if we collect information by selecting some students like 100, then this will be called Sampling Method. On the basis of sampling method, it is possible to study the monthly expenditure of all the students of the college. Sampling method has three main stages (i) to select a sample (ii) to collect information from it and (iii) to make inferences regarding the population.

Merits of Sampling Method

- **Saving of Money:** Sampling method is less expensive. It saves money and labour because only a few units of the population are studied.
- **Saving of Time:** In sampling method, data can be collected more quickly as these are obtained from some items of the universe. Thus, much time is saved.

- **Organisational Convenience:** In this method, research work can be organised and executed more conveniently. More skilled and competent investigators can be appointed.
- **More Scientific:** Sampling method is more scientific because data can be inquired with other samples.
- **Only Method:** In some field where inquiry by census method is impossible, then in such situation, sampling method alone is more appropriate. If the population is infinite or too widespread or of perishable nature then in such cases sampling method is used.

Demerits of Sampling Method

- **Less Accurate:** Sampling method has less accuracy because rather than making inquiry about each unit of the universe, partial inquiry or inquiry relating to some selected units only is made.
- **Wrong Conclusions:** If method of selecting a sample is not unbiased or proper caution has not been taken, then results are definitely misleading.
- **Less Reliable:** Compared to census method, there is more likelihood of the bias of the investigator, which makes the results less reliable.
- **Need of Specified Knowledge:** This is a complex method as specialised knowledge is required to select a sample.
- **Not Suitable:** If all units of a population are different from one another, then sampling method will not prove to be much useful.

Q7. State the various stages involved in planning and organising censuses and surveys. [June-2011, Q.No.-5]

Ans. Various stages in planning censuses and surveys are as follows:

(1) Scope and Objectives of Inquiry: A successful conduct of a census or a survey, that is, an inquiry, calls for careful planning and a good deal of preparatory work. 'Statistical inquiry' refers to some investigation wherein relevant information is collected, analysed and interpreted by the application of statistical methods.

The object and scope of a statistical inquiry will have to be clearly outlined before undertaking the actual work of collecting data. This enables the investigator to avoid collecting unnecessary and irrelevant data and concentrate only on obtaining information that is directly connected with the object of his inquiry. The most important thing to remember while planning an inquiry is that one should obtain the most reliable and maximum information relevant to the purpose of inquiry with the minimum use of time, money and energy.

An inquiry may be either a general-purpose inquiry or a specific-purpose inquiry. For instance, an inquiry regarding the educated unemployed in India, or into the working condition of college teachers in India, has its own set object and purpose, hence it is a specific purpose inquiry. The population census, which is general and exhaustive and is undertaken once in ten years, is a general-purpose inquiry. These enquiries are undertaken at certain regular intervals of time, conditions, or circumstances, without materially altering their general structure and purpose.

(2) Preparation of sampling frame of the inquiry: This is important while taking a view on the kind of information we wish to collect as this has a bearing on the details to be collected. We, therefore, have to decide on the respondent units from which we should collect the data. This would of course depend on the inquiry in question and the choice would be such as to ensure a complete coverage of the universe in question (or the sample to be selected from it) and the kind of data we need. For instance, the respondent units will be the household in the tuberculosis inquiry, even though our interest is in measuring the proportion of people who are affected by the disease. This is because the households together cover almost the entire population and the data required would be collected about all the individuals in the household. We also need information about the characteristics of the household to relate the incidence of the disease to certain household characteristics, the location of the household and so on. The study on milk yield would have to cover both households and enterprises (like dairies) to cover the entire cow population in the State. We can then move on to the task of preparing the list of the responding units, called the frame of the inquiry. This is also called the sampling frame, as this will be used to draw the sample required for a survey. This list may be readily available and can be updated -for example, the house list from the Census Organisation, if the Population Census has recently been undertaken. Otherwise, the sampling frame will have to be prepared by the organisers of the survey.

(3) Finalisation of the schedule or questionnaire of the Inquiry: We then move on to the task of translating the requirements of data and the tabulation plan to items of information to be collected from the respondent units and organise these items of information into a logical format that can be used to collect information from each of the respondent unit covered by the inquiry. Such a format, setting out the items of information to be collected from each unit, is called the schedule or questionnaire of the inquiry. The feedback from such pretesting of the schedule/questionnaire is made use of in revising and finalising the schedule or the questionnaire. Part of the process of pretesting and the feedback from it is also to tabulate the data collected through the schedule/questionnaire during pretesting.

The question whether the questionnaire approach or the schedule approach should be adopted for the inquiry is important. The respondents are asked a set of pre specified questions in the questionnaire approach and their replies to these questions are recorded either by themselves or by investigators. This approach assumes that the respondent is capable of understanding and answering the questions all by him/herself, as the investigator is not supposed, in the questionnaire approach, to influence the response in anyway by interpreting the terms used in the question. The questionnaire approach is also used in mail survey methods.

(4) Manual of Instructions to Field Staff and Training: The schedule is not complete without an accompanying document, namely, Manual of Instructions to Field Staff that contains the following:

- concepts and definitions of the terms used in the schedule (or questionnaire), those relevant to the inquiry and items of information sought in the schedule, instructions regarding identification of (responding) units;
- instructions about the manner in which information should be collected from the responding units; and
- methods of cross checking answers provided by the units for different items in the schedule to ensure accuracy of the information recorded in the schedule.

The field staff consists (a) investigators, who collect information from the responding units, (b) supervisors, one each for a group of investigators, and (c) higher layers of direction and control, depending upon the size and complexity of the inquiry.

(5) Scrutiny Note and Coding Plan: Other items of preparatory work relate to scrutiny and coding of the filled-in schedules as soon as these reach the processing centres from the field. A Scrutiny Note has to be prepared for the guidance of those employed for scrutiny work. The scrutiny staff has to be trained in scrutiny work. The Scrutiny Note indicates (a) the manner in which the schedules have to be checked for errors, (b) the different types of mistakes that may be found in the filled up details against different items and (c) the interrelationships between different items in the schedule and so on.

The entries in the filled-in schedules against different items have to be coded to facilitate tabulation of the data collected in the schedules. A coding plan detailing the code structures proposed to be adopted for different items in the schedule along with the concepts and definitions involved has to be prepared for the purpose.

The coding plan for the inquiry at hand may make use of existing standardised code structures for some items and adopt its own structures for others, depending upon its requirements. The staff to be entrusted with coding work has also to be trained intensively in the use of the coding plan.

(6) Recruitment and Training: The conduct of an inquiry calls for the deployment of a large number of people with professional expertise and technical skills. The manpower requirements will be low in the initial stages of planning and the number deployed will rise to a peak during the fieldwork and taper off to lower levels after the fieldwork and data processing operations are completed. The manpower requirements will have to be estimated by taking in to account the workload involved in the inquiry at different stages and at different levels of supervision and control. For instance, the number of locations of field work, the number of respondent units to be listed/identified, the optimum workload per day in terms of data collection from these units that can be efficiently handled by an investigator will determine the number of investigators required. Norms of workload of the supervising staff at different layers of supervision and control in terms of the number of people supervised at the next lower level will help in assessing the staff needs at these levels. The requirements of the scrutiny, coding, data entry and tabulation staff can be likewise estimated with the use of norms of daily output. The recruitment and training of the different types of staff will have to be planned and organised in such a way as to minimise delays in the progress of the inquiry and wastage of resources due to staff waiting for work or work waiting for staff. This can be done if we take due note of the time ordinarily taken for different components of the process of recruitment and posting, namely, advertisement, processing of applications, selection, dispatch of offers and joining time, training and posting, and plan accordingly. There should also be an adequate component of leave reserve in the stock of staff to be able to tackle contingencies of leave, staff turnover, etc.

(7) Organisation of the fieldwork: This is the next task. The allocation of the workload, in terms of the number of responding units and time required for identification and collection of information from these units, among investigators is one aspect.

The second is a similar allocation of the workload of supervision and allocation of the same among supervisors.

The third is the organisation of the supply of the requisite number of schedules and related stationery to the field staff in such a way that there is zero idle time in the field. (While the requisite material is supplied to the field staff initially while they set out to the field, the needs arising while they are in the field have to be met immediately.)

The fourth relates to arrangements being in place to ensure quick response to quests from the field for clarifications, on technical, administrative, personnel and personal issues that come up during fieldwork.

The fifth is the provision for a leave reserve for personnel and an administrative system that ensures replacements taking up, with the least possible delay in the fieldwork, field positions falling vacant due to members of the field staff leaving for any reason.

The sixth is the safe dispatch of the filled-in schedules, after the necessary checking up in the field, to the main office for processing of the schedules.

(8) Scrutiny, Coding, Data Entry and Tabulation: The filled-in schedules received from the field are processed further in the main office. This work can also be distributed at one or more places, depending upon the size of the inquiry, and the results combined at the main office. The filled-in schedules have to be subjected to scrutiny making use of the Scrutiny Note. This stage of processing gives us an idea of the quality of the fieldwork, the quality of field supervision and in fact the quality of preparatory work like the training of field staff and the instruction manual. The work of the scrutiny staff should of course be checked by supervisors appointed for the purpose. The entries in the schedules against different items have then to be coded by trained coding staff to facilitate tabulation of the data collected in the schedules. The coding work will also have to be checked by coding supervisors. Errors in coding lead to errors of classification of data. The data in the schedules are then ready for 'data entry' by trained data entry operators into the computers. Errors can arise during data entry and there should, therefore, be supervision and checking of this process too.

The work on scrutiny, coding and data entry need not wait for the fieldwork to be over: It can be initiated as soon as the flow of filled-in schedules start and these three stages of work can be organised in the fashion of an assembly line, linked at one end to the arrival of filled-in schedules from the field and at the other end to the tabulation domain.

This set of tables for the area can then be examined to see whether any modification needs to be made in the tabulation plan to suit our analytical needs.

Now we are ready to generate the tables as per the tabulation plan. The tables can then be checked for dimensional reliability.

(9) Analysis and Report: The data classified into a set of tables is now available to us for analysis. We may analyse the data with the help of appropriate economic and statistical analytical techniques and interpret the data collected to arrive at conclusions relevant to the objectives with which we embarked on the inquiry. The report on the inquiry is then drafted.

Q8. What do you know about sampling and non-sampling errors?

Ans. The results obtained from a sample survey may contain two types of errors: sampling and non-sampling errors. The sampling error is also called the chance error, and non-sampling errors are also called the systematic errors.

Sampling or Chance Error

Usually, all samples taken from the same population will give different results because they contain different elements of the population. Moreover, the results obtained from any one sample will not be exactly the same as the ones obtained from a census. The difference between a sample result and the result we would have obtained by conducting a census is called the sampling error, assuming that the sample is random and no non-sampling error has been made.

Definition

The sampling error is the difference between the result obtained from a sample survey and the result that would have been obtained if the whole population had been included in the survey.

The sampling error occurs because of chance, and it cannot be avoided. A sampling error can occur only in a sample survey. It does not occur in a census.

Sampling errors can be of two types–biased and unbiased. Biased errors arise on account of any bias in selection, estimation, etc. One may adopt a wrong process of selection or during the survey one may record wrong data. Further, after the survey is over, wrong methods of analysis may be used. As long as there is some bias, the survey results cannot be regarded as objective conclusions. These may turn out to be misleading. In view of this, the statistician should endeavour to make the survey as objective as possible. One way to do so is to draw a sample of adequate size on completely random basis. However, in some cases some restrictions may have to be imposed while choosing a random sample. In such cases, one should ensure that such restrictions do not introduce bias in the results. A point worth emphasising here is that sampling errors can be minimised by increasing the sample size. Of course, there is substantial reduction initially when the sample size is increased, subsequently the reduction in sampling error is not much. As such one may choose sample size in such a way that the survey results are within the permissible limits of error.

Non-sampling Errors

Even when a census survey is undertaken, there may arise several types of errors, which are known as non-sampling errors. Such errors can occur both in the census and sample survey though they are likely to be more in the census survey. These errors can occur at any stage of the survey–right from the planning stage to the execution of the survey. For example, the survey may use a defective method of data collection, or on account of entry of wrong data in the tabulation an error may occur.

Causes of Non-sampling Errors

There can be numerous causes which contribute to non-sampling errors. Some of these are:

- Using imprecise definition or wrong concepts while launching the survey.
- Entrusting the survey work to untrained and inexperienced investigators.
- Dispatching a defective mail questionnaire to respondents who may not clearly understand certain questions.

- Errors that may arise on account of non-response from respondents.
- Poor supervision of the field staff.
- Faulty tabulation while transferring the questionnaire data to tabulation sheets.
- Calculation mistakes in the processing and analysis of data.
- Committing mistakes while oral or written presentation of the survey results.

It will be seen that these are several causes responsible for non-sampling errors. Those responsible for organising and conducting a survey, whether census or sample, must be quite vigilant in carrying out their jobs. Adequate instruction must be given pointing out the possible areas where errors may occur, to the concerned staff. In this way, one can minimise the occurrence of the sampling and non-sampling errors.

Q9. Write a short note on the cost of inquiry.

Ans. Time and funds, which are not unlimited resources, act as constraints on the scope and size of an inquiry. Cost and time considerations enter at almost every stage of the inquiry and determine the scope of every aspect of the study. Preparing estimates of the cost of conducting the inquiry is part of the preparatory work relating to the inquiry. After all, the sponsor or the agency launching the inquiry should be aware of the financial implications of the inquiry and mobilise the resources needed for it. Factors that impact on the cost and duration of the inquiry are as follows:

- The decision whether the inquiry would be a census or a survey;
- The number of respondent units to be covered and their spread over space and time;
- The amount of data to be collected from each of the respondent units;
- The manner of collecting data from the respondent units- by visiting respondent units, by mail, by telephone or by extraction of information from sampled records.

Each of the factors at (1), (2), (3) and (4) above individually and together impact on the size of listing operations, the size of the schedule, the related paper and printing cost, staff cost, communication cost, processing cost (scrutiny, coding, data entry and tabulation), office expenses and other costs like analysis and report. One could derive summary measures of cost as cost per respondent unit and cost per item of data collected for each of the method of collection of data listed in (4) above as a rough guide for decisions on covering additional units or collecting additional items of data.

Items of cost

(1) Preparatory work relating to the inquiry, namely,

- preparation of the frame of the inquiry and, in the case of a sample survey, drawing a sample from it,
- finalisation of the schedule for the inquiry in consultation with data users after pretesting and pretabulation,
- recruitment of personnel required for the different stages of the inquiry,
- training programme for the field staff and scrutiny, coding and data entry staff, preparation of the training manual and manual of instructions to field workers,
- printing of schedules and related material like the training manual, instructions to different layers of field workers.

(2) Fieldwork (salaries and remuneration, traveling allowance, etc. of field staff and others involved in the field work);

(3) Stationary and office equipment and other office expenses, like postage, telephone and fax;

(4) Processing charges (remuneration/salaries of scrutiny, coding, data entry and tabulation staff, software, cost of computer time or computers, computer stationery. This work can also be got done by an outside agency, in which case the cost of getting it done);

(5) Supervision, direction and report (salaries, office expenses, stationery, word processing and so on); and

(6) Printing of the report.

Q10. Define the following terms:

(a) Population

Ans. We have a collection of units relevant for a particular inquiry. A unit, in this collection, is an entity on which we can make observations according to a well-defined procedure. The entire collection of such units is called a *population* or *universe*.

(b) Parameter

Ans. In a statistical inquiry, our interest lies in one or more characteristics of the population. A measure of such a characteristic is called a *parameter*.

For example, we may be interested in the mean income of the people of some region for a particular year. We may also like to know the standard deviation of these incomes of the people. Here, both mean and standard deviation are parameters.

(c) Statistic

Ans. Sometimes it is difficult to obtain information about the whole population. In other words, it may not be always possible to compute a population parameter. In such situations, we try to get some idea about the parameter from the information obtained from a sample drawn from the population. This sample information is summarised in the form of a *statistic*. For example, sample mean or sample median or sample mode is called a statistic. Thus, a statistic is calculated from the values of the units that are included in the sample. So, a *statistic can be defined as a function of the sample values*.

(d) Estimator and Estimate

Ans. The basic purpose of a statistic is to estimate some population parameter. The procedure followed or the formula used to compute a statistic is called an *estimator* and the value of a statistic so computed is known as an *estimate*.

(e) Inference

Ans. The purpose of drawing a sample from population is to arrive at some conclusion about the parent population from the results of the sample. This process of drawing conclusion or making inferences about the population from the information contained in the sample chosen from the sample is called inference.

Q11. Describe the various kinds of non-random sampling method.

Ans. The non-random sampling methods are often called non-probability sampling methods. In a non-random sampling method, the probability of any particular unit of the population being chosen is unknown. Here, the method of selection of sampling units is quite arbitrary as the researchers rely heavily on personal judgment. Non-random sampling methods usually do not produce samples that are representative of the general population from which they are drawn. The greatest error occurs when the researcher attempts to generalise the results on the basis of a sample to the entire population. Such an error is insidious because it is not at all obvious from merely looking at the data, or even from looking at the sample. The easiest way to recognise whether a sample is representative or not and determine whether the sample is selected randomly or not.

Nevertheless, there are occasions where non-random samples are best suited for the researcher's purpose. The various non-random sampling methods commonly used are:

(1) Convenience Sampling: Convenience sampling refers to the method of obtaining a sample that is most conveniently available to the researcher. For example, if we are interested in finding the overtime wage paid to employees working in call centres, it may be convenient and economical to sample employees of call centres in a nearby area. Also, on various issues of public interest like budget, election, price rise, etc. the television channels often present on-the-street interviews with people to reflect public opinion. It may be cautioned that the generalisation of results based on convenience sampling beyond that particular sample may not be appropriate. Convenience samples are best used for exploratory research when additional research will be subsequently conducted with a random sample. Convenience sampling is also useful in testing the questionnaires designed on a pilot basis. Convenience sampling is extensively used in marketing studies.

(2) Judgment Sampling: Judgment sampling method is also known as purposive sampling. In this method of sampling, the selection of sample is based on the researcher's judgment about some appropriate characteristic required of the sample units. For example, the calculation of consumer price index is based on a judgment sample of a basket of consumer items, and other related commodities and services which are expected to reflect a representative sample of items consumed by the people. The prices of these items are collected from selected cities which are viewed as typical cities with demographic profiles matching the national profile. In business, judgment sampling is often used to measure the performance of salesmen/saleswomen. The salesmen/saleswomen are grouped into high, medium or low performers based on certain specified qualities. Then the sales manager may actually classify the salesmen/saleswomen working under him/her who in his/her opinion will fall in which group. Judgment sampling is also often used in forecasting election results. We may often wonder how a pollster can predict an election based on only 2 to 3 per cent of votes covered. It is needless to say the method is biased and does not have any scientific basis. However, in the absence of any representative data, one may resort to this kind of non-random sampling.

(3) Quota Sampling: The quota sampling method is commonly used in marketing research studies. The samples are selected on the basis of some parameters such as age, sex, geographical region, education, income, occupation, etc. in order to make them as representative samples. The investigators, then, are assigned fixed quotas of the sample meeting these population characteristics. The purpose of quota sampling is to ensure that various sub-groups of the population are represented on pertinent sample characteristics to the extent that the investigator desires. The stratified random sampling also has this objective but should not be confused with quota sampling. In the stratified sampling method, the researcher selects a random sample from each group of the population, whereas, in quota sampling, the interviewer has a quota fixed for him/her to achieve. For example, if a city has 10 market centres, a soft drink company may decide to interview 50 consumers from each of these 10 market centres to elicit information on their products. It is entirely left to the investigator whom s/he will interview at each of the market centres. The interview may take place in the morning, mid day, or evening or it may be in the winter or summer.

Quota sampling has the advantage that the sample confirms the selected characteristics of the population that the researcher desires. Also, the cost and time involved in collecting the data are also greatly reduced. However, quota sampling has many limitations, as given below:

- In quota sampling, the respondents are selected according to the convenience of the field investigator rather than on a random basis. This kind of selection of sample may be biased. Suppose in our example of soft drinks, after the sample is taken it was found that most of the respondents belong to the lower income group then the purpose of conducting the survey becomes useless and the results may not reflect the actual situation.
- If the numbers of parameters, on which basis the quotas are fixed, are larger then it becomes difficult for the researcher to fix the quota for each sub-group.
- The field workers have the tendency to cover the quota by going to those places where the respondents may be willing to provide information and avoid those with unwilling respondents. For example, the investigators may avoid places where high income group respondents stay and cover only low income group areas.

(4) Snowball Sampling: This method is used when dealing with rare characteristic. In such cases, contacting respondent units would be difficult and costly. This method relies on referrals from initial respondents to generate additional respondents. This technique enables one to access social groups that are relatively invisible and vulnerable. This method can lower search costs substantially but this saving in cost is at the expense of the representative character of the sample. An example of this method of sampling is to find a rare genetic trait in a person and to start tracing his linkage to understand the origin, inheritance and etiology of the disease.

Q12. Define the term 'representative sample', indicate how is 'random sampling' principally different from that of 'non-random sampling?

Ans. A sample is simply a small group drawn from the survey population. Taking a sample is a way of making general statements about the whole survey population based on the responses of only a small percentage of the total survey population.

If the results obtained from the sample are to be used to make valid (true) generalisations about the whole survey population, it is important that the sample is representative. A representative sample is one that contains a good cross-section of the survey population, such as the right proportions of people of different ethnic origins, ages, social classes and sexes. The information obtained from a representative sample should provide roughly the same results as if the whole survey population had been questioned.

Difference

A conscious or subjective selection of units introduces a bias that erodes the sample's capacity to be a true representative of the characteristics of the population. It is for this reason that a random sampling procedure is preferred. Although non-random sampling is drawn without any regard to the rigours of a random sampling procedure, it gives a rough idea of the unknown features of the population under focus.

Q13. Write a short note on random sampling.

Ans. A probability/random sampling is a method of sampling that ensures that every unit in the population has a known non-zero chance of being selected. Please note that every potential sample need not have the same chance of selection. Practitioners have been using various forms of random selection, the most popular being a random number table. Today, computers have replaced the random number table and the software generates the random numbers in a scientific manner very fast.

There are quite a few variant of random sampling:

- Simple Random Sampling (With Replacement) [SRSWR],

- Simple Random Sampling (Without Replacement)[SRSWOR],
- Interpenetrating Sub-Samples (I-Pss),
- Systematic Sampling (SYS),
- Sampling with Probability Proportional to Size (PPS),
- Stratified Sampling (STs),
- Cluster Sampling(CS), and
- Multi-Stage Sampling (MSS).

Q14. What is Simple Random Sampling With Replacement (SRSWR)? Explain the procedure for drawing sample by SRSWR method with the help of example. How will you estimate the population mean and variance of sample drawn by SRSWR method?

[June-2012, Q.No.-3] [Dec-2011, Q.No-3]

Or

What is systematic sampling? Explain the procedure for drawing sample by systematic sampling. How will you estimate the population mean of the sample drawn by systematic sampling?

[June-2011, Q.No.-3]

Or

What is Simple Random Sampling without replacement (SRSWOR)? State the procedure for drawing sample by SRSWOR. How will you estimate the population mean of the sample drawn by SRSWOR? [Dec-2012, Q.No.-3]

Ans. Simple random sampling is said to be "with replacement". When the sample member are drawn from the population one by one, and after each drawing, the selected population unit is noted and then returned to the population before the next one is drawn. This means that at each stage of the sampling process all the population units (including those obtained in earlier drawings) are considered for selection with equal probability. Thus, the population remains the same before each drawing and any of the population units may appear more than once in the sample.

Operational procedure for selecting the sample by SRSWR Method

We can assign one card to each unit in the population with the necessary identification particulars (or just the identification number) specified on it. These are then put into a bowl or a suitable container and shuffled thoroughly. Thereafter, a card is drawn, its identification noted. The card is placed back into the container and the contents thoroughly shuffled again before the second card is drawn as before. In this way n (the sample size) cards are drawn. The identification numbers noted down indicate the units included in the sample. Such a procedure is tedious especially when a large sample is to be drawn and the population is also large. The shuffling of the cards cannot also be done thoroughly enough to ensure random selection of units. It is better to make use of tables of random numbers for drawing random samples. These tables contain a series of four-digited (or five-digited or ten-digited) random numbers. Supposing a sample of 30 units is to be selected out of a population of 3000 units. First, allot one number from the set of numbers to 0001 to 3000 as the identification number to each one of the population units. The problem of drawing the sample of size 30 then reduces to that of selecting 30 random numbers, one after another, from the random number tables. Turn a page of the Tables at random and start noting down, from the first column of (four or five or ten-digit) random numbers, the first four digits of the numbers from the top of the column downwards. Continue this operation on to the second column till the required sample size of 30 is selected. If any of these random numbers is more than 3000, it should be rejected. Some numbers (<3000) would be repeated in the process, and this means that a unit of the population would be selected more than once, this being sampling with replacement.

Estimation of the Population Mean

Let us look at the estimates of the population mean and other parameters. Let us first select a sample of one unit, say, 'u_1', from the population of N units U_i, i = 1,2,...,N by the simple random sampling method. Let y_1 be the value of the variable Y for the selected unit u_1. This single sample observation y_1 is itself the sample mean m and is an estimate of the population mean $M = \frac{1}{N}\sum_{i=1}^{N} Y_i$. Since any of the N units could be selected with the probability of selection $\left(\frac{1}{N}\right)$, the single sample observation 'y_1' is a random variable assuming values Y_i, i=1,2,3,.....,N with probability $\frac{1}{N}$. Hence,

$$E(y_1 = m) = \sum_{i=1}^{N} Y_i \frac{1}{N} = \frac{1}{N}\sum_{i=1}^{N} Y_i = M$$

$$E(y_1) = \frac{1}{N}\sum_{i=1}^{N} Y_i = M \qquad ...(i)$$

Let us now take up the case of a sample of n units $[u_i]$ i = 1,2,...,n being drawn by SRSWR from the population $\{U_i\}$ i = 1,2,....,N. Let y_i, i = 1,2,...,n be the sample observations and Y_i, i = 1,2,....,N be the population values of the characteristic y. Each sample observation y_i is a random variable which assumes values Y_i, i = 1,2,....,N with equal probability and is, therefore, an unbiased estimator of the population mean M as shown above. The sample mean $m=\frac{1}{n}\sum_{i=1}^{n}y_i$ is the mean of n unbiased estimates of M and is, therefore, also an unbiased estimator of M. Denoting the sample mean in SRSWR as m_{srswr} we have,

$$E(m_{srswr})=E\left[\frac{1}{n}\sum_{i=1}^{n}y_i\right]=\frac{1}{n}\sum_{i=1}^{n}E(y_i)=\frac{1}{n}\sum_{i=1}^{n}M=\frac{1}{n}nM=M$$

$$m_{srswr}=\frac{1}{n}\sum_{i=1}^{n}y_i \text{ is an unbiased estimator for M} \qquad \text{...(ii)}$$

If a unit gets selected in the sample more than once, the corresponding value of y_i will also have to be repeated as many times in the summation for calculating m_{srswr}.

Sampling Variance of the Sample Mean

Let us take the case of a sample of one unit

The Sampling Variance

$(y_1 = m) = E[y_1 - E(y_1)]^2 = E[m - E(m)]^2 = E[m - M]^2 = \sigma^2$

This can also be expressed further in two different ways [see A-1(i) in the Annexure]:

$$V(y_1)=\sigma^2 = E(y_1^2)-M^2 = \frac{1}{N}\sum_{i=1}^{N}Y_i^2 - M^2 \qquad \text{...(iii)}$$

Let the sample be of size 'n'. The sampling variance of the sample mean from a sample of size 'n' in SRSWR can be shown to be [see A-1(ii) in the Annexure for derivation]

$$\text{Sampling Variance of } m_{srswr}, V(m_{srswr})=\frac{\sigma^2}{n}. \qquad \text{...(iv)}$$

$$\text{Then, Standard Error of } m_{srswr} \; SE(m_{srswr})=\frac{\sigma}{\sqrt{n}} \qquad \text{...(v) \&}$$

$$\text{CV or RSE of } m_{srswr} \; C(m_{srswr})=\left(\frac{1}{\sqrt{n}}\right)\left(\frac{\sigma}{M}\right)=\frac{C(y)}{\sqrt{n}} \qquad \text{...(vi)}$$

The sampling variance, SE and CV (RSE) of the sample mean in SRSWR is much less than the corresponding population parameters for the variable y. These decrease as the sample size increases. The precision of the sample mean in SRSWR, as an estimator of M increases as the sample size increases. However, the extent of decrease in the standard error will not be commensurate with the size of the increase in the sample size.

Other useful expressions for $V(y_i)=\sigma^2$ and $V(m_{srswr})=\frac{\sigma^2}{n}$ are [see A-1(ii) in the Annexure for derivation]:

$$\sigma^2=E(y_i^2)-M^2 \quad ...(vii)$$

$$\frac{\sigma^2}{n}=E(m^2)-M^2 \quad ...(viii)$$

We must also try and get **an unbiased estimator of** $V(m_{srswr})=\frac{\sigma^2}{n}$, as σ^2 may not be known. We can expect that a function of sample observations similar to the functional form of variance, namely, the sample variance $S^2=\frac{1}{n}\sum_{i=1}^{n}(y_i-m_{srswr})^2$ could be an unbiased estimator of σ^2. While the details of this derivation is presented in A-2 of the Annexure, we may note from the result there that $E(s^2)$ turns out to be $\frac{n-1}{n}\sigma^2$ and, therefore, an unbiased estimator of

$$\sigma^2 \text{ is } v(y)=\left\{\frac{1}{n-1}\right\}\sum_{i=1}^{n}(y_i-m_{srswr})^2=\left[\frac{1}{n-1}\right][ss]^2 \quad ...(ix)$$

and an unbiased estimator of $\frac{\sigma^2}{n}=v(m_{srswr})=\frac{v(y)}{n}$ ...(x)

Q15. What is systematic sampling without replacement? How will you estimate the population mean and of the sample drawn by systematic sampling?

Ans. In this selection procedure, if a unit from a population of size N is selected, it is not returned to the population. Thus, for any subsequent selection, the population size is reduced by one.

Obviously, at the time of the first selection, the population size is N and probability of a unit being selected randomly is 1/N, for the second unit to be randomly selected, the population size is (N-1) and the probability of selection of any one of the remaining is 1/(N-1), similarly at the third draw, the probability of selection is 1/(N-2) and so on. Here no member of the population can occur more than once in the sample.

Estimation of Population Mean

Having drawn a random sample of n units (u_i) (i = 1,2,.........n) from a population $\{U_i)$ (i = 1,2,.............N) by SRSWOR, we should like to estimate the population mean $M=\frac{1}{N}\sum_{i=1}^{N}Y_i$. Let us use the sample mean $m_{srswor}=\frac{1}{n}\sum_{i=1}^{n}y_i$. The derivation of $E(m_{srswor})$ in A-3 of the Annexure shows that m_{srswor} is an unbiased estimator of M.

Sampling Variance of the Sample Mean in SRSWOR

What is the precision of the estimator m_{srswor}? How does it compare with that of m_{srswr}? The variance of m_{srswor} is derived in A-4 in the Annexure. Two results derived there are:

$$V(m_{srswor})=E\left[m_{srswor}{}^{2}\right]-M^2 \qquad ...(i)$$

$$V(m_{srswor})=\frac{N-n}{N-1}\frac{\sigma^2}{n}=\frac{N-n}{N-1}\cdot\frac{1}{n}\cdot\frac{1}{N}\sum_{i=1}^{N}(Y_i-M)^2 \qquad ...(ii)$$

Compare equation (eq-2) with equation $\left(m_{srswr},V(m_{srswr})=\frac{\sigma^2}{n}\right)$ under SRSWR. Since (N - n)/(N – 1) is less than 1 for n> 1,

$$\frac{N-n}{N-1}\frac{\sigma^2}{n}<\frac{\sigma^2}{n}, \text{or } V(m)_{srswor}<V(m_{srswr}). \qquad ...(iii)$$

$$V(m_{srswor})=\frac{N-n}{N-1}\frac{\sigma^2}{n}=\frac{N-n}{N-1}\cdot\frac{1}{n}\cdot\frac{1}{N}\sum_{i=1}^{N}(Y_i-M)^2 \qquad ...(iv)$$

Compare equation (iv) with equation $\left(m_{srswr},V(m_{srswr})=\frac{\sigma^2}{n}\right)$ under SRSWR.

Since (N – n)/(N – 1) is less than 1 for n> 1,

$$\frac{N-n}{N-1}\frac{\sigma^2}{n}<\frac{\sigma^2}{n}, \text{or } V(m)_{srswor}<V(m_{srswr}). \qquad ...(v)$$

The sample mean based on SRSWOR and SRSWR is an unbiased estimator of the population mean M but the one based on SRSWOR is a more efficient estimator of M than the one based on SRSWR. The sampling variance of the sample mean under SRSWOR is smaller than the sampling variance under SRSWOR by a factor $\frac{N-n}{N-1}$. This is because an SRSWOR sample has 'n' distinct units while an SRSWR sample has less than 'n' distinct units. The factor $\frac{N-n}{n-1}$ is called the ***finite population correction or finite population multiplier.*** Such a correction factor becomes necessary when the population is finite. The finite population correction gets closer to one as N becomes large, that is for large populations, and when the population size is large relative to the sample size. For instance, the finite population correction need not be used when the sampling fraction $\frac{n}{N}$ is less than 0.05.

Sampling by SRSWOR method is, therefore, a better sampling method than SRSWR, from the point of view of precision of the sample mean as an estimator of M, especially when the population is not large and the sampling fraction is larger than 0.05.

Unbiased Estimate of Sampling Variance of the Sample Mean

We find that the expression for V (m) contains the population variance. We cannot find the value of the sampling variance of the sample mean m if the value σ^2 is not known. We would then need an estimate of V (m) based on the sample. Such an unbiased estimate is (see the derivation in A-5 in the Annexure):

$$v\left(m_{srswor}\right)=\frac{N-n}{N}\cdot\frac{1}{n}\cdot\frac{1}{n-1}\sum_{i=1}^{n}\left(y_i-m\right)^2=\frac{N-n}{N}\cdot\frac{1}{n}\cdot\frac{1}{n-1}[ss]^2 \qquad \text{...(vi)}$$

Estimates of Total and Proportion

Unbiased estimates of total, or, Y, can be obtained by multiplying unbiased estimates of M by N. V(Y*) (Y* is the estimate of Y) and an unbiased estimate of V(Y*), namely, v(Y*) can be obtained by multiplying the corresponding expressions for 'm' by N^2. C of Y* is the same as that of 'm'.

The sample proportion 'p' is an unbiased estimate of the population proportion 'P' in SRSWOR also. The expressions for V(p) and v(p) can easily be derived for SRSWOR as follows using the technique we adopted in SRSWR.

$$V(P)=\frac{N-n}{N-1}\frac{PQ}{n}, \text{where } P+Q=1 \qquad \text{...(vii)}$$

$$C(p)=\sqrt{\frac{N-n}{N-1}}\cdot\sqrt{\frac{1}{n}}\cdot\sqrt{\frac{Q}{P}} \quad \text{and} \qquad \text{...(viii)}$$

$$v(p)=\frac{N-n}{N}\cdot\frac{pq}{n-1} \text{where } p+q=1 \qquad \text{...(ix)}$$

Q16. Discuss the method of interpenetrating sub-samples.

Ans. When two or more samples are taken from the same population by the same process of selection the samples are called interpenetrating samples. Suppose a sample is selected in the form of $k(\geq 2)$ subsamples, each subsample being selected by the same sampling procedure. If each subsample gives a valid estimate of the population parameter θ, then this network of subsamples forms interpenetrating subsamples. If the subsamples are drawn independently then an unbiased variance estimator is readily obtained.

Suppose the subsamples produce estimates $t_1,...,t_k$ when $E(t_i)=\theta, i=1,........k$. An overall unbiased estimate of $=k(k-1)V(\bar{t})$. and an unbiased estimator of $V(\bar{t})$ is

$$V(\bar{t})=\frac{1}{k(k-1)}\sum_{i=1}^{k}\left(t_i-\bar{t}\right)^2 \qquad ...(i)$$

because

$$E\left(\sum_{i=1}^{k}(t_i-\bar{t})^2\right)=\sum_{i=1}^{k}E\left(t_i^2\right)-kE(\bar{t}^2)=\sum_{i=1}^{k}\{V(t_i)+\theta^2\}-k\{V(\bar{t})+\theta^2\}$$

$$=\sum_{i=1}^{k}V(t_i)-kV(\bar{t}) =k(k-1)V(\bar{t}).$$

The explicit formulae for $V(\bar{t})$ and its unbiased estimator may often be very complex. Equation (1) gives a ready estimator of $V(\bar{t})$. However, $V(\bar{t})$ may not be as precise an estimator as the one based on explicit expression for $V(\bar{t})$.

The method of interpenetrating sub-samples is thus useful in arriving at unbiased estimates of (a) the population parameter, (b) the sampling variance of the estimator and (c) a confidence interval for the parameter in diverse situations because of its operational convenience. It is also useful in assessing non-sampling errors.

Q17. Describe the method of drawing a systematic sample. What problem do you face in selecting the sample? Is the sample mean unbiased parameter of population mean M. How do you overcome these problems? What is the sampling variance of m_{sys}, and how do you get $v(m_{sys})$?

Ans. Systematic sampling is very convenient in practice and is often used in field surveys. The scheme is operationally more convenient than simple random sampling and ensures at the same time equal probability of inclusion of each unit in the sample. Suppose that the units are numbered 1 through N and n units are to be selected. Assume N/n = k, an integer. Arrange the population units into an $n \times k$ array as shown in Table 2.1 and select a random number, say, r between 1 to k. The sample consists of the unit r and every kth unit thereafter, that is, the sample is $\{r, r+k, r+2k, ..., r+(n-1)k\}$. The number r is called the random start and k the sampling interval. Denoting the columns of the array as $S_1, ..., S_k$, it is seen that there are k systematic samples, each having the probability of selection 1/k. Hence, inclusion probability of any particular unit in the sample is 1/k = n/N. In this case, sample size is always fixed at n.

Table 2.1

1	2	...	r	...	k
$(k+1)$	$(k+2)$	...	$k+r$	...	$2k$
		...		...	
$\underbrace{(n-1)k+1}_{S_1}$	$\underbrace{}_{S_2}$	...	$\underbrace{}_{S_r}$	...	$\underbrace{nk}_{S_k}$
		...		...	

Some difficulty, however, arises if N is not an integral multiple of n.

Estimation of Population Mean

Let Y_i be the values assumed by the variable associated with the unit U_i, i =1,2........N. An unbiased estimator of the population mean M based on a systematic sample is given by a slight variant of the sample mean. It is

$m_{sys}* = \left(\frac{k}{N}\right)\sum_{i=1}^{n^*} y_i$, where n^* is the size of the selected sample and k the sampling interval.

If N=nk, n*=n and the estimator m* =m, the sample mean $\frac{1}{n}\sum_{i=1}^{n} y_i$.

What is the bias in using the sample mean as the estimator for M? Let us consider the difference between m and m^* for a sample with size n^*.

$$m^* - m = \frac{k}{N}\sum_{i=1}^{n^*} y_i - \left(\frac{1}{n^*}\right)\sum_{i=1}^{n^*} y_i$$

$$= \left(\frac{k}{N} - \frac{1}{n^*}\right)\sum_{i=1}^{n^*} y_i = \left(\frac{k}{N} - \frac{1}{n^*}\right) n^* m = \left(\frac{kn^*}{N} - 1\right) m$$

The bias $\left(\frac{kn^*}{N} - 1\right)$ is likely to be negligible if 'n' (or n^*) is not very small and N is very large. The bias is thus likely to be small in the case of systematic samples selected from a large population.

Circular Systematic Sampling

Linear systematic sampling does not always lead to the desired sample size n if N/n is not an integer, in which case $\bar{y}$ is not unbiased for $\overline{Y}$. This difficulty is overcome by the use of circular systematic sampling (css), first suggested by Lahiri (1954b). Here k is taken as $[N/n]^*$, the integer nearest to N/n. A random number is chosen from 1 to N and the units corresponding to this random number is chosen as the random start. Thereafter every kth unit is chosen in a cyclical manner till a sample of n units is selected. Thus, if r is a number selected at random from 1 to N, the sample consists of units corresponding to these numbers,

$$\{r+jk\} \text{ if } r+jk \leq N$$

$$(r+jk-N) \text{ if } r+jk>N,\ j=0,1,\ldots,(n-1).$$

As an example, if N = 37, n =5, r =26, the sample is {26, 33, 3, 10, 17}. Clearly, there are N possible samples. One corresponding to each random start r (= 1, ...,N) and each sample is chosen with the same probability 1/N. Hence, the inclusion probability of each unit in the sample is n/N, because a unit may occur in the sample either in the first position, second position, ..., or the nth position. Unlike in an Iss, a sample mean in css is always an unbiased estimator of a population mean.

$$E(\bar{y})=\frac{1}{N}\sum_{r=1}^{N}\left(\frac{1}{n}\sum_{i=1}^{n}y_i\right)_r=\frac{1}{Nn}\sum_{r=1}^{N}\left(\sum_{i=1}^{n}y_i\right)_r\bar{Y}$$

where r stands for the sample selected with the random start r.

$$V(\bar{y})=\frac{1}{N}\sum_{r=1}^{N}(\bar{y}_r-\bar{Y})^2.$$

An Unbiased Estimate of Sampling Variance of the Sample Mean

Let nk = N. Then $m^*=m$. There are k possible samples each with a probability of $\frac{1}{k}$. Let the sample mean of the r-th systematic sample be $m_r=\frac{1}{n}\sum_{i=1}^{n}y_{ir}$, where y_{ir} is the value of the characteristic under study for the i-th unit in the r-th systematic sample. Since $E(m_r)=M$. Denoting the mean in systematic sampling as m_{sys}, the sampling variance of m_{sys} is derived in A-6, the results of interest are:

$$V(m_{sys})=\sigma_b^2 \text{ (the between-sample variance)} \quad \text{...(i)}$$

$$V(m_{sys})=V(y)-\sigma_w^2, \text{ where } \sigma_w^2 \text{ is within-sample variance} \quad \text{...(ii)}$$

It is clear from equation 1 that the variance of the sample mean is less than the variance of the variable (characteristic) under study or the population variance, since σ_w^2 is a positive quantity. Further, V(m) can be reduced by increasing σ_w^2, or by increasing the within-sample variance. This would happen ***if the units within each systematic samples are as heterogeneous as possible.*** Since we select a sample of n units from the population of N units by selecting every k-th element from the random start 'r', the population is divided into 'n' groups and we select one unit from each of these 'n' groups of population units. Units within a sample would be heterogeneous if there is heterogeneity between the 'n' groups. This would imply that units within each of the n groups would have to be as homogeneous as possible. All these suggest that the sampling variance of the sample mean is related to the arrangement of the units in the population. This is both an advantage and disadvantage of systematic sampling. An arrangement that conforms to the conditions mentioned above would lead to a smaller sampling variance or an efficient estimate of the population mean while a 'bad' arrangement would lead estimates that are not as efficient.

How does $V(m_{sys})$ compare with $V(m_{srswr})$ and $V(m_{srswor})$? This depends on the correlation between pair of units in the systematic sample (called intraclass correlation coefficient). It can be shown that $V(m_{sys})$ is less than $V(m_{srswr})$ if this correlation is negative. $V(m_{sys})$ is less than $V(m_{srswor})$ if this correlation is less than $-\frac{1}{N-1}$.

There is another aspect that needs to be noted in respect of systematic sampling. Systematic sampling is not recommended when there is a periodic or cyclic variation in the population. We get inefficient samples in such cases if the sampling interval k is equal to the period of the cycle or a multiple of the period. If the period of the cycle is known, we should choose the sampling interval k as **an odd multiple of one-half of the period** to overcome the problem of periodic and cyclic variation. An example of periodic variation is easily given from the population census. The individual slips of the members of a household will usually occur in a certain order-head of the household, his wife and children according to their age. If the sampling interval is equal to or a multiple of the average household size, then the sample selected will be one with similar characteristics-predominantly wives or mainly heads of households or mostly children.

An Unbiased Estimate of the Sampling Variance of the Sample Mean

It is not possible to get an unbiased estimate of the variance of the sample mean of a systematic sample. This is because this involves the estimation of the sum $\sum\Sigma Y_i Y_j$ or the sum of the product of pairs of the values of the N units in the population. It is not possible to estimate this sum as some of these pairs have no chance of getting selected in a sample when we draw systematic samples. This is a disadvantage of systematic sampling. However, there is a method of getting an unbiased estimate of the sampling variance of the sampling mean in systematic sampling by drawing interpenetrating sub-samples (I-P sub-samples). Suppose we need to select a systematic sample of size 'n'. Instead of selecting one sample of size 'n' as a single systematic sample, let us select the sample of size 'n' in two or more systematic samples of the same size, say, p sub-samples of size $\frac{n}{p}$ each, drawing each of these sub-samples with an independent random start. We thus have p independent sub-samples and the corresponding unbiased estimators of the population mean M, namely, $\{m_i\} i=1,2,.....p$. A combined unbiased estimator of M and an unbiased estimator of the variance of the sampling variance of m_{sys} are given by:

$$m_{sys-IP} = \frac{1}{p}\sum_{i=1}^{p} m_i \qquad ...(iii)$$

$$v(m_{sys-IP}) = \frac{1}{p(p-1)}\sum_{i=1}^{p}(m_i - m)^2, p = \text{no. of I-P sub-samples} \qquad ...(iv)$$

Q18. Discuss the method of PPS in detail.

Or

What is done in the PPS method of suitably weight the sample observation (at the estimation stage) so as to obtain unbiased estimates of population parameters.

Or

How to take a random sample with PPSWR? What are the operational steps involved in drawing a PPS sample with replacement?

Ans. Probability proportional to size (PPS) is a sampling technique for use with surveys or mini-surveys in which the probability of selecting a sampling unit (e.g. village, zone, district, health center) is proportional to the size of its population. It gives a probability (i.e. random, representative) sample.

It is most useful when the sampling units vary considerably in size because it assures that those in larger sites have the same probability of getting into the sample as those in smaller sites, and vice verse. This method also facilitates planning for field work because a pre-determined number of respondents is interviewed in each unit selected, and staff can be allocated accordingly.

Suitably weight the sample observation (at the estimation stage) so as to obtain unbiased estimates of population parameters. The weights are the probabilities of selection of the units.

Let the population units be $\{U_1, U_2, ... U_N\}$. Let the main variable Y and the related size variable X associated with these units be $\{Y_1, X_1; Y_2, X_2; ..... Y_N, X_N\}$. The probability of selecting any unit, say, U_i in the sample will be

$$P_i = \left(\frac{X_i}{X}\right), \text{ where } \sum_{i=1}^{N} X_i = X.$$

Let us select one unit by PPS method. Let the unit selected thus have the values y_1 and x_1 for the variables y and x. The variables y and x are random variables assuming values Y_i and X_i respectively, with probabilities $P_i, i = 1, 2, ... N$. An unbiased estimator of the population total $Y = \sum Y_i$, summation being from $i = 1$ to N is given by

$$Y^*_{(1)pps} = \frac{Y_1}{P_1} \qquad ...(i)$$

$$\text{as } E(Y_1^*) = E\frac{y_1}{P_1} = \sum_{i=1}^{N} \frac{Y_i}{P_i} P_i = \sum_{i=1}^{N} Y_i = Y$$

Let K be a constant. What is $E(KY_1{}^*)$?

$$E\left\{K\left(\frac{Y_1}{P_1}\right)\right\} = KE\left(\frac{y_1}{p_1}\right) = KY_1^*$$

$$\text{If } K = \frac{1}{N},$$

we get an unbiased estimate of the population mean M as

$$m^*_{(1)pps} = \left(\frac{1}{N}\right) Y^*_{(1)pps} = \frac{1}{N}\frac{y_1}{p_1} \qquad ...(ii)$$

The variance of $Y^*_{(1)PPS}$ is given by (see A-7 in the Annexure for the derivation)

$$V\left[Y^*_{(1)pps}\right]=\sum_{i=1}^{N}\frac{Y_i^2}{P_i}-Y^2 \qquad ...(iii)$$

It would be clear from the expression for the variance that the variance of the estimate will be small if the P_i are proportional to Y_i. The variance of KY_1* being $K^2V(Y_1*)$, the variance of the unbiased estimator of the population mean m^*_{1-PPS} will be $(1/N^2)V(Y_1*)$.

$$V\left[m^*_{(1)pps}\right]=\frac{1}{N^2}\left(\sum_{i=1}^{N}\frac{Y_i^2}{P_i}-Y^2\right) \qquad ...(iv)$$

PPS Sampling With Replacement (PPSWR)

A sample of n units with PPS can be drawn with or without replacement. Let us first deal with PPSWR. Let a sample of n units be drawn by PPS with replacement (PPSWR) method. Let $\{y_i, p_i\}$ be respectively the sample observation on the selected unit and the initial probability of selection at the i-th draw, i = 1,2,.....n.. The quantities $\frac{y_i}{p_i}$ are independent random variables, each taking the N values $\frac{Y_1}{P_1},\frac{Y_2}{P_2},.....\frac{Y_N}{P_N}$ with probabilities $P_1,P_2,.......,P_N$ respectively. Each $\frac{y_i}{p_i}, i=1,2,...,n$ in the sample is an unbiased estimate of the population total $Y=\sum Y_i$, the summation being from $i=1 \text{ to } N$ and denoted by Y_i*. The sampling variance of Y_i* is

$$V\left(Y^*_{(i)pps}\right)=\sum_{r=1}^{N}\left(\frac{Y_r^2}{P_r}\right)-Y^2.$$

An unbiased estimator of Y based on the sample of size n will be the average of the n independent unbiased estimators, namely,

$$Y^*_{ppswr}=\frac{1}{n}\sum_{i=1}^{n}\frac{y_i}{p_i}=\frac{1}{n}\sum_{i=1}^{n}Y^* \qquad ...(v)$$

The sampling variance of $V(Y^*)$ will be $V\left[\frac{1}{n}\sum_{i=1}^{n}\frac{y_i}{p_i}\right]$. As shown in A-8 in the Annexure, it reduces to

$$V\left(Y^*_{ppswr}\right)=\frac{1}{n}\left[\sum_{r=1}^{N}\left(\frac{Y_r^2}{P_r}\right)-Y^2\right] \qquad ...(vi)$$

$$V\left(m_{ppswr}\right) \text{ will then be } =\left(\frac{1}{N^2}\right)\left(\frac{1}{n}\right)\sum\left(\frac{Y_r^2}{P_r}\right)-Y^2 \qquad ...(vii)$$

This expression for sampling variance of the estimator $Y*$ contains the population parameter Y and can be of little use if Y is not known. We should, therefore, be interested in arriving at an unbiased estimator of $V(Y*)$ which does not depend on any population parameter. We have now a sample of size n drawn by PPSWR method and we, therefore, have n independent unbiased estimates of $Y*$. An unbiased estimate of the sampling variance of $Y*$ as shown in A-9 in the Annexure is given by:

$$v\left(Y^*_{ppswr}\right)=\frac{1}{n(n-1)}\left[\sum\frac{y_i^2}{p_i^2}-nY^{*^2}\right] \quad ...(viii)$$

Operational Procedure for Drawing a PPSWR Sample

There are N units in the population $\{U_i\}$, with size $\{X_i\}, i=1,......., N$.

- We first cumulate the sizes of the units and arrive at the cumulative totals of the unit sizes. Thus $T_{i-1}=X_1+X_2+......+X_{i-1}; T_i=X_1+X_2+..+X_{i-1}+X_i=T_{i-1}+X_i; i=1,2...,N.$
- We then choose a random number R between 1 and $T_N=X_1+X_2+....+X_N=X.$
- We choose the unit U_i if R lies between T_{i-1} and T_i, that is, if $T_{i-1}<R\le T_i$. The probability $P(U_i)$ of selecting the i-th unit will thus be
$$P(U_i)=\frac{T_i-T_{i-1}}{T_N}=\frac{X_i}{X}=P_i.$$
- We repeat the operation n times for selecting a sample of size n with PPSWR.

Q19. Discuss the method of stratified sampling in detail.

Ans. Sometimes it may be necessary or desirable to classify the universe into a number of groups and treat each of these groups as a separate universe for purposes of sampling. Each of these groups is called a **stratum.** The process of grouping is called **stratification.** Estimates obtained from each stratum can then be combined to arrive at estimates for the entire universe. This method is very useful as (i) it gives estimates not only for the whole universe but also for the sub-universes and (ii) it affords the choice of different sampling methods for different strata as appropriate. This method is known as **Stratified Sampling.** This method is useful in several situations like.

- a survey organisation has regional field offices,
- valid estimates are required at sub-population levels like regions, groups of population and so on, and

- different sampling methods can be used for different groups, depending on the availability of additional information regarding variables related to the variable under study.

The population (universe) of N units is divided into k strata. Let N_s be the number of units in the s-th stratum and Y_{si} be the value of the i-th unit in the s-th stratum. Let the population mean of the s-th stratum be M_s.

$M_s = \frac{1}{N_s}\sum_{i=1}^{N_s} Y_{si}$ (that is over the units within the s-th stratum) and the population M is $= \frac{1}{N}\sum_{s=1}^{k} N_s M_s = \sum_{s=1}^{k} W_s M_s$, where $W_s = \frac{N_s}{N}$. Suppose that we select random samples from each stratum and the sampling method for different strata are different. Let the unbiased estimate of the population mean M_s of the s-th stratum be m_s. Denoting 'st' for stratified sampling an unbiased estimator of M is given by

$$m_{st} = \sum_{s=1}^{k} W_s m_s = \frac{1}{N}\sum_{s=1}^{k} N_s m_s \qquad \text{...(i)\&}$$

Sampling var. of

$$m_{st} = V(m_{st}) = \sum W_s^2 \, V(m_s) = \frac{1}{N^2}\sum_{s=1}^{k} N_s^2 \, V(m_s) \qquad \text{...(ii)}$$

[Cov.$(m_s, m_r) = 0$ for $s \neq r$, as the samples from different strata are independently chosen]

The estimator for the population total Y is given by

$Y_{st}{}^* = Nm_{st} = \sum N_s m_s = \sum Y_s$ and

$V(Y_{st}^*) = V(Nm_{st}) = N^2 V(m_{st}) = \sum N_s^2 V(m_s) = \sum V(Y_s^*)$. Thus

$$Y_{st}^* = \sum_{s=1}^{k} Y_s^* \qquad \text{...(iii)\&}$$

$$V(Y_{st}^*) = \sum_{s=1}^{k} V(Y_s^*) \qquad \text{...(iv)}$$

Thus, efficient estimators, that is, estimators with smaller variance can be obtained in stratified sampling if we form the strata in such a way as to minimise intra-strata or within-strata variation. This would mean maximising between-strata or inter-strata variation, since the total variation is made up of within-strata and between-strata variation. In other words, units in a stratum should be homogeneous.

Stratified sampling enables us to choose the sample we wish to select by drawing independent samples from each of the different strata into which we have grouped the universe. How do we allocate the total sample size 'n' among the different strata? One way is to allocate the sample size to different strata in proportion to the size of individual strata measured by the number of units in these strata, namely,

$N_s, [\sum_{s=1}^{k} N_s = N]$. This method is especially appropriate in situations where no information is available except the sizes of the strata. The sample size for the samples from the stratum, say, the s-th stratum, would then be $n_s = n\frac{N_s}{N}$ and $\sum n_s$ can easily seen to be equal to 'n'. There are other methods like allocation of the sample size among strata in proportion to the stratum totals of the variable under study, that is, Y_s, the stratum total of the s-th stratum, 's' varying from 1 to k. We can determine the optimum stratum-wise-sample-size by minimising the sampling variance of the sample mean (eq-2) subject to the constraint that the cost of the survey is fixed. As derived in A-10 in the Annexure, the stratum-wise optimum sample size will then be

$$n_s = \left[(F - F_0)\right]\left[\frac{W_s\sqrt{\frac{V_s}{F_s}}}{\sum_{s=1}^{k} W_s\sqrt{V_s F_s}}\right] \qquad \text{...(v)}$$

The stratum sample size should, therefore, be proportional to $W_s\sqrt{\frac{V}{F_s}}$. The minimum variance with the n_s so determined is, from equations (b) and (c) of the Annexure,

$$\text{Min } V(m_{st}) = \frac{\left[\sum_{s=1}^{k} W_s\sqrt{V_s F_s}\right]^2}{F - F_0} \qquad \text{...(vi)}$$

Q20. Write a short note on the multistage sampling.

Ans. Multi-stage sampling refers to a sampling technique, which is carried out in various stages. Under this method, the population is regarded as made of number of first stage units also called primary units, each of which consists of a number of secondary stage units, each of which further composed of third stage units and so on, till we arrive with the desired sampling unit. The book you can believe most – GPH Book.

In multistage sampling, sampling is carried out stage by stage within the selected clusters, instead of enumerating all units in the sampled clusters, as in cluster sampling.

Multistage sampling consists in sampling first stage units by a suitable method of sampling. From among, the selected first stage units, a sub sample of secondary stage units is drawn by suitable method of sampling. Further stages of selection may be carried out till we reach the desired sampling units. Same or different methods of sampling may be followed for various stages of sampling. For example, if an education information team which attempts to study the preference of courses in universities wishes to collect preferences from 5000 students. The team considers universities in India as first stage units, then the number of colleges as the second stage units, branches of study (Arts, science, Management) as third stage units and selection of students as the fourth stage. Each stage serves as a mechanism of reduction in the sample size.

Q21. What are basis of choice of an appropriate sampling method?

Ans. Sampling efficiency and precision of the estimate are not only factor, which determine the type of sampling method to use for a study. The availability of relevant information on which to draw the sample and the cost in time and travel to locate the respondents must also be considered in choosing a practical sampling method.

(1) Suppose we do not have any a priori information about the nature of the population variable under study. SRSWR and SRSWOR would then be the appropriate methods. Both are operationally simple. However, since $V(m_{srswor}) < V(m_{srswr})$, SRSWOR is to be preferred. SRSWOR provides a more precise estimate of M than SRSWR for the sample size (and, therefore, more or less the same cost). The extent of reduction in variance of m being (n – 1)/(N – 1), the advantage of SRSWOR over SRSWR holds only when the sampling fraction is not small, or N and n are not large.

(2) Systematic sampling is operationally even simpler than SRSWR and SRSWOR, but it should not be used for sampling from population where periodic or cyclic trends/variations exist. This difficulty can be overcome if the period of the cycle is known, by choosing the sampling interval to be equal to an odd multiple of one-half of the period. $V(m_{sys})$ can be reduced if the units chosen in the sample are as heterogeneous as possible. But this will call for a rearrangement of the population units before sampling.

(3) Sometimes, additional information is available about the variable 'y' under study, say, on a variable (size variable) 'x' related to 'y'. The PPS

method is designed to make use of such information and should be preferred in such a case. The sampling variance of Y* (or m) gets reduced when the probability of selection of units $P_i = (X_i / N)$ are proportional to Y_i, that is, the size X_i is proportional to Y_i or the variables x and y are linearly related to each other and the regression line passes through the origin. In such cases PPS is more efficient than SRSWR. An added advantage is that this method can be utilised along with other sampling methods and their relative efficiencies. PPS is also operationally simple. PPS-WOR combines the efficiency of SRSWOR and the efficiency increasing capacity of PPS. However, most of the procedures of selection available, estimators and their variance for PPS-WOR are complicated and are not commonly used in practice. This is particularly so in large-scale sample surveys with a small sampling fraction, as in such cases sampling without replacement does not result in much gain in efficiency. Hence, unless the sample size is small, we should prefer PPSWR.

(4) Stratified sampling comes in handy when we wish to get estimates at the level of sub-populations or regions or groups. This method also gives us the freedom to choose different sampling methods/designs in different strata as appropriate to the group (stratum) of the population and the opportunity to utilise available additional information relating to the stratum. The sampling variance of estimators can also be brought down by forming the strata in such a way as to ensure homogeneity of units within individual strata. In fact, the stratum sizes can be so chosen as to minimise the variance of estimators, when there is a ceiling on the cost of the survey. Stratified sampling with SRS, SRSWOR or PPSWR presents a set of efficient sampling designs.

(5) Sometimes, sampling of groups of individual units than direct sampling of units might be found to be operationally convenient. Suppose it is easier to get a complete frame of clusters of individual units than that of units (or only such a frame, and not that of the units is available. In such circumstances, cluster sampling is adopted. This is in general less efficient than direct sampling of individual units, as clusters usually consist of homogeneous units. A compromise between operational convenience and efficiency could be made by adopting a two-stage sampling design, by selecting a sample of individual units (second stage units) from sampled clusters (the first stage units). A multi-stage design would be useful in cases where clusters have to be selected at more than one stage of sampling.

(6) Finally, we can use the technique of independent I-Pss in conjunction with the chosen sampling design to get at (i) an unbiased estimate of the sampling variance of, say, 'm' for any sampling design or estimator of the sampling variance, however completed, (ii) a confidence interval for the population parameter, say, 'M' based only on the I-Pss estimates and (iii) a tool for monitoring the quality of work of the staff and agencies drafted for field work in the sample survey.

(7) SRSWOR, stratified sampling with SRSWOR and, when available information permits, PPSWR and stratified sampling with PPSWR, turn out to be a set of more efficient and operationally easy designs to choose from. I-Pss can also be used in these designs where possible and necessary.

The main aim of GPH book is to provide knowledge as well as good marks in exams.

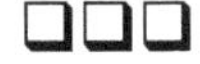

3 Quantitative Methods-I

An Overview

There are two types research design: quantitative and qualitative. Hardcore economists mostly rely on the quantitative method, which they deem scientific, hard, and objective as compared to qualitative research design which they perceive to be soft and subjective. The statistical tools employed as a quantitative method are correlation and regression. The concepts of correlation and regression form the core of regression models. Before applying the regression model to an empirical situation, an essential primary step is to examine whether, there exist any relation between the different variable under inquiry. The observed correlation between a set of variables has to be examined for their functional relationship.

Q1. Define correlation between two variables. How do you measure linear correlation between two variables?

Ans. In our day to day life, we find many examples when a mutual relationship exists between two variables, i.e. with fall or rise in the value of one variable, the fall or rise may take place in the value of other variable. For example, price of commodity rises as the demand for the commodity goes up. Upto a certain time-period, weight of a person increases with the increase in age. Similarly, the temperature rises with the rise in the sunlight. These facts indicate that there is certainly some mutual relationship that exists between the demand for commodity and its price, the age of a person and his weight, and the sunlight and temperature. The correlation refers to the statistical technique used in measured the closeness of the relationship between the variables.

Several measures of correlation are available, the selection of which depends mostly on the level of data being analysed. Ideally, researchers would like to solve for ρ, the population coefficient of correlation. However, because researcher virtually always deal with sample data, this section introduces a widely used sample coefficient of correlation, r. This measure is applicable only if both variables being analysed have at least an interval level of data.

The statistic r is the Pearson product-moment correlation coefficient, named after Karl Pearson (1857-1936), an English statistician who developed several coefficients of correlation along with other significant statistical concepts. The term r is measure of the linear correlation of two variables. It is a number that ranges from – 1 to 0 to +1, representing the strength of the relationship between the variables. An r value of +1 denotes a perfect positive relationship between two sets of numbers. An r value of –1 denotes a perfect negative correlation, which indicates an inverse relationship between two variables: as one variable gets larger, the other gets smaller. An r-value of 0 means no linear relationship is present between the two variables.

Q2. Explain the following:

(a) How two independent variables have zero correlation but the converse in not true?

Ans. Statistically independent variables have a zero correlation coefficient. The converse, however, is not true, because the correlation coefficient measures only the linear association between two variables. A zero correlation coefficient only indicates that a linear relation is not present.

Other types of dependence may be present and not be reflected in the numerical value of the correlation coefficient.

(b) Does the presence of strong correlation between two variables necessarily imply the existence of a meaningful relationship between them?

Ans. Sometimes, two variables, even when seem to be not related in any manner, may display a high degree of correlation. Yule called this kind of correlation as 'nonsense correlation'. If we measure two variables at regular time intervals, both the variables may display a strong time-trend. As a result, the two variables may display a strong correlationship even when they are unrelated. Thus, one should be very careful while using such a source of data.

Another situation when two, seemingly unrelated, variables may display a high degree of correlation is the result of the influence of a third variable on both of them. Thus, the existence of a correlation between two variables does not necessarily imply a relationship between them. It only indicates that the data are not inconsistent with the possibility of such a relationship. The reasonableness of a possible relationship must be established on theoretical considerations first, and then we should proceed with the computation of correlation.

Q3. Explain the concept of regression.

Or

Explain how regression is not primarily concerned with primarily analysis.

Ans. Regression is the study of nature of relationship between the variables, so that one may be able to predict the unknown value of one variable for a known value of another variable.

If two variables are significantly correlated, and if there is some theoretical basis for doing so, it is possible to predict values of one variable from the other. This observation leads to a very important concept known as 'Regression Analysis'.

According to M. M. Blair, "Regression analysis is a mathematical measure of the average relationship between two or more variables in terms of the original units of the data."

Although regression analysis deals with the dependence of one variable on other variables, it does not necessarily imply causation. In the words of Kendall and Stuart, "A statistical relationship, however strong and however suggestive can never establish causal connection: our ideas of causation must come from outside statistics, ultimately from some theory or other." For example, there is no statistical reason to assume that rainfall does not depend on crop yield. The fact that we treat crop yield as dependent on rainfall (among other things) is due to non-statistical considerations: Common sense suggests that the relationship cannot be reversed; we cannot control rainfall by varying crop yield. Thus, a statistical relationship in itself cannot logically imply causation. To ascribe causality, one must appeal to a priori or theoretical considerations.

Q4. Bring out the difference between correlation and regression.

Ans. Differences between correlation and regression are given below:

No.	Correlation	Regression
(1)	Correlation means the relationship between the variables.	Regression means stepping back to the average value and is a mathematical measure expressing the average relationship between two variables.
(2)	Correlation do not indicate the cause and effect relationship between the variables.	Regression indicates the cause and effect relationship between the variable.
(3)	In correlation any variable can be x or y	In regression independent variable is considered as x and dependent variable as y.
(4)	There may be non-sense correlation between two variable.	There is no such non-sense regression between two variables.
(5)	Correlation coefficient measures the degree and direction of the linear relationship.	Regression analysis establishes the functional relationship between the two variables.
(6)	For a given value of one variable we cannot estimate the value of other variable using correlation analysis.	In regression analysis, we can estimate the value of dependent variable for given value of independent variable.
(7)	Correlation coefficient is always less than one.	One regression coefficients can be greater than one.
(8)	Correlation coefficient is independent of change of origin and scale.	Regression coefficient is independent of change of origin but not scale.
(9)	R(x, y)=r(y, x)	$b_{yx} \neq b_{xy}$

Q5. What are the properties of regression coefficient?

Ans. The main properties of the regression coefficients are as follows:

- Coefficient of correlation is the geometric mean of the regression coefficients, i.e.

  $r=\sqrt{b_{xy}\times b_{yx}}$

  This property can be proved in the following manner:

  Regressio coefficient of X on Y $b_{xy}=r.\frac{\sigma_x}{\sigma_y}$ ...(i)

  Regression coefficient of Y on X $b_{yx}=r.\frac{\sigma_y}{\sigma_x}$ ...(ii)

  Multiplying (i) and (ii)

  $b_{xy}.b_{yx}=r.\frac{\sigma_x}{\sigma_y}r.\frac{\sigma_y}{\sigma_x}$

  or $r=\sqrt{b_{xy}\times b_{yx}}$

  Hence, $r=\pm\sqrt{b_{xy}.b_{yx}}$

- Both the regression coefficients must have the same algebraic signs. In other words, when one regression coefficient is negative, the other would be also negative. It is never possible that one regression coefficients is negative while the other is positive.
- The coefficient of correlation will have the same sign as that of regression coefficients. If both regression coefficients are negative, then the correlation coefficients would be negative. And b_{xy} if b_{yx} and have positive signs, the r will also take plus sign.
- Both the regression coefficients cannot be greater than unity: If one regression coefficient of y on x is greater than unity, then the regression coefficient of x on y must be less than unity. This is because

  $r=\pm\sqrt{b_{xy}.b_{yx}}=\pm1$

  and never greater than one. If both the regression coefficients happen to be more than 1 then their geometric mean will exceed 1 which will not give the correlation coefficients whose value never exceeds 1.

- Arithmetic mean of two regression coefficients is either equal to or greater than the correlation coefficient. In terms of the formula:

  $$\frac{b_{yx}+b_{xy}}{2} \geq r$$

- Shift of origin does not affect regression coefficients but shift in scale does affect regression coefficients. Regression coefficients are independent of the change of origin but not of scale. This means if some common factor is taken out from the items of the series, then in that case, we will have to make adjustment in the regression coefficients formula which is shown below:

  $$b_{yx} = b_{vu} \cdot \frac{i_y}{i_x} \text{ and } u = \frac{X-a}{h}$$

  where, $u = \frac{X-a}{h}$ and $v = \frac{Y-b}{k}$

  i_y and i_x are common factors of Y and X series respectively.

Q6. Explain the method of least square.

Ans. Least Square Method is a statistical technique to determine the line of best sit for a model. It is also known as straight line method. This method is most commonly used in research to estimate the trend of time series data, as it is mathematically designed to satisfy two conditions. They are:

- sum of $(Y-Y_c)=0$, and
- sum of $(Y-Y_c)^2 =$ least

The straight line method gives a line of best fit on the given data. The straight line, which can satisfy the above conditions and make use of the regression equation is given by:

$$Y_c = a + bX$$

Where, 'Y_c' represents the trend value of the time series variable Y, 'a' and 'b' are constant.

Values of which 'a' is the trend value at the point of origin and 'b' is the amount by which the trend value changes per unit of time, and 'X' is the unit of time (value of the independent variable).

The values of constants, 'a' and 'b', are determined by the following two normal equations.

$$\sum Y = Na + b\sum X \quad \text{...(i)}$$

$$\sum XY = a\sum X + b\sum X^2 \qquad \text{...(ii)}$$

The process of finding values of constants a and b can be made simple by using a shortcut method, that is, by taking the origin year in such a way that it gives the total of 'X' $\sum X$ equal to 'zero'. This becomes possible if we take the median year as origin period. Thus, the negative values in the first half of the series balance out the positive values in the second half. Thus, the normal equation shall be changed as follows, with reference to $\sum X = 0$.

$$\sum Y = a \left(\text{as } b\sum X \text{ becomes zero}\right)$$

$$\sum XY = b\sum X^2 \left(\text{as } a\sum X \text{ becomes zero}\right)$$

Therefore, the values of two constants are obtained by the following formula:

$$a = \frac{\sum Y}{N} \text{ and } b = \frac{\sum XY}{\sum X^2}$$

It is to be noted that when the number of time units involved is even the point of origin will have to be chosen between the two middle time units.

Q7. Explain the concept of reverse regression.

Ans. In a simple regression model with variables (Y,X), direct regression refers to the regression of Y on X, where reverse regression refers to the regression of X on Y.

The regression of X on Y is in fact intrinsically different from that of Y on X. Geometrically speaking, in regression of X on Y, we minimise the sum of the squares of the horizontal distances against the minimisation of the sum of the squares of the vertical distances in Y on X, for obtaining the least square estimates. If our regression equation of X on Y is given by

$$X = a' + b'Y,$$

Then its least square estimates are given by the criterion:

Minimise

$$\sum_{i=1}^{n}\left(X_i - \hat{X}_i\right)^2$$

with respect to a' and b'

By applying the usual minimisation procedure, we obtain the following two normal equations:

$$\sum X = na' + b'\sum Y$$

and

$$\sum XY = a'\sum Y + b'\sum Y^2.$$

We can simultaneously solve these two equations to get the least square estimates

$$\hat{b}' = \frac{\sum(X-\bar{X})(Y-\bar{Y})}{\sum(Y-\bar{Y})^2} = r\frac{\sigma_X}{\sigma_Y}$$

and

$$\hat{a}' = \bar{X} - \hat{b}'\bar{Y}$$

The slope b′ of the regression of X on Y is called the regression coefficient of X on Y. It measures the rate of change of X with respect to Y, in order to distinguish it clearly from the regression coefficient of Y on X; we also use the symbol b_{xy} for it.

Putting the values of a′ and b′, the regression equation of X on Y can be written as

$$X - \bar{X} = b_{XY}(Y-\bar{Y}) = r\frac{\sigma_X}{\sigma_Y}(Y-\bar{Y})$$

To highlight the inherent difference between the two kinds of regression, the regression of Y on X is sometimes termed as the direct regression and that of the X on Y is called the reverse regression.

Q8. Explain the different types of data that are used in economic models.

Ans. The data that economic model builders use to generate forecasts can be divided into three principal categories: time-series, cross-section, and panel data.

Time Series data: Most forecasting models use time-series data. A time series is a sequence of data at equidistant intervals where each point represents a certain time period (e.g. monthly, quarterly, or annually). Examples include quarterly data for consumption, monthly data for industrial production or housing starts, daily data for the stock market, annual data for capital spending, quarterly data for individual company sales and profits, or monthly levels of production and inventories.

Cross-section data: represent a snapshot of many different observations taken at a given time. The decennial census of population data are often used for cross-section analysis; for any given census year, statistical relationships can be used to estimate the correlation between income and education, location, size of family, race, age, sex, and a whole host of other variables.

Panel data: refers to the reexamination of cross-section data with the same sample at different periods of time, for example, the problem with the June 1995 data might be that individuals buy a new car on average only once every four years (say), so that month might not have been typical. Thus, the same people could be asked about their income, saving and consumption in January 1997, and at other periods. Over a longer period of time, the spending patterns of these individuals could be tracked to help determine how much is saved at different levels of income, whether upper-income people spend a larger proportion of their income on housing, transportation, or medical care, or a host of other items. Panel data could also be used to determine whether individuals who started smoking cigarettes at a young age continued to smoke throughout their lives, whereas those who started smoking later found it easier to quit.

Q9. Discuss the meaning of linearity in regression model.

Ans. Linearity is the main principal assumption, which justifies the use of linear regression model for purpose of prediction. Linearity is the relationship between dependent and independent variables.

Violations of linearity are extremely serious--if you fit a linear model to data which are nonlinearly related, your predictions are likely to be seriously in error, especially when you extrapolate beyond the range of the sample data.

Detect: nonlinearity is usually most evident in a plot of the *observed versus predicted values* or a plot of *residuals versus predicted values,* which are a part of standard regression output. The points should be symmetrically distributed around a diagonal line in the former plot or a horizontal line in the latter plot. Look carefully for evidence of a "bowed" pattern, indicating that the model makes systematic errors whenever it is making unusually large or small predictions.

Fixation: consider applying a *nonlinear transformation* to the dependent and/or independent variables-if you can think of a transformation that seems appropriate. For example, if the data are strictly positive, a log transformation may be feasible. Another possibility to consider is adding another regression, which is a nonlinear function of one of the other variables. For example, if you have regressed Y on X, and the graph of residuals versus predicted suggests a parabolic curve, then it may make sense to regress Y on both X and X^2 (i.e. X-squared). The latter transformation is possible even when X and/or Y have negative values, whereas logging may not be.

Q10. How regression model is non-deterministic in nature?

Ans. In contrast to the deterministic relationships, we have many problems where variables are found to be associated, interdependent or one variable dependent on a number of independent variables, but such dependence or inter-relationships are not governed by any well defined physical laws. For example, a plot of observed values of the variables on a graph paper indicates the presence of some relationship in a rather crude form interwoven with chance variations. In particular situations, there may be some partial theoretical foundation available indicating some plausible form of the relationship but the theoretical basis is not as precise or universally acceptable as in the case of deterministic relations.

Suppose a factory manufactures items in batches and the production manager is interested in studying the relationship between the cost of production (Y) of a batch with the batch size (X) of the production run. In any production process, it is well known that a certain component of the production cost is fixed regardless of batch size. The overhead costs and some other administrative costs belong to this category and the veriable cost which is directly proportional to the number of units produced including raw material and labour costs. Assuming the absence of any other costs, we can develop a deterministic cost size relationship of the form

$$Y = F + bX$$

Where F is the fixed cost and b is the unit variable cost. It should be noted that unforeseen costs such as cost due to machine breakdowns or cost due to inferior raw material, etc. are not taken into this model, and these factors make the model non-deterministic.

Q11. What is the difference between disturbance term and intercept?

Or

What do understand by the population regression function? Define the term the disturbance in this regard and differentiate with the intercept.

Ans. The population regression function (PRF) is a description of the model that is thought to be generating the actual data and it represents the true relationship between the variables. The population regression function is also known as the data generating process (DGP). The PRF embodies the true values of α and β, and is expressed as

$Y = \alpha + \beta X + U$

In this population regression function, the variable U deserves some attention. In our formulation, in fact, Y is stochastic or random, but X is non–stochastic or deterministic in nature. Consequently, a random variable like U is introduced in the population regression function to incorporate this element of randomness of a statistical relationship. The random variable U is also called the **disturbance term.** It is a sort of catch–all variable that represents all kinds of indeterminacies of an inexact relationship. Thus, it may represent follows:

- **Inherent randomness in human behaviour:** The unpredictability of human psyche is also reflected in the human behaviour. As a result, even after taking into account all possible factors, a regression equation cannot fully explain the value of the dependent variable for the given values of all possible explanatory variables.
- **Effect of omitted variables:** Sometimes for the sake of parsimony, all the explanatory variables are not included in a regression model. The disturbance term can be taken as a representative variable of all such omitted variables.
- **Effect of measurement error:** Sometimes, it is not possible to measure the values of the dependent variable accurately. Consequently, the disturbance term is introduced in the regression model to represent the combined effect of all such possible sources of measurement error.
- **Error in the formulation:** Often, the functional form of the regression model proves to be far from a correct depiction of the underlying relationship between the dependent variable and the independent variables. We incorporate the disturbance term to correct the distortions that may arise from a wrong specification of the regression model.

Difference between the Disturbance Term and the Intercept

There is a difference between the interpretation of the disturbance term and that of the intercept term α in our regression term. As we have noted, that the disturbance represents the random effects of the known and unknown variables that have not been included in the regression model. The intercept term, on the other hand, stands for all such variables, that are known to have some definite non–random effects on the dependent variable. For example, in the demand function, if we just formulate a two variable regression equation between the quantity demanded and the price instead of a multiple regression equation, then we are consciously not including variables like prices of other commodities and the income of the consumer. And all these variables affect the quantity demanded in a known fashion. So, the intercept term here represents the average effect of all such known factors that are not explicitly included in the model.

It should be clear now that it is the disturbance term that makes the relationship statistical in nature and renders the entire procedure so rich in content.

Q12. State the assumptions of the classical linear regression model.

Ans. The CLR model consists of five basic assumptions about the way in which the observations are generated.

- The first assumption of the CLR model is that the dependent variable can be calculated as a linear function of a specific set of independent variables, plus a disturbance term. The unknown coefficients of this linear function form the vector β and are assumed to be constants.
- The second assumption of the CLR model is that the expected value of the disturbance term is zero; i.e. the mean of the distribution from which the disturbance term is drawn is zero.
- The third assumption of the CLR model is that the disturbance terms all have the same variance and are not correlated with one another.
- The fourth assumption of the CLR model is that the observations on the independent variable can be considered fixed in repeated samples; i.e. it is possible to repeat the sample with the same independent variable values.
- The fifth assumption of the CLR model is that the number of observations is greater than the number of independent variables and that there are no exact linear relationships between the independent variables. Although this is viewed as an assumption for the general case, for a specific case it can easily be checked, so that it need not be assumed. The problem of multicollinearity (two or more independent variables being approximately linearly related in the sample data) is associated with this assumption.

Q13. State the Gauss-Markov theorem.

Ans. The least square estimators $\hat{\alpha}$ and $\hat{\beta}$ can be taken as the estimators of the unknown population parameters α and β because they satisfy certain desirable properties. We can state them without proofs below:

(1) Least square estimators are linear.

(2) Least square estimators are unbiased i.e. $E(\hat{\alpha})=\alpha$ and $E(\hat{\beta})=\beta$.

This means, if we consider different values of the least square estimates obtained from a number of random samples for a given population on the average, they will be equal to the unknown population parameters. They will not be systematically overestimating or underestimating the population parameters.

(3) Among all the linear unbiased estimators, least square estimators have the minimum variance. In this sense, they are termed as the efficient estimators.

All these properties of the least square estimators lead to what is known as the Gauss-Markov Theorem. The theorem states:

Under the assumptions of the classical regression model, among all the linear unbiased estimators, the least square estimators have the minimum variance. In other words, the least square estimators are the best linear unbiased estimators or in short, BLUE.

Q14. Discuss in detail about Standard Error of the Regression Estimate.

Ans. The standard deviations of the least square estimates are known as the standard errors of the estimates. It should be clear that the standard errors are the standard deviations of the sampling distributions of the least square estimates. The standard deviations or standard errors are obtained by taking the positive square root of the variances of $\hat{\alpha}$ and $\hat{\beta}$. The expressions for both the variance and standard of the least square estimators are given below:

$$\text{var}(\hat{\alpha})=\frac{\sum X^2}{n\sum(X-\bar{X}^2)}\sigma^2$$

$$\text{se}(\hat{\alpha})=\sqrt{\frac{\sum X^2}{n\sum(X-\bar{X}^2)}\sigma^2}$$

$$\text{var}(\hat{\beta})=\frac{\sigma^2}{\sum(X-\bar{X})^2}$$

$$\text{se}(\hat{\beta})=\frac{\sigma}{\sqrt{\sum(X-\bar{X})^2}}$$

It should be recollected that σ is the standard deviation of the error term U in our population regression model and we assume that it is a constant. However, since the population regression model is unknown, it follows that σ is also unknown. As a result, for the calculation of variance and standard error of the least square estimates $\hat{\alpha}$ and $\hat{\beta}$, we need to estimate σ. It can be proved that an unbiased estimator of

σ is $\sqrt{\frac{\sum \hat{U}^2}{n-2}}$. Here, $n-2$ is what is known as the degrees of freedom in statistics.

This concept you must have studied in your compulsory course in statistic. Now, $\hat{U} = Y - \hat{Y}$ is the sample regression error term and accordingly we can calculate it. Thus by replacing σ by its unbiased estimator we can compute the standard error of both $\hat{\alpha}$ and $\hat{\beta}$. It should be noted here that we can write the unbiased estimator of σ as

$$\hat{\sigma} = \sqrt{\frac{\sum \hat{U}^2}{n-2}} = \sqrt{\frac{\sum \left(\hat{U} - \bar{\hat{U}}\right)^2}{n-2}}$$

This is, because, $\bar{\hat{U}}$ is the mean of the sample regression errors. Now, while calculating it, the positive errors will tend to cancel the negative errors and as a result, it will be reduced to zero. From above expression of the estimator of σ, it can easily be interpreted as the standard deviation of the sample observations about the estimated sample regression line. The sample estimator $\hat{\sigma} = \sqrt{\frac{\sum \hat{U}^2}{n-2}}$ is known as the standard error of estimate or the standard error of the regression.

Q15. What is goodness of fit? How does coefficient of determination act as a measure of goodness of fit? [Dec-2012, Q.No.-7]

Ans. Once such a regression line is fitted, we may be interested in examining how good has been the fit in the sense how faithfully it can describe the unknown population regression line. This is known as the issue of goodness of fit. In this matter, the regression error term or residual $\hat{U}$ plays an important role. Small quantities of residuals imply that a large proportion of variation in the dependent variable has been explained by the regression equation and consequently, the fit is good. Similarly, large quantities of residuals obviously point to a poor fit. At this stage, what we are interested in is to obtain a quantitative measure of the goodness of fit that is free of any unit for the purpose of comparability. Coefficient of determination, which is the square of the correlation coefficient, can be shown that this coefficient of determination acts as a measure of goodness of it. The variation in the dependent variable Y about its mean can be conceptualised as:

$$\text{var}(Y) = \sum (Y - \overline{Y})^2$$

We can decompose it into two components. The first is the variation explained by the regression. The second is the portion that remains unexplained by the regression. Thus, we can write:

$$(Y - \overline{Y}) = (Y - \hat{Y}) + (\hat{Y} - \overline{Y})$$

Squaring and applying summation on both the sides:

$$\sum (Y - \overline{Y})^2 = \sum (\hat{Y} - \overline{Y})^2 + \sum (Y - \hat{Y})^2 + 2\sum (\hat{Y} - \overline{Y})(Y - \hat{Y})$$

Now, let us try to find the value of $\sum (\hat{Y} - \overline{Y})(Y - \hat{Y})$. We have the regression equation

$$Y = \hat{\alpha} + \hat{\beta}X + \hat{U} \text{ or } \overline{Y} = \hat{\alpha} + \hat{\beta}\overline{X} + \overline{\hat{U}}$$

Subtracting the second equation from the first equation:

$$Y - \overline{Y} = \hat{\beta}(X - \overline{X}) + \hat{U}, \text{ because } \overline{\hat{U}} = \frac{\sum \hat{U}}{n} = 0, \text{ as } \sum \hat{U} = 0.$$

Writing lower case letters for the deviations of the variables from their mean, we have the sample regression equation in the form:

$$y = \hat{\beta}x + \hat{u}$$

Now

$$\sum (\hat{Y} - \overline{Y})(Y - \hat{Y})$$

$$= \sum (\hat{Y} - \overline{Y})\hat{U} = \sum \hat{Y}\hat{U} - \overline{Y}\sum \hat{U} = \sum \hat{Y}\hat{U}, \text{ because } \sum \hat{U} = 0$$

$$= \sum (\hat{\alpha} + \hat{\beta}X)\hat{U} = \hat{\alpha}\sum \hat{U} + \hat{\beta}\sum X\hat{U} = \hat{\beta}\sum X\hat{U}$$

We have

$$x = X - \overline{X}$$

$$\Rightarrow \sum x = \sum (X - \overline{X}) \text{ or } \sum x\hat{U} = \sum (X - \overline{X})\hat{U} = \sum X\hat{U} - \overline{X}\sum \hat{U} = \sum X\hat{U}$$

Now

$$\sum x\hat{U} = \sum x(y - \hat{\beta}x) = \sum xy - \hat{\beta}\sum x^2$$

We know, $\hat{\beta} = \frac{\sum(X-\bar{X})(Y-\bar{Y})}{\sum(X-\bar{X})} = \frac{\sum xy}{\sum x^2}$

Putting the value of $\hat{\beta}$ in the above expression for $\sum x\hat{U}$,

$$\sum x\hat{U} = \sum xy - \frac{\sum xy}{\sum x^2}\sum x^2 = \sum xy - \sum xy = 0$$

Hence,

$$\sum(\hat{Y}-\bar{Y})(Y-\hat{Y}) = 0$$

Thus,

$$\sum(Y-\bar{Y})^2 = \sum(\hat{Y}-\bar{Y})^2 + \sum(Y-\hat{Y})^2$$

If $\sum(Y-\bar{Y})^2$ is defined as the total sum of squares (TSS), $\sum(\hat{Y}-\bar{Y})^2$ as the explained sum of squares (ESS) and $\sum(Y-\hat{Y})^2$ as the residual sum of squares (RSS),

We have

TSS = ESS + RSS

Dividing both the sides by TSS,

$$\frac{TSS}{TSS} = \frac{ESS}{TSS} + \frac{RSS}{TSS}$$

Defining the ratio of ESS to TSS as R^2, we have

$$R^2 = 1 - \frac{RSS}{TSS} = \frac{ESS}{TSS}$$

Now it is clear that R^2 or coefficient of determination can be interpreted as the proportion of total variation in Y explained by the regression of Y on X.

Q16. Explain the various functional forms of regression model. For the measurement of growth rate, which form of regression model is suitable? [June-2012, Q.No-6]

Ans. There are mainly four forms of regression models:

(1) Linear model

This functional form is the most common one. Its equation is given by

$$Y = \alpha + \beta X + U$$

It is both linear in parameter and linear in variable. This model can be estimated by the ordinary least square (OLS) method. The least square estimators $\hat{\alpha}$ and $\hat{\beta}$ are the unbiased estimators of the unknown population parameters α and β.

Here, the regression coefficient β measures the rate of change of Y per unit change of X.

(2) Log-linear Model

This model is also known as log-log, double-log or constant elasticity model. Its original form is given by

$Y = \alpha X^{\beta} e^{U}$, Where, e is the base of **natural log** (e is approximately equal to 2.718). In the original form, the model is non linear in nature. However, by applying the log transformation, the model is transformed to

$\ln Y + \ln \alpha + \beta \ln X + U$

If we put $\ln Y = y, \ln \alpha = a, \beta = b$ and lnX=x the model reduces to

$y = a + bx + U$

From the above transformation, it is very clear that the model now becomes linear in parameter and linear in log of the variables; and thus, can be estimated by the ordinary least square method. Here, a will be estimating $\ln \alpha$ and then by taking the antilog of a, we shall obtain the estimate for α. The regression coefficient b=β deserves our special attention. It measures a change in log Y per unit of a change in log X. In the language of calculus, $\beta = \frac{d \ln Y}{d \ln X}$. Now, a change in the log of some variable implies a proportional change in it. Thus, β is the ratio of a proportional change in Y to a proportional change in X. In other words, β measures the elasticity of Y with respect to X. This is the rationale for the log linear regression model being termed as the constant elasticity model.

(3) Semi-Log Model

One of the common forms of semi-log regression models is the so-called growth rate model. The model is expressed as:

$\log Y = \alpha + \beta t + U$

In this model, the dependent variable is expressed in log, whereas, the independent variable is the time period, and it is measured in absolute term. Since, log operator is applied only to the left hand side of the equation, the model is called the semi-log model. In this model, the slope coefficient β is a measure of the proportional change in the dependent variable for a unit change in the time period. Thus, it measures the growth rate of the dependent variable.

(4) Reciprocal Model

In the reciprocal model, the dependent variable is regressed on the reciprocal of the independent variable. Its functional from is:

$$Y=\alpha+\beta\frac{1}{X}+U$$

Although the model is non-linear in variable (because the power of X is -l), it is linear in parameter. Hence, it can be estimated by the OLS method. The model has an important characteristic. As the independent variable X increases indefinitely, the term $\beta\frac{1}{X}$ approaches zero, β being a constant. Consequently, the dependent variable Y approaches a limiting value or an asymptote equal to the intercept α. An application of this model can be in the relationship between per capita GNP and the child mortality. As per capita GNP increases, the infant mortality rate is expected to fall but we cannot expect it to fall independently if per capita GNP continues to increase indefinitely. In such a situation, in all probability, the mortality rate will tend to a limiting value.

Another application of the reciprocal model can be in the estimation of the Phillips curve. This curve proposes an inverse relationship between the change in unemployment rate and that in inflation rate. With a growth in unemployment rate, the growth in inflation rate is expected to fall. In fact, Phillips curve postulates that if the unemployment rate increases beyond its so-called natural rate, the growth in the inflation rate should become negative. However, with an indefinite increase in the unemployment rate, the inflation growth cannot be expected to fall indefinitely. It should stabilise at some negative limiting value. Thus, Phillips Curve can be an appropriate case for the use of the reciprocal model.

Q17. What is classical normal regression model? Explain its uses.

[Dec-2011, Q.No-7]

Ans. A two variable classical regression model can be presented as:

$$Y=\alpha+\beta X+U$$

In this model, U is the population disturbance term. We can estimate the unknown parameters of this regression model from the sample information by using the least square or, as it is sometimes called, ordinary least square method. The least square estimates possess some desirable properties if the population disturbance U satisfies some five assumptions of classical regression model. These five assumptions are adequate for the estimation purposes. But the scope of a regression model is just not restricted to the estimation of the parameters. An important purpose of the sample estimates is to test some hypotheses about the unknown population regression parameters with their help. And we can do this if we make some assumption about the distribution of U. This we do by making the assumption of normality for U. The assumption essentially means that the population regression disturbance term follows normal distribution with mean zero, a constant variance equal to σ^2 and a zero covariance. In fact U has a conditional distribution, in the sense that, for each of the given values of the non–stochastic independent variable X, we might have a distribution of different values of U.

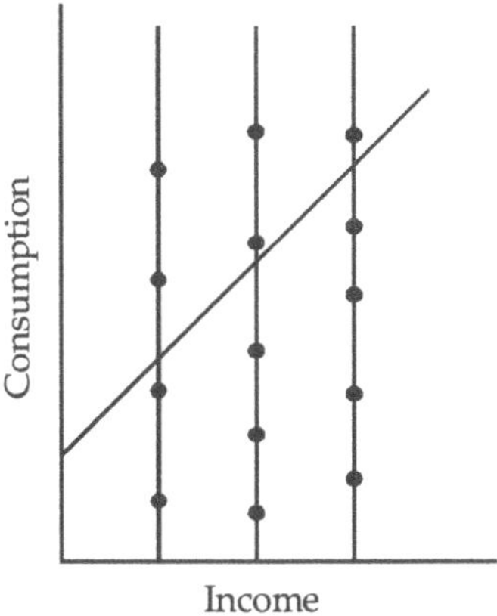

Fig. 3.1: Bi–Variate Population with the Unknown Regression Line

In Figure 3.1, we can see that for a given observed value of income we can have different observed values of consumption represented by the bold dots on each of the vertical lines. The vertical distance between an observed value of consumption and the corresponding estimated value from the regression line for a given income level measures the value of the disturbance term. Thus, there are many possible values of U for each of the given income levels. As a result, there are conditional distributions of U for different levels of income.

The significance of the normality assumption is that these conditional distributions of U should all be independently normally distributed with the same mean equal to zero and the same variance equal to σ^2. Mathematically speaking:

$E(U_i) = 0$ for all i's

$V(U_i) = \sigma^2$ for all i's

$Cov(U_iU_j) = 0 \quad$ for $i \neq j$

In other words, the population disturbance variable should have independent and identical normal distribution.

If we make this additional normality assumption along with the five assumptions of classical regression model about the disturbance term U, then the regression model is called the classical normal regression model.

Q18. Discuss the concept of Hypothesis testing.

Ans. Considering the two variable regression model:

$$Y = \alpha + \beta X + U$$

We might be interested in examining whether the unknown parameter α or β assumes a particular value or not. This is what is known as hypothesis testing in statistics. We can conduct such a test from the sample estimate of α or β as the case might be. Although we may test some hypothesis about the intercept α, our main concern in regression model is the slope coefficient β. We have the estimated sample regression function:

$$\hat{Y} = \hat{\alpha} + \hat{\beta}X + \hat{U}$$

Here, $\hat{\beta}$ is the sample estimate of β and we shall use it for estimating the unknown β. $\hat{\beta}$ might vary from sample to sample collected from the same population. As a result, $\hat{\beta}$ is a random variable with some probability distribution. Now, for the purpose of hypothesis testing, we need to know the form of this distribution of $\hat{\beta}$.

It is here, that the assumption of normality helps us. We know that $\hat{\beta} = \sum kY$ and thus, it is a linear function of the observed values of Y. But, $Y = \alpha + \beta X + U$. Consequently, we can see, $\hat{\beta} = \sum k(\alpha + \beta X + U)$. Now, we already know that the ks, the Xs and the parameters are all given. As a result, finally, $\hat{\beta}$ becomes a linear function of the random disturbance variable U. Thus, $\hat{\beta}$ has the same distribution as U. Therefore, the assumption of normality $U, \hat{\beta}$ implies that $\hat{\beta}$ is distributed as normal.

We know that $E(\hat{\beta}) = \beta$ and $se(\hat{\beta}) = \frac{\sigma}{\sqrt{\sum(X - \bar{X})^2}}$. It follows then that:

$$\hat{\beta} \sim N\left(\beta, \frac{\sigma}{\sqrt{\sum(X - \bar{X})^2}}\right).$$

We know that an unbiased estimate of σ is given by $\hat{\sigma}^2 = \frac{\sum \hat{U}^2}{n-2}$,

where, $\hat{U}$ is the sample regression error term and, as is, therefore, result computable, and n is the size of the sample. When we standardise $\hat{\beta}$ by subtracting its mean from it and divide it by its estimated standard deviation, it no longer follows normal distribution and it in fact follows a student-t distribution with $n-2$ degrees of freedom. This student-t distribution has a mean equal to zero and a standard deviation equal to one. Thus, it is standard student-t distribution that is used for testing of hypothesis about β. we have a table for such a standard student-t distribution for different degrees of freedom. And like the standard normal table, this table is put into use for such tests of hypotheses.

Q19. What is a multiple regression? Explain with an example.

Ans. Multiple linear regression is in some ways a relatively straightforward extension of simple linear regression that allows for more than one independent variable. The objective of multiple regression is the same as that of simple regression; that is, we want to use the relationship between a response (dependent) variable and factor (independent) variables to predict or explain the behaviour of the response variable. However, the computations are considerably more complicated and must be performed by computers, and the inferential procedures may be more difficult to interpret, primarily because there may be relationships among the independent variables.

Some examples of analyses using the multiple regression model include the following:

- Estimating weight gain of children using various levels of a dietary supplement, exercise, and behaviour modification
- Predicting scholastic success (GPA) of college freshmen based on scores on an aptitude test, high school grades, and IQ level
- Estimating changes in sales associated with increased expenditures on advertising, increased number of sales personnel, increased number of management personnel, and various types of sales strategies
- Predicting daily fuel consumption for home heating based on daily temperature, daily wind velocity, and previous day's temperature.

Q20. Discuss the multiple linear regression.

Ans. In multiple regression, we try to predict the value of one variable given the values of other variables. Let us consider the case of three variables y, x_1 and x_2. We assume there exists linear relationship between them. Thus, $y = a + bx_1 + cx_2$

where, a, b and c are constants.

We apply the same method of ordinary least square to obtain the estimates $\left(\hat{a}, \hat{b} \text{ and } \hat{c}\right)$ of a, b and c to minimise the sum of the square of errors.

Thus, our task is to $\underset{\hat{a},\hat{b},\hat{c}}{\text{Min}}\ E = \sum e_i^2 = \sum_{i=1}^{n}\left(y_i - \hat{a} - \hat{b}x_{1i} - \hat{c}.x_{2i}\right)^2$

Differentiating E with respect to $\hat{a}, \hat{b} \text{ and } \hat{c}$ we get following three normal equations:

$$\sum\left(y_1 - \hat{a} - \hat{b}x_{1i} - \hat{c}.x_{2i}\right) = 0 \quad \text{...(i)}$$

$$\sum\left(y_i - \hat{a} - \hat{b}x_{1i} - \hat{c}.x_{2i}\right)x_{1i} = 0 \quad \text{...(ii)}$$

$$\sum\left(y_i - \hat{a} - \hat{b}x_{1i} - \hat{c}.x_{2i}\right)x_{2i} = 0 \quad \text{...(ii)}$$

Dividing (i) by n (total number of observations), we get,

$$\bar{y} = \hat{a} + \hat{b}\bar{x}_1 + \hat{c}.\bar{x}_2 \quad \text{or} \quad \hat{a} = \left(\bar{y} - \hat{b}\bar{x}_1 - \hat{c}.\bar{x}_2\right)$$

Substituting $\hat{a} = \left(\bar{y} - \hat{b}\bar{x}_1 - \hat{c}.\bar{x}_2\right)$ in equation (ii) and (iii), we get

$$\sum y_i x_{1i} = \left(\bar{y} - \hat{b}x_1 - \hat{c}.x_2\right)\sum x_{1i} + \hat{b}\sum x_{1i}^2 + \hat{c}\sum x_{2i}x_{1i} \quad \text{...(iv)}$$

$$\sum y_i x_{2i} = \left(\bar{y} - \hat{b}x_1 - \hat{c}.x_2\right)\sum x_{2i} + \hat{b}\sum x_{2i}.x_{1i} + \hat{c}\sum x_{2i}^2 \quad \text{...(v)}$$

$$\text{From(4)}, \sum y_i x_{1i} - x\bar{y}.\bar{x} = \hat{b}\left(\sum x_{1i}^2 - x\bar{x}_1^2\ \hat{b}\sum x_{1i}^2\right) + \hat{c}\left(\sum x_{2i}.x_{1i} - x\bar{x}_1\bar{x}_2\right)$$

Dividing both sides by n, we get

$$\text{cov}(y, x_1) = \sigma^2_{x_1}.\hat{b} + \text{cov}(x_1, x_2)\hat{c} \quad \text{...(vi)}$$

Similarly, from Equation (v), we get

$$\text{cov}(y, x_2) = \text{cov}(x_1, x_2).\hat{b} + \sigma^2_{x_2}.\hat{c} \qquad \text{...(vii)}$$

Solving (v) and (vi), we get

$$\hat{b} = \frac{\text{cov}(y, x_1)\sigma^2_{x_2} - \text{cov}(x_1, x_2).\text{cov}(y, x_2)}{\sigma^2_{x_1}\sigma^2_{x_2} - \text{cov}(x_1, x_2)^2}$$

$$= \frac{\sigma^2_{x_1}\sigma^2_{x_2}\left\{\frac{\sigma_y}{\sigma_{x_1}}\frac{\text{cov}(y, x_1)}{\sigma_{x_1}\sigma_y} - \frac{\sigma_y}{\sigma_{x_2}}\frac{\text{cov}(x_1, x_2)}{\sigma_{x_1}\sigma_{x_2}}\frac{\text{cov}(y, x_2)}{\sigma_y\sigma_{x_2}}\right\}}{\sigma^2_{x_1}\sigma^2_{x_2}\left\{1 - \left(\frac{\text{cov}(x_1, x_2)}{\sigma_{x_1}\sigma_{x_2}}\right)^2\right\}}$$

$$= \frac{\frac{\sigma_Y}{\sigma_{x_1}}\left(\gamma_{yx_1} - \gamma_{x_1x_2}.\gamma_{yx_2}\right)}{1 - \gamma^2_{x_1x_2}}$$ [γ_{xy} = correlation coefficient between variables x and y]

and $$\hat{c} = \frac{\sigma^2_{x_1}.\text{cov}(y, x_2) - \text{cov}(x_1, x_2).\text{cov}(y, x_2)}{\sigma^2_{x_1}\sigma^2_{x_2} - \text{cov}(x_1, x_2)^2}$$

which can be further simplified as $$\hat{c} = \frac{\frac{\sigma_Y}{\sigma_{x_2}}\left(\gamma_{yx_2} - \gamma_{yx_1}.\gamma_{x_1x_2}\right)}{1 - \left(\gamma_{x_1x_2}\right)^2}$$

Note: $\hat{b}$ and $\hat{c}$ give the effect of x_1 and x_2 on y respectively.

Since $\hat{b}$ is the per unit effect of x_1 on y after eliminating the effects of x_2, it give the partial regression coefficient of y and x_1 eliminating the effects of x_2. It is often denoted by $b_{12.3}$. Similarly, $\hat{e}$ is often denoted by $b_{13.2}$.

The general multiple linear regression takes of the form:

$$Y_i = B_1X_{1i} + B_2X_{2i} + B_3X_{3i} + ... + +B_kX_{ki} + u_i \qquad i = 1, 2, ..., n$$

where u_i is the error term.

Q21. How do you interpret the coefficient of multiple regression model?

Or

What do you understand by the coefficient of multiple determination?

Ans. The coefficient of multiple determination (R^2) is analogous to the coefficient of determination (r^2). R^2 represents the proportion of variation of the dependent variable, y, accounted for by the independent variables in the regression model. As with r^2, the range of possible values for R^2 is from 0 to 1. An R^2 of 0 indicates no relationship between the predictor variables in the model and y. An R^2 of 1 indicates that 100 per cent of the variability of y has been accounted for by the predictors. Of course, it is desirable for R^2 to be high, indicating the strong predictability of a regression model. The coefficient of multiple determination can be calculated by the following formula:

$$R^2 = \frac{SSR}{SS_{yy}} = 1 - \frac{SSE}{SS_{yy}}$$

R^2 can be calculated in the real estate example by using the sum of squares regression (SSR), the sum of squares error (SSE), and sum of squares total (SS_{yy}) from the ANOVA portion of Figure 3.2.

SSR, SSE, Ss_{yy}

Analysis of Variance

Source	DF	SS	MS	F	P
Regression	2	8189.7	4094.9	28.63	.000
Error	20	2861.0	143.1		
Total	22	11050.7			

Fig. 3.2: Analysis of Variance

$$R^2 = \frac{SSR}{SS_{yy}} = \frac{8189.7}{11050.7} = 0.741 \text{ or } R^2 = \frac{SSR}{SS_{yy}} = 1 - \frac{2861.0}{11050.7} = 0.741$$

In addition, virtually all statistical software packages print out R^2 as standard output with multiple regression analysis. A reexamination of Figure 3.2 reveals that R^2 given as

$R-sq=74.1\%$

This result indicates that a relatively high proportion of the variation of the dependent variable, house price, is accounted for by the independent variables in this regression model.

Q22. Explain the problem of multi-co-linearity. How can it be detected? What are its Practical consequences?

Or

What is multi-colinerity? What are its consequences?

[June-2012, Q.No.-7]

Ans. Multi-co-linearity is a problem in multiple regression that develops when one or more of the independent variables is highly correlated with one or more of the other independent variables. If one independent variable is a perfect linear combination of the other independent variables; that is, if it is regressed on the other independent variables and the resulting R^2=1.0, then the matrix of inter correlations among the independent variables is singular and there exists no unique solution for the regression coefficients. If, however, the independent variables are not perfectly correlated, but only highly correlated, there exists a solution for the regression coefficients but the estimates, while unbiased, are unstable, and their standard errors are typically large.

Multi-co-linearity is a multivariate problem, not a bivariate problem. That means that a simple perusal of the bivariate correlation matrix is not sufficient to eliminate consideration of the problem of Multi-co-linearity. The problem is not only that, two independent variables are highly correlated, but that one independent variable is highly correlated with all of the other independent variables. That means we need to examine the R^2's of each independent variable regressed on the other independent variables.

The practical consequences of multi-co-linearity: Gujarati, D.N. has listed the following consequences of multiplicity of linear relationships:

- Large variances/SEs of OLS estimates.
- Wider confidence intervals.
- Insignificant 't' ratios for β parameters.
- A high R^2 despite few significant t values.
- Instability of OLS estimators: The estimators and their standard errors (SEs) become very sensitive to small changes in data.
- Sometimes, even signs of some of the regressions may turn out to be theoretically unacceptable like a rise in income having negative impact on demand for milk.
- When many regressions have insignificant coefficients, their individual contributions to the explained sum of squares cannot be assessed properly.

The multi-co-linearity can be detected by:

- High R^2 but few significant 't' ratios.
- High pair wise correlation between explanatory variables. One can try partial correlations, subsidiary or auxiliary regressions as well. But each such technique increases burden of calculations.

Q23. What is Hetero-scedasticity? How can it be detected? What are its consequences? [Dec-2012, Q.No.-12]

Or

What is Hetero-scedasticity? What are its consequences? How will you tackle it. [June-2011, Q.No.-7]

Ans. One assumption underlying regression analysis is that the error term e_1 given by $y_i - y_c$ has a constant variance, i.e. it should stay the same regardless of the value of the independent variable. For example, take the case where the amount of money saved by individuals is related to income levels. If the variation in the amount saved stays the same across all income groups then the assumption is satisfied and the error term is said to be homoscedastic. However, if the variance of savings is not constant across all levels of income (e.g. if individuals at high-income levels save more than those at low-income levels) then we have the problem of heteroscedasticity.

The consequences of hetero scedasticity:

If the assumption of homoscedasticity does not hold, we observe the following impact on OLS estimators:

- They are still linear.
- They are still unbiased.
- But they no longer have minimum variance – that is we cannot call them BLUE: the Best Linear Unbiased Estimators. In fact, this point is relevant both for small as well as large samples.
- Reason for this problem hinted at in (3) above is that generally, OLS estimators have some bias built into their formulae. We try to rectify that by making use of degrees of freedom.

  For instance $\hat{\sigma}^2$, (the estimator for true population σ^2) given by $\sum e_1^2 / df$ no longer remains unbiased. And this very $\hat{\sigma}^2$ enters into calculation of standard errors of OLS estimates.
- Since, estimates of standard errors are themselves no longer reliable, we may end up drawing wrong conclusions, using conventional reasoning based on procedures for testing the hypothesis.

Detection of Hetero Scedasticity

In applied regression analysis, plotting the residual terms can give us important clues about whether or not one or more assumptions underlying our regression model hold. The pattern exhibited by e_i^2 plotted against the concerned variable can provide important clue. If no pattern is detected-homoscedasticity holds or hetero scedasticity is absent. On the other hand, if errors form a pattern with variable-expanding, increasing linear or changing in some non-linear manner, hetero scedasticity is certainly present.

Some tests have been designed to detect presence of Hetero scedastcity, using various statistical techniques. Prominent ones are: Park Test, Glejser Test, Whites General Test, Spearman's Rank correlation Test, Goldfeld-Quandt Test, etc.

Tackling the Hetero Scedasticity

Our ability to tackle the problem will depend upon the assumptions, we can really make about error variance. Thus, the following situations may emerge:

(1) When σ_1^2 is known

Here, the CLRM $Y_i = \beta_0 + \beta_1 X_i + U_i$ can be transformed, dividing each value by corresponding σ_i thus,

$$\frac{Y_i}{\sigma_1} = \beta_0\left(\frac{1}{\sigma_i}\right) + \beta_1\left(\frac{X_i}{\sigma_i}\right) + \frac{U_i}{\sigma_i}$$

This effectively transforms error terms to $\mu_i = \frac{U_i}{\sigma_i}$ which is homo-scedastic and therefore, the OLS estimators will be free of disability caused by hetero scedasticity. The estimates of β_0 and β_1 in this situation are called **Weighted Least Squares Estimators (WLSEs)**.

(2) When σ^2 is unknown: we make some further assumptions about error variance

(a) Error variance is proportional to the X_i s. Here, the Square Root transformation is enough. We divide on both sides by $\sqrt{X_i}$. Thus, our regression line looks like: $\frac{Y_i}{\sqrt{X_i}} = \frac{\beta_0}{\sqrt{X_i}} + \beta_1 \frac{X_i}{\sqrt{X_i}} + \frac{U_i}{\sqrt{X_i}}$

$= \beta_0 \frac{1}{\sqrt{X_i}} + \beta_1 \sqrt{X_i} + \mu_i$ here $\mu_i = \frac{U_i}{\sqrt{X_i}}$ and this is sufficient to address the problem.

(b) Error variance proportional to X_1^2. Here, instead of division by $\sqrt{X_i}$, we divide by X_i on both the sides and estimate

$$\frac{Y_i}{X_i} = \beta_0 \frac{1}{X_i} + \beta_1 \frac{U_i}{X_i} = \beta_0 \frac{1}{X_i} + \beta_1 + U_i$$

The error term will be $\mu_i = \frac{U_i}{\sigma_i}$ and this will be free of hetero scedasticity, facilitating use of CLS techniques.

(3) Respecification of Model

Assigning a different functional form to the model, in place of speculating about the nature of variance may be found expedient. We can estimate this model:

$$\ln Y_i = \beta_0 + \beta_1 \ln X_i + U_i$$

This loglinear model is usually adequate to address our concerns.

Q24. What is auto-correlation? What are its consequences? Which technique would you apply to detect auto-correlation?

[Dec-2010, Q.No-7]

Ans. Autocorrelation refers to the correlation of a time series with its own past and future values. Autocorrelation is also sometimes called "lagged correlation" or "serial correlation", which refers to the correlation between members of a series of numbers arranged in time.

Sometimes, the sequence of observations is such that the error terms associated with each observation are correlated. This situation may arise when the regression equation is estimated using time-series data. When the error terms are serially correlated, the ordinary least squares (OLS) estimation yields unbiased estimates, which are not efficient. Sometimes, the sampling variances may be seriously underestimated and result in exaggerated values of R_2 and t statistic. This would result in over-confidence of the forecasts.

If autocorrelation is present in the regression analysis, it creates a problem for the validity of the t-test. Simply stated, autocorrelation tends to increase the likelihood that the null hypothesis will be rejected. This is because autocorrelation gives a downward bias to the standard error of the estimated regression coefficient ($SE_{\hat{b}}$). Thus, in the presence of autocorrelation, researchers may well declare that certain independent variables have a statistically significant impact on the dependent variable when in fact they do not. From a policy standpoint, suppose the estimated coefficient of the advertising variable in a regression model of demand passed the t-test when it really should not have. A firm might then be led to increase its advertising expenditures when in fact it should be looking at other ways to expand demand (e.g. through promotions, alternative channels of distribution, or price actions).

A widely used test for detecting autocorrelation or serial correlation in the error terms is the Durbin-Watson test, which is, based on the least squares residuals. When the error terms are serially independent, the d-statistic has a theoretical distribution with mean 2; but sampling fluctuations may lead to a different computation of the d-statistic even when the true errors are serially independent. Durbin and Watson computed a table of critical values for 95 per cent confidence levels to test the null hypothesis that the error terms are serially independent against the alternative that the null hypothesis is false. Most of the computer software packages for multiple regression analysis provide the computed Durbin-Watson (DW) statistic for the estimated regression equation.

Q25. Discuss the concept of Maximum Likelihood Estimators.

Ans. Sometimes another class of estimators is used in place of OLS. This class of estimators is called maximum likelihood estimators (MLEs). The MLEs possess some stronger theoretical properties. But it also requires a stronger assumption about distribution of error terms. Moreover, when errors follow normal distribution, we find that OLS and MLE methods give identical estimates of β parameters, both in simple and in multiple regressions. However, MLE estimate of σ^2 is biased. Hence, if one uses assumption of normal distribution of U_is and persists with OLS, one does not miss out on anything that may be advantageous in MLE.

The Method: Simple Regression Illustration

In the model $Y_1 = \beta_0 + \beta_1 X_1 + U_i$, the Y_1 is normally and independently distributed with means $\beta_0 + \beta_1 X_i$ and variance σ^2. Therefore, the joint probability density function of $Y_1, Y_2, Y_3 \ldots\ldots\ldots\ldots\ldots\ldots Y_n$ with above mean and variance will be

$$f\left(Y_1 \ldots\ldots\ldots\ldots Y_n / \beta_0 + \beta_1 X_i, \sigma^2\right) \qquad \ldots(i)$$

But given the independent of Y_s, this function can be written as product of 'n' individual density functions, or

$$f\left(Y_1 \ldots\ldots\ldots\ldots Y_n / \beta_0 + \beta_1 X_i + U_i, \sigma^2\right)$$

$$= \pi\left[Y_i / \beta_0 + \beta_1 X_i + U_i, \sigma^2\right] \qquad \ldots(ii)$$

$$\text{where } f\left(Y_i\right) = \frac{1}{\sigma\sqrt{2\pi}} . e^{\left[-Y_2 \frac{\left(Y_i - \beta_0 - \beta_1 X_i\right)^2}{\sigma^2}\right]} \qquad \ldots(iii)$$

Putting this value for each Y_i in eq-(ii), we get the likelihood function (LF):

$$LF\left(\beta_0, \beta_1, \sigma^2\right) = \frac{1}{\sigma^n\left(\sqrt{2\pi}\right)^n} . e^{\left[\frac{1}{2}\sum \frac{\left(Y_i - \beta_0 - \beta_1 - U_i\right)^2}{\sigma^2}\right]} \qquad \ldots(iv)$$

The method of maximum likelihood estimation is nothing but maximisation of the (LF) given in eq-(iv) above. We can differentiate logarithms of (LF) with respect to β_0, β_1 and σ^2 and equate the respective partials to zero to get the requisite estimation relations. So as

$$\ln(LF) = -n/n\sigma^2 - \frac{n}{2}\ln(2\pi) - \frac{1}{2}\sum\frac{(Y_i - \beta_0 - \beta_1 X_1 - U_i)^2}{\sigma^2} \quad ...(v)$$

therefore,

$$\frac{\partial \ln(LF)}{\partial \beta_0} = \frac{-1}{\sigma^2}\sum(Y_i - \beta_0 - \beta_1 X_i)(-1) = 0 \quad ...(vi)$$

$$\frac{\partial \ln(LF)}{\partial \beta_1} = \frac{-1}{\sigma^2}\sum(Y_i - \beta_0 - \beta_1 X_1)(-X_i) = 0 \quad ...(vii)$$

$$\frac{\partial \ln(LF)}{\partial \sigma^2} = \frac{-n}{2\sigma^2} + \frac{1}{2\sigma^4}\sum(Y_i - \beta_0 - \beta_1 X_i)^2 = 0 \quad ...(viii)$$

Simplification of eq-(vi) and eq-(vii) gives us

$$\sum Y_1 = n\beta_0 + \beta_1 \sum X_i \quad ...(ix)$$

$$\sum X_i Y_i = \beta_0 \sum X_i + \beta_1 \sum X_1^2 \quad ...(x)$$

Which are same as OLS normal equations.

Substituting values of ML (=OLS) estimates obtained by simultaneously solving eq-(ix) and eq-(x) into eq-(vii) gives us

$$\tilde{\sigma}^2 = \frac{1}{n}\sum(Y_i - \beta_0 - \beta_1 X_i)^2$$

$$= \frac{1}{n}\sum U_i^2 \quad ....(xi)$$

Expectation of $\tilde{\sigma}^2, E(\tilde{\sigma}^2) = \frac{1}{n}E(\sum U_i^2) = \left(\frac{n-2}{n}\right)\sigma^2 = \sigma^2 - \frac{2}{n}\sigma^2$

or $\tilde{\sigma}^2$ is biased downwards.

Q26. Given the following regression results:

$$\hat{Y}_t = 2.6911 - 0.4795X_t$$

$$\Delta e = (0.1216) \qquad (0.1140)$$

$$RSS = 0.1491, \; r^2 = 0.6628$$

Where

Y = Consumption of cups of mile per day.

X = retail price of milk in India for the year 1970-80.

(a) Interpret the results

(b) Whether the slope coefficient is statistically significant at 5 per cent level. [Dec-2011, Q.No-12]

Ans. We know that

$\hat{Y}_t = \hat{\alpha} + \hat{\beta}X_t$

Here,

$\hat{\alpha} = 2.6911$ $\hat{\beta} = -0.4795$

$s.e(\hat{\alpha}) = 0.1216$ $s.e(\hat{\beta}) = 0.1140$

$RSS = 0.1491$ $r^2 = 0.6628$

The regression line estimates the average consumption(Y) for a given level of price (X). The slope coefficient $\hat{\beta} = -0.4795$ estimates the rate of change of consumptions with respect to particular level of price. For example, 100 or more persons try to consume milk about 48 of them are consuming the milk.

The intercept $\hat{\alpha} = 2.6911$ can be interpreted as the average combined effect of all those variables that affect the consumption of milk. Here RSS= 0.1491. We know that small quantities of residual imply that a large proportion of variation in the dependable variable has been explained by the regression equation and consequently, the fit is good.

The coefficient of regression r^2=0.6628 indicates that about 66 per cent of the variation in the consumption can be explained by a variation in the price of milk, definitely its not high but indicates a good fit to the given sample. From the interpretation, it is proved that the coefficient is not statistically significant at 5 per cent level.

To get success in your studies, read only GPH Book.

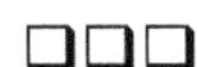

Feedback is the breakfast of Champions.

Ken Blanchard

You can Help other students.
"Inform any error or mistake in this book."

We and Universe
will reward you for Your Kind act.

Email at : feedback@gullybaba.com
or
WhatsApp on 9350849407

4 Quantitative Methods-II

An Overview

The process of economic growth entails changes in the level of income and prices. This is a process in continuum. However, the change in income and price levels needs to be studied closely in order to understand its effect on the economy. For analysis of comparison of economic situation overtime and to assess and measure the disparity in income level, statistical techniques like inequalities measures, time series analysis and index numbers are needed.

Economic growth is the single most important factor in reducing inequality. It generated additional goods and services in the economy, which in an equitable and just society should translate into better social opportunities, especially for disadvantaged people. In reality, however, economic growth does not always translate into better development prospects for the poor and disadvantaged people and inequality still remains a major problem that needs to assessed and tackled. Broadly these measures can be put under two categories positive measure and normative measures.

Q1. Explain the various positive measure of inequality.

Ans. If all values in a distribution are not equal, which means that there is dispersion in the distribution, there exists inequality in the distribution. If a measure is developed to capture this non-equality in values without giving explicit consideration to its consequences with respect to social well-being or economic significance in a particular context, the measure is known as positive. These include the followings:

(1) Relative Range

A measure of relative dispersion can be taken a measure of inequality. It is defined as the relative range by

$$RR_1 = \frac{Max_i\, x_i - Min_i\, x_i}{\mu} \qquad ...(i)$$

that is, the relative difference between the highest income and the lowest income. If income is equally distributed, then $RR_1 = 0$ and if one person received all the income, then RR_1 is maximum if one wants to make the index lie in the interval between 0 and 1, one can define it as

$$RR_2 = \frac{Max_i\, x_i - Min_i\, x_i}{N\mu} \qquad ...(ii)$$

which means it is the gap between the maximum share and the minimum share.

That is,

$$RR_2 = Max_i\, q_i - Min_i\, q_i \qquad ...(iii)$$

Though Cowell has suggested division of range by $Min_i x_i$, which does not serve, in our view, any purpose. Two other normalisation or standardisation procedures that make it unit-free and contain it in (0,1) interval are suggested below:

$$RR_3 = \frac{Max_i\, x_i - Min_i \overline{x}_i}{Max_i\, x_i} \qquad ...(iv)$$

and

$$RR_4 = \frac{Max_i\, x_i - Min_i x_i}{Max_i\, x_i + Min_i x_i} \qquad ...(v)$$

The basic weaknesses of these range-based measures are that they are not based on all values and therefore they do not reflect the change in inequality if there is any transfer of income between two non-extreme recipients.

Instead of considering extreme values at either end, which may not be even known, some scholars have toyed with the idea of the ratio between the mean income of the highest fractile (percentile, quintile or decile) and that of the lowest counterpart.

They term it as the extreme disparity ratio (EDR). Naturally, this ratio is not contained in the interval (0.1). This ratio is independent of μ as well. The measure will not reflect the transfer of income that does not involve the extreme fractiles.

(2) Relative Inter-Quartile Range

Sometimes, extremism of the relative range is sought to be moderated by restricting the distribution between the 10th and 90th percentile or sometimes to interquartile range. Bowley (1937) suggested relative quartile deviation as the index of inequality:

$$B=\frac{x^{q^3}-x^{q^1}}{x^{q^3}+x^{q^1}} \qquad \text{...(vi)}$$

where x^{q^3} represents the income level which divides the population in r and (4-r) quartiles. B is zero for degenerate distribution where everybody has the same income and unity if the lowest 75 per cent people have no income at all.

Though the extremes are moderated in comparison to the measure of range, it has an obvious weakness that the measure takes into account only 50 per cent of the distribution. Further, a transfer of income between two persons without causing either or both of them cross x^{q^1} or x^{q^3} would not change the measured level of inequality. Thus, the index suffers from all weaknesses of the earlier proposals except that of extremism. Its highest value reaches when the lowest 75 per cent people do not possess any income.

A variant of this measure is inter-quartile ratio, which can be defined as the 75th percentile (3rd quartile) income minus 25th percentile (1st quartile) income divided by the median (x^{q^2}) income.

(3) Relative Standard Variation

The standard deviation divided by the mean can be used as one measure of dispersion. It is:

$$RSD=\frac{\sigma}{\mu} \qquad \text{...(vii)}$$

where σ and μ are standard deviation and mean of the distribution.

It can be equivalently defined as the standard deviation of relative incomes. Using definition of σ, one can find out that it lies in the interval of

0 and $(N-1)^{1/2}$, not in (0,1). The highest value depends on the size of distribution.

Since the measure uses all values, any transfer of income would be reflected in the measure. However, it should be noted that the measure is equi-sensitive to transfers at all levels. Whether a given amount d is transferred between

x_j=₹400 and x_k=₹500, or between x_j=₹10,000 and x_k=₹10,100, the change in RSD is exactly the same.

(4) Standard Deviation of Logarithms

One way of attaching greater importance to transfers at lower end (as required by Sen) is to consider some transformation of incomes. This transformation can easily be attained by considering the logarithms that stagger the income at lower levels.

This measure is defined in either of the following two ways:

$$SDL_1 = \left(\frac{1}{N}\sum_{i=1}^{N}(\log\mu - \log x_i)^2\right)^{1/2} \quad \text{...(viii)}$$

$$SDL_2 = \left(\frac{1}{N}\sum_{i=1}^{N}(\log\hat{\mu} - \log x_i)^2\right)^{1/2} \quad \text{...(ix)}$$

where μ and $\hat{\mu}$ are the arithmetic and geometric means respectively. While standard statistical literature prefers use of geometric mean the more common practice in literature on income inequality is one of using arithmetic means.

Cowell (1995) prefers to define these in terms of variance and calls the square of SDL_1 as the logarithm variance (V_1) and the square of SDL_2 as the variance of logarithms (V_2). Name of the second is clear from the expression but that of the first is derived from the fact that $(\log x - \log\overline{x})$ could be written as $\log(x/\overline{x})$. One can see that V_1 is equal to V_2 plus $\log(\hat{\mu}/\mu)$.

As these measures are in terms of ratios of incomes, any proportionate change in incomes would leave the magnitude of inequality unchanged when measured by these indices. But, unfortunately, a transfer from a richer person to a poorer person may raise the magnitude of inequality, particularly if the poorer person has income more than 2.72 times the mean of the distribution.

While the lower limit, irrespective of formula, is zero when everybody has the same income, the upper limit depends on the size of distribution and approaches infinity when N is large and when everybody except the richest, receives income equal to one unit (as zero is inadmissible in logarithmic transformation.) Further, if we face grouped data, it is convenient to use μ in place of $\hat{\mu}$ and μ_i in place of x_i.

The variance of logarithms is however, decomposable. It is a property that is being given emphasis of late. It can be shown that V_2 is the sum of between group component and within group component, latter being population-weighted sum of within-group V_2's.

(5) Champernowne Index

Champernowne (1973) makes use of the idea of geometric mean. It is a well known fact of an unequal distribution that its geometric mean is smaller than the arithmetic mean. The additive inverse of the ratio of geometric mean to arithmetic mean can duly be considered as an index of inequality. Formally, the index could be written as:

$$CII = 1 - \frac{\hat{\mu}}{\mu} \qquad ...(x)$$

where μ and $\hat{\mu}$ are arithmetic and geometric means of the income distribution. It is easy to see that its value is bound between 0 and 1.

These measures are sensitive to transfer to income and change is greater when the transfer takes place at lower end of the distribution. They are sensitive to transfer of income between two persons.

(6) Hirschman-Herfindahl Indices

These indices were developed in the course of studying the commodity concentration in trade by Hirschman (1945) and in characterising market monopoly in industry by Herfindahl (1950). Later, they were more used in capturing autonomy and dependence of units in a federation.

If each unit is a class in itself, $p_i = 1/N, i = 1,2...,N$. Then concentration could be captured through use of q_i's. As the sum of q_i's is always 1, Hirschman devised a measure which would capture the inequality among them. He proposed square root of the sum of squares of shares q_i $i = 1,2...,N$. That is

$$H_1 = \left(N \sum_{i=1}^{N} q_i^2 \right)^{1/2} \qquad ...(xi)$$

which could be generalised as

$$H^*_1 = \left(N \sum_{i=1}^{N} q_i^a \right)^{1/a}, a > 1$$

Herfindahl devised a very similar measure, which has been more popular than the original (eq-xi). This is just the sum of share squares:

$$H_2 = \sum_{i=1}^{N} q_i^2 \qquad ...(xii)$$

$$H^*_2 = \sum_{i=1}^{N} q_i^a, a \geq 1. \qquad ...(xiii)$$

It is clear that, besides inequality among the shares, the values of these measures depends on N – the fewness or largeness of the number of units. For N = 2, it has been suggested that (1/N) could be subtracted from (eq-xii)

$$H_3 = \sum_{i=1}^{N} q_i^2 - \frac{1}{N} \qquad ...(xiv)$$

The minimum value of H_3 is zero. But it serves no great purpose. When N = 2, for $q_1 = 0.99$ and $q_2 = 0.01$, while $H_2 = 0.98$, $H_3 = 0.48$. H_2 scores definitely better than H_3 in characterising the scene of monopoly.

(7) Kolm's Index

Let there be N incomes such that N= nm where n is the number of different incomes and each income has m recipients. The number of equal pairs with a given income would be m(m-1)/2 and total number of equal pairs would be n.m(m-1)/2. Total number of all pairs would obviously be N(N–1)/2-nm (nm-1)/2. One can think of an 'equality' index in terms of nm(m–1)/nm(nm–1)=(m-1)/(N-1). The inequality index could then be constructed by subtracting it from 1:1-(m-1)/(N-1)-(N-m)/(N-1)=m (n-1)/(nm-1)=(nm-m)/(nm-1). In case, income x_1 has f_i recipients, the measure is:

$$K = 1 - \frac{\sum f_i^2 - N}{N(N-1)} = \frac{N^2 - \sum f_i^2}{N(N-1)} \qquad ...(xiv)$$

The purpose of developing this curiosum due to Kolm (1996) is just to make one feel that there could be a variety of simple ways to approach the issue of measurement of inequality.

Q2. What do you understand by the Gini index and Gini coefficient? Discuss its relative advantage and disadvantage as a measure of inequality. Explain its relationship with the Lorenz curve.

Or

State the computation device of Gini coefficient index.

[Dec-2010, Q.No-10]

Or

What is Gini ratio? How can you compute it? [June-2011, Q.No.-8]

Or

State the relationship between Lorenz curve and Gini coefficient. [June-2012, Q.No.-8]

Ans. The Gini coefficient is a measure of inequality of a distribution. It is defined as a ratio with values between 0 and 1: the numerator is the area between the Lorenz curve of the distribution and the uniform distribution line; the denominator is the area under the uniform distribution line. It was developed by the Italian statistician Corrado Gini.

The Gini index is the Gini coefficient expressed as a percentage, and is equal to the Gini coefficient multiplied by 100. (The Gini coefficient is equal to half of the relative mean difference.)

The Gini coefficient can also be used to measure wealth inequality. This use requires that no one has a negative net wealth. It is also commonly used for the measurement of discriminatory power of rating systems in the credit risk management.

The Gini coefficient is defined as a ratio of the areas on the Lorenz curve figure. If the area between the line of perfect equality and Lorenz curve is A, and the area under the Lorenz curve is B, then the Gini coefficient is A/(A+B). Since A+B = 0.5, the Gini coefficient, G = 2A = 1-2B. If the Lorenz curve is represented by the function Y = L(X), the value of B can be found with integration and:

$$G=1-2\int_0^1 L(x)dx$$

In some cases, this equation can be applied to calculate the Gini coefficient without direct reference to the Lorenz curve. For example:

- For a population with values $y_i, i=1$ to n, that are indexed in non-decreasing order $(y_i \leq y_{i+1})$:

$$G=\frac{1}{n}\left(n+1-2\left(\frac{\sum_{i=1}^{n}(n+1-i)y_i}{\sum_{i=1}^{n}y_i}\right)\right)$$

- For a discrete probability function f(y), where $y_i, i=1$ to n, are the points v nonzero probabilities and which are indexed in increasing order $(y_i < y_{i+1})$

$$G=1-\frac{\sum_{i=1}^{n}f(y_i)(S_{i-1}+S_i)}{Sn} \quad \text{where, } S_i=\sum_{j=1}^{i}f(y_j)y_j \text{ and } S_0=0$$

- For a cumulative distribution function F(y) that is piecewise differentiable a mean μ, and is zero for all negative values of y:

$$G = 1 - \frac{1}{\mu}\int_0^\infty (1 - F(y))^2 \, dy$$

Since the Gini coefficient is half the relative mean difference, it can also be calculated using formulas for the relative mean difference.

For a random sample, S consisting of values $y_i, i = 1$ to n, that are indexed in non-decreasing order $(y_i \leq y_{i+1})$, the statistic:

$$G(S) = \frac{1}{n-1}\left(n+1-2\left(\frac{\sum_{i=1}^{n}(n+1-i)y_i}{\sum_{i=1}^{n} y_i}\right)\right)$$

is a consistent estimator of the population Gini coefficient, but is not, in general, unbiased. Like the relative mean difference, there does not exist a sample statistic that is in general an unbiased estimator of the population Gini coefficient. Confidence intervals for the population Gini coefficient can be calculated using bootstrap techniques.

Sometimes the entire Lorenz curve is not known, and only values at certain intervals are given. In that case, the Gini coefficient can be approximated by using various techniques for interpolating the missing values of the Lorenz curve. If (X_k, Y_k) are the known points on the Lorenz curve, with the X_k indexed in increasing order $(X_{k=1} < X_k)$, so that:

- X_k is the cumulated proportion of the population variable, for $k = 0,\ldots,n$, with $X_0 = 0, X_n = 1$.
- Y_k is the cumulated proportion of the income variable, for $k = 0,\ldots,n$, with $Y_0 = 0$, $Y_n = 1$.

If the Lorenz curve is approximated on each interval as a line between consecutive points, then the area B can be approximated with trapezoids and:

$$G_1 = 1 - \sum_{k=1}^{n}(X_k - X_{k-1})(Y_k + Y_{k-1})$$

is the resulting approximation for G. More accurate results can be obtained using other methods to approximate the area B, such as approximating the Lorenz curve with a quadratic function across pairs of intervals, or building an appropriately smooth approximation to the underlying distribution function that matches the known data. If the population means and boundary values for each interval are also known, these can also often be used to improve the accuracy of the approximation.

While most developed European nations tend to have Gini coefficients between 0.24 and 0.36, the United States Gini coefficient is above 0.4, indicating that the United States has greater inequality. Using the Gini can help quantify differences in welfare and compensation policies and philosophies. However it should be borne in mind that the Gini coefficient can be misleading when used to make political comparisons between large and small countries.

Advantages as a measure of inequality

- The Gini coefficient's main advantage is that it is a measure of inequality by means of a ratio analysis, rather than a variable unrepresentative of most of the population, such as per capita income or gross domestic product.
- It can be used to compare income distributions across different population sectors as well as countries, for example the Gini coefficient for urban areas differs from that of rural areas in many countries (though the United States' urban and rural Gini coefficients are nearly identical).
- It is sufficiently simple that it can be compared across countries and be easily interpreted. GDP statistics are often criticised as they do not represent changes for the whole population; the Gini coefficient demonstrates how income has changed for poor and rich. If the Gini coefficient is rising as well as GDP, poverty may not be improving for the majority of the population.
- The Gini coefficient can be used to indicate how the distribution of income has changed within a country over a period of time, thus it is possible to see if inequality is increasing or decreasing.
- The Gini coefficient satisfies four important principles:
    - Anonymity: it does not matter who the high and low earners are.
    - Scale independence: the Gini coefficient does not consider the size of the economy, the way it is measured, or whether it is a rich or poor country on average.
    - Population independence: it does not matter how large the population of the country is.
    - Transfer principle: if income (less than the difference), is transferred from a rich person to a poor person the resulting distribution is more equal.

Disadvantages as a measure of inequality

- The Gini coefficient measured for a large economically diverse country will generally result in a much higher coefficient than each of its regions has individually. For this reason, the scores calculated for individual countries within the EU are difficult to compare with the score of the entire US.
- Comparing income distributions among countries may be difficult because benefits systems may differ. For example, some countries give benefits in the form of money while others give food stamps, which may not be counted as income in the Lorenz curve and therefore not taken into account in the Gini coefficient.
- The measure will give different results when applied to individuals instead of households. When different populations are not measured with consistent definitions, comparison is not meaningful.
- The Lorenz curve may understate the actual amount of inequality if richer households are able to use income more efficiently than lower income households. From another point of view, measured inequality may be the result of more or less efficient use of household incomes.
- As for all statistics, there will be systematic and random errors in the data. The meaning of the Gini coefficient decreases as the data become less accurate. Also, countries may collect data differently, making it difficult to compare statistics between countries.
- Economies with similar incomes and Gini coefficients can still have very different income distributions. This is because the Lorenz curves can have different shapes and yet still yield the same Gini coefficient. As an extreme example, an economy where half the households have no income, and the other half share income equally has a Gini coefficient of ½; but an economy with complete income equality, except for one wealthy household that has half the total income, also has a Gini coefficient of ½.
- Too often, only the Gini coefficient is quoted without describing the proportions of the quantiles used for measurement. As with

other inequality coefficients, the Gini coefficient is influenced by the granularity of the measurements. For example, five 20 per cent quantiles (low granularity) will yield a lower Gini coefficient than 25 per cent quantiles (high granularity) taken from the same distribution

Q3. Explain Lorenz Curve as a geometrical device to measure inequality. Describe its properties. [Dec-2011, Q.No.-8]

Ans. It is a graphical method of studying dispersion. Lorenz curve was given by famous statistician Max O Lorenz. Lorenz curve has great utility in the study of degree of inequality in the distribution of income and wealth between the countries. It is also useful for comparing the distribution of wages, profits, etc. over different business groups. Lorenz curve is a cumulative percentage curve in which the percentage of frequency (persons of workers) is combined with the percentage of other items such as income, profits, wages, etc.

The Lorenz curve of concentration of incomes is the relationship between the cumulative proportions of recipients, usually plotted on the abscissa, and the corresponding cumulative shares of total income with the recipients, usually plotted on the ordinate. If population proportions and income shares of class j are denoted by p_j and q_j cumulative proportions and shares upto class i, by P_i and Q_i then

$$P_i = \sum_{j=1}^{i} P_j, \qquad 1 \geq P_j \geq 0 \qquad \text{...(i)}$$

and $$Q_i = \sum_{j=1}^{i} q_j, \qquad 1 \geq q_j \geq 0 \qquad \text{...(ii)}$$

The relationship between P_i and Q_i is given by the curve

$$Q_i = L(P_i), \qquad 1 \geq P_i \geq 0, \qquad 1 \geq Q_i \geq 0 \qquad \text{...(iii)}$$

and the point on the curve by (P_i, Q_i). Naturally, the first point is (0,0) and the last one on the curve, (1, 1). It is also clear that $Q_i \leq P_i \; i = 1, 2, \ldots, N-1$ if there are N classes of incomes. It means no point will make an angel of more than 45° with the abscissa at the origin. Then, one can be sure that the Lorenz curve lies in the lower triangle of Lorenz Box of the unit square. See Figure 4.1 in which OLB shows the Lorenz curve (Figure 4.1).

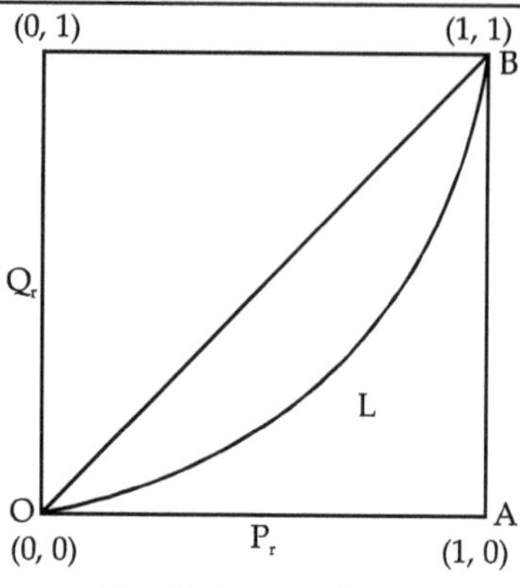

Fig. 4.1: Lorenz Curve

Properties of the Lorenz Curve

Now it easy to see that the extreme case of perfect equality is given by the diagonal OB which represents $P_i = Q_i, i = 1, 2, ..., N$. The other extreme of perfect inequality will be given by a curve OAB. The diagonal OB is often designate as the egalitarian line or line of equality. The other diagonal CA is known as the alternative diagonal and is useful to study the symmetry of the curve. The line OAB with sharp kink of 90° at A can be said to be the line of perfect inequality.

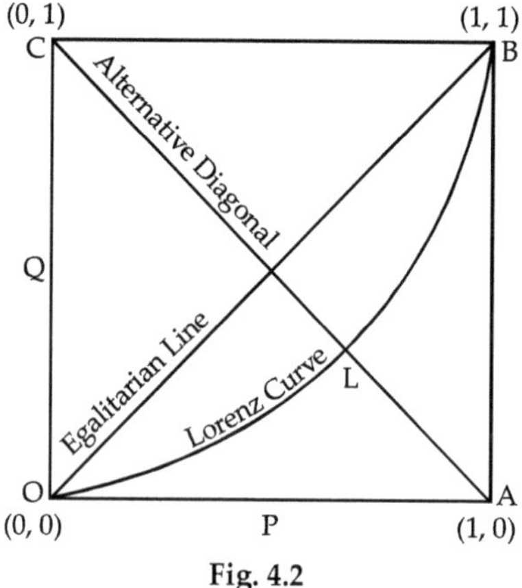

Fig. 4.2

We can finally note the following properties:

- $1 \geq p_i \geq 0; 1 \geq q_i \geq 0, i = 1, 2, ..., N$
- $1 \geq P_i \geq 0; 1 \geq Q_i \geq 0, i = 1, 2, ..., N-1$
- $P_0 = Q_0 = 0; P_N = Q_N = 1$
- $P_i \geq Q_i, i = 1, 2, ..., N-1$

By drawing a Lorenz Curve, we can know whether a given distribution is equal or unequal. We do not yet know how much unequal a given distribution is. When we draw two or more Lorenz Curves, we can compare the distributions as regards their levels of inequality. And even this comparison is possible only when the curves do not intersect (Figure 4.4).

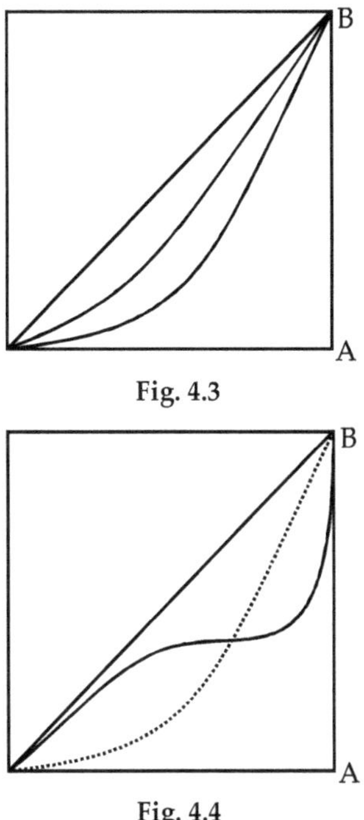

Fig. 4.3

Fig. 4.4

However, we can devise some measures, which are based on the Lorenz curve. In case the Lorenz curves intersect, reducing the distributions into single real number is the only option. So we shall discuss only two such proposals.

A Measure Based on Area

If Lorenz curve coincides with the diagonal of equality, the inequality is nil and if Lorenz curve coincides with the two sides of the square, the inequality is full. In the case of non-intersecting Lorenz curves, it is clear that the curve closer to the diagonal of equality will circumscribe smaller area between itself and the diagonal of equality than the one, which is farther. We can therefore devise a measure of inequality by dividing the area OLB by the area of triangle OAB, which is the maximum possible area between the diagonal of equality and Lorenz curve. As the area of OAB is (1/2), the measure turns out to be twice the area between the diagonal of equality and the Lorenz curve. In other words, Lorenz coefficient of concentration (LCC) is:

$$LCC=\frac{\text{Area OLB}}{\Delta OAB}=2\text{Area OLB}$$

Since this turns out to be exactly equal to Gini coefficient.

A Measure Based on Length

This measure is proposed by Kakwani (1980). The length of the Lorenz curve, denoted by l, cannot fall below $\sqrt{2}$, which is the length of the egalitarian line and cannot exceed 2, which is the sum of the lengths of the two arms of the lower triangle. In order to produce a measure with the minimum value 0 and the maximum value 1, following exercise can be suggested:

Table 4.1

	Minimum	Actual	Maximum
Length of the Curve	$\sqrt{2}$	l	2
Length of the Curve $-\sqrt{2}$	0	$l-\sqrt{2}$	$2-\sqrt{2}$
$\frac{\text{Length of the Curve}-\sqrt{2}}{\text{Maximum length}-\sqrt{2}}$	0	$\frac{l-\sqrt{2}}{2-\sqrt{2}}$	1

So this measure is clearly:

$$LK=\left(l-\sqrt{2}\right)/\left(2-\sqrt{2}\right)$$

In both the cases, one can draw actual graphs and actually measure the area and the length and calculate the indices for level of inequality.

Q4. Discuss the following normative measures:

(a) Dalton Index

Ans. For each individual, Dalton assumes, marginal economic welfare diminishes as income increases. It means income-welfare function

$$U_i=U_i(x_i), i=1,2,...N \qquad ...(i)$$

(where U_i is welfare of person i possessing income x_i is concave, suggesting that $(\partial U_i/\partial x_i)>0$ but $(\partial^2 U_i/\partial x_i^2)<0$. Dalton further assumes that economic welfare of different persons is additive. Thus, in his scheme, social welfare is a simple aggregation of personal welfares. In other words, social welfare W is given by

$$W=\sum_{i=1}^{N}U_i(x_i) \qquad ...(ii)$$

He further assumes that the relation of income to economic welfare is the same for all members of the community. That is,

$$U_i = U(x_i), i = 1, 2, ... N \quad ...(iii)$$

In that case, the relation (ii) can be expressed as

$$W = \sum_{i=1}^{N} U(x_i) \quad ...(iv)$$

which makes it clear that whosoever gains in welfare, the addition to the social welfare is the same. For any given level of social welfare, any distribution of welfare among the members of the society is permissible. However, one must remember that the relation of individual income to their welfares is concave. Therefore, transfer of income from A to B will not lead to symmetric change in welfares of those two persons involved in the transaction. The result is some impact on W the measure of social welfare.

From Figure 4.5, we may compare the situation when two individuals, both possessing the same relation, have two different income levels, with that when they have the same (mean) income. We may note that the sum of the welfare of person 1(BB') and the welfare of person 2(DD') is less than the twice of CC' which is the level of welfare enjoyed by both the persons when they have equal income. It is easy to see that the loss suffered by person 2, that is D' E, is overcompensated by the gained by person 1, which is C' F.

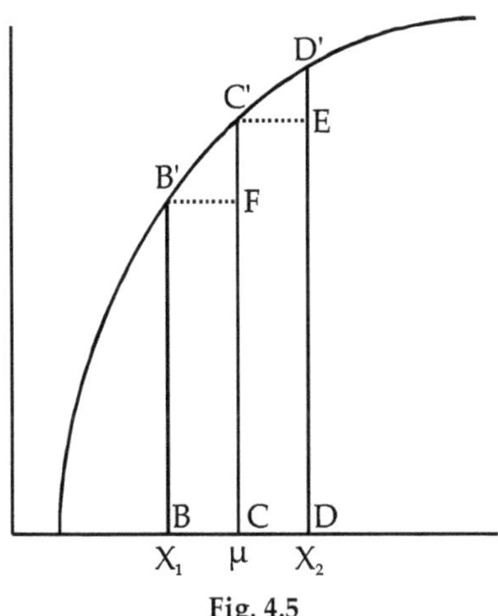

Fig. 4.5

This demonstrates that, under assumptions by Dalton, an equal distribution is preferable to an unequal one for a given amount of total income from the viewpoint of social welfare. In fact, for a given total income, the economic welfare of the society will be maximum when all incomes are equal. The inequality of any given distribution may therefore be defined as:

$$D_1 = \frac{\sum_{i=1}^{N} U(\mu)}{\sum_{i=1}^{N} U(x_i)} = \frac{NU(\mu)}{\sum_{i=1}^{N} U(x_i)} \quad ...(vii)$$

which is equal to unity for an equal distribution and greater than unity for an unequal one. It may therefore, be preferred to define the Dalton's index as

$$D_2 = \frac{NU(\mu)}{\sum_{i=1}^{N} U(x_i)} \quad ...(viii)$$

which is obviously zero for an equal distribution. How large can it be? It will depend on the values $U(0), U(\mu)$ and $U(N\mu)$ when N and μ are given, not necessarily 1. Later writers have therefore, preferred to define Dalton's index in the following form, which inverts the arguments of D_2 subtract it from 1:

$$D = 1 - \frac{\sum_{i=1}^{N} U(x_i)}{NU(\mu)} = 1 - \frac{\bar{U}}{U(\mu)} \quad ...(ix)$$

It looks as if the index is contained in the interval (0, 1). However, there are many valid concave functions where it may not hold true. For example, if we have $U(x_i) = \log x_i$, then $D = 1 - \{\log\hat{\mu} / \log\mu\}$. Given the fact that $\hat{\mu} < \mu$, D would turn out to be a negative number for $\hat{\mu} < 1$. And μ could be less than 1 as x can be measured in any unit. It would be the same case $U(x_i) = 1/x_i$.

However, in order to obtain numerical magnitude, it is not sufficient to define the index. Dalton (1920) points out that though defined in terms of economic welfare, inequality has to be measured in terms of income. Then, no unique measure of inequality will emerge. It will verily depend on the particular functional relationship assumed. Dalton himself considered two such functions for the purpose of illustration. The first is related to Bernaulli's hypothesis. It holds that proportionate additions to income (in excess of that required for bare subsistence-poverty line) make equal additions to personal welfare, That is,

$$dU_i = \frac{dx_i}{x_i} \text{ or } U_i = \log x_i + c_i \quad ...(x)$$

Under the assumption that every person has the same functional relationship, the Dalton's index can be given as:

$$D=1-\frac{\log\hat{\mu}+c}{\log\mu+c} \qquad \text{...(xi)}$$

where $\hat{\mu}$ is the geometric mean of personal incomes. The other formulation be discusses is given as

$$dU_i=\frac{dx_i}{x_1^2} \text{ or } U_i=c-\frac{1}{x_i} \qquad \text{...(xii)}$$

where c is the maximum welfare one can obtain when $x \to \infty$. Dalton's index in this case would turn out to be:

$$D=1-\frac{c-(1/\tilde{\mu})}{C-(1/\mu)} \qquad \text{...(xiii)}$$

where $\tilde{\mu}$ is the harmonic mean.

(b) Atkinson Index

Ans. One of the most popular inequality measures, named after the Welsh economist Anthony Barnes Atkinson, the index has been extensively used in the normative measurement of inequality. Atkinson (1970) set out the approach to constructing social inequality indices based on the loss of equivalent income. In an initial contribution, another Welsh economist, Edward Hugh Dalton (1887–1962), used a simple utilitarian social welfare function to derive an inequality measure. The same utility function was taken to apply to all individuals, with diminishing marginal utility from income. An equal distribution should maximise social welfare. Inequality should be estimated as the shortfall of the sum–total of utilities from the maximal value. In an extended way, the Atkinson index measures the social loss resulting from unequal income distribution by shortfalls of equivalent incomes. Inequality is measured by the percentage reduction of total income that can be sustained without reducing social welfare, by distributing the new reduced total exactly. The difference of the equally distributed equivalent income with the actual income gives Atkinson's measure of inequality.

The social welfare function considered by Atkinson has the form

$$U(y)=A+B\frac{y^{1-\varepsilon}}{1-\varepsilon}, \varepsilon \neq 1$$

$$U(y)=\log_e(y), \varepsilon=1$$

and the index takes the form

$$A_\varepsilon = 1 - \left[\frac{1}{n}\sum_{i=1}^{n}\left(\frac{y_i}{\mu}\right)^{1-e}\right]^{\frac{1}{1-e}} \quad \varepsilon \geq 0, \varepsilon \neq 1$$

$$A_1 = 1 - \exp\left[\frac{1}{n}\sum_{i=1}^{n}\text{Ln}\left(\frac{y_i}{\mu}\right)\right] \quad \varepsilon = 1$$

where ε is a measure of the degree of inequality aversion or the relative sensitivity of transfers at different income levels. As ε rises, we attach more weight to transfers at the lower end of the distribution and less weight to transfers at the top. The limiting cases at both extremes are $\varepsilon \to \infty$, which only takes account of transfers to the very lowest income group and $\varepsilon \to 0$, giving the linear utility function, which ranks distribution solely according to total income.

(c) Sen Index

Ans. There are people who feel rather strongly that the social valuation of the welfare of individuals should depend crucially on the incomes of their neighbours too. Then, why should society add simply individual welfares? One may also question the assumption of one welfare function for all individuals. If we do so, we should go for broad social welfare function such as

$$W = W(x_i, x_2, \ldots, x_N) \quad \ldots(i)$$

which is just symmetric, quasi-concave and increasing in individual income levels. Then, a more general normative measure of inequality can be defined by devising the concept of 'generalised equally distributed equivalent income'. This is obviously the level of per capita income x^* which, if shared by all, would produce the same level of W as is generated by the present actual distribution. That is,

$$x^* = x | W(x^*, x^*, \ldots, x^*) = W(x_1 x_2, \ldots, x_N) \quad \ldots(ii)$$

Under the assumption that (S. 1) is quasi-concave, $x^* \leq \mu$ for every distribution of income. The index S would then be

$$S = 1 - \frac{x^*}{\mu} \quad \ldots(iii)$$

which is but a generalised version of A. if utilitarian framework is employed, then S and A turn out to be indistinguishable.

These measures, it may be noted, clearly suggest that there exists a redistribution equivalent of growth so far as the concern is about raising the welfare.

(d) Theil Entropy Index

Ans. Theil (1967) poses a question: Does information theory supply us with a 'natural' measure of income inequality among N individuals, which is based on income shares? He answers: Yes. Here is a short introduction.

Let us start with income share of individual i:

$$q_i = \frac{x_i}{N_\mu} > 0 \quad \text{such that} \sum_{i=1}^{N} q_i = 1 \qquad ...(i)$$

When $x_i = \mu, i = 1, 2, ..., N$ that is, when distribution is equal, we have

$$q_i = \frac{1}{N} \quad i = 1, 2, ... N \qquad ...(ii)$$

We have complete inequality when some $x_i N\mu$ and $x_j = 0, j \neq i$. It implies that

$q_i = 1$ for some i and $q_j = 0, i \neq j$.

In information theory, one way of defining entropy of probabilities p_i is

$$H = \sum_{i=1}^{N} p_i \log \frac{1}{P_i} \qquad ...(iii)$$

Replacing probabilities by shares, we have

$$H = \sum_{i=1}^{N} q_i \log \frac{1}{q_i}. \qquad ...(iv)$$

which can be taken as a measure of equality. For the situation of complete equality, we can see that H is equal to logN and for that of complete inequality H is zero. We can therefore define Theil index T as

$$T = \log N \sum_{i=1}^{N} q_i \log \frac{1}{q_i}. = \sum_{i=1}^{N} q_i \log N - \sum_{i=1}^{N} q_i \log \frac{1}{q_i}$$

$$= \sum_{i=1}^{N} q_i \log N.q_i \qquad ...(v)$$

This measure is motivated by the notion of entropy in information theory. But one can see that it can be interpreted in the traditional normative framework with

$$U_i = q_i \log \frac{1}{q_i} \qquad ...(vi)$$

and

$$W = \sum_{i=1}^{N} U_i(q_i). \qquad ...(vii)$$

We may note that eq-(vi) depends on x_i as well as on μ along with N and U that it is concave with respect to $x_{i.}$

While the lower limit of T is zero, its upper limit log N increases as the number of individuals increases. To many people, it is objectionable. However, Theil (1967) chooses to defend it. When society consists of two crore persons and one grabs all and when society consists of two persons and one grabs all, cannot have the same level of inequality. The former case is equivalent to the situation in which one crore out of two crore people have nothing and the other one crore have equal income. Maximum value for two-person society is log 2, and that for two crore-person society is 7 log 2. Some researchers still insist that the measure should be normalised by dividing it by log N.

(e) Kakwani Index

Ans. Enlightened by Sen Index, Kakwani put forward another index in 1980:

$$K = \frac{\mu}{1+G} \qquad ...(i)$$

In the formula, K represents Kakwani Index, μ average income, and G Gini Coefficient.

Indexes based on social welfare theory to measure income inequality are problematic mainly in two aspects: first, in the process of adding overall social utility function, the heterogeneity of individual utility is ignored; second, how to construct a utility function, which can be accepted by the whole society? All the social welfare indexes are limited in that they suppose individual welfare is dependent on economic entity alone, and social welfare is dependent on individual welfare determined by individual income of economic entity. However, in practice, another significant feature of income inequality is that the individual welfare of economic entity relies on not only his own income, but also a comparison with his peers.

Q5. What is time series analysis? Discuss its utility in Research work.

Or

Define the concept of time series.

Or

What is the utility of the analysis of Time Series in research?

Or

Write short note on "Time Series".

Ans. The set of data collected on the basis of time (such as days, months, years) is called as time series. Time series data have a natural temporal ordering. This makes time series analysis distinct from other common data analysis problems, in which there is no natural ordering of the observations (e.g. explaining people's wages by reference to their education level, where the individual's data could be entered in any order). Time series analysis is also distinct from spatial data analysis where the observations typically relate to geographical locations (e.g. accounting for house prices by the location as well as the intrinsic characteristics of the houses). A time series model will generally reflect the fact that observations close together in time will be more closely related than observations further apart. In addition, time series models will often make use of the natural one-way ordering of time so that values for a given period will be expressed as deriving in some way from past values, rather than from future values.

Methods for time series analyses may be divided into two classes: frequency-domain methods and time-domain methods. The former include spectral analysis and recently wavelet analysis; the latter include auto-correlation and cross-correlation analysis.

Definition

A time series consists of statistical data which are collected, recorded over successive increments.

"When quantitative data are arranged in the order of their occurrence, the resulting statistical series is called a time series".

Utility of Time series

The study of time series has great importance in economic and business world which is illustrated by the following points:

- **To study the Past Behaviour of the Data:** With the help of time series, changes occurred in the past are studied. Only by analysing the various sorts of changes occurred in the past, economists and businessmen can frame their present policies by taking advantage of the past experience.
- **To Forecast Future Behaviour:** With the help of time series anticipation of changes going to occur in the future becomes possible because studies about past prove to be very useful for forecasting about future.
- **Estimation of Trade Cycles:** Cyclical fluctuations in a time series give idea about the changes taking place in the business

like boom, recession, depression and recovery. Businessman can apply this knowledge to rationalise his course of action, by way of which potential losses can be avoided.

- **Comparison with other Time Series:** Time series analysis is also important for the comparison of various time series. By comparing different time series together, their cause and effect can be more elaborately analysed.
- **Study of Present Variations:** Time series analysis is also helpful in studying the present variations in different economic variables like national income, export-import, price, output, etc.
- **Universal Utility:** Time series analysis benefits all classes like businessmen, farmers, consumers, economists and government and accordingly they plan and direct their activities.

Q6. What are the components of time series?

Ans. Many types of changes collectively exert influence on time series. Some are natural or institutional, while others are socio-economic in character. Some of them may be responsible for short-term variation, while others effect long-run variation. Such changes are called as components of time series. Thus, a time series is made up of a variety of elements, or components, which account for the observed variations over a period of time.

Components of time series are usually classified into four components, namely:

- **Secular Trend:** The general tendency of the time series data to increase or to decrease or to remain segregated during a long period of time is called secular trend.

  Trend values are helpful in studying the behaviour pattern of the phenomenon under study. In enables us to make comparisons between two times and draw meaningful conclusions from them.
- **Seasonal Variations:** Seasonal variations refer to such movements in a time series, which are due to forces, rhythmic in nature, and repeat themselves periodically every season. These variations repeat themselves in less than one year time. Seasons could be weekly, monthly, quarterly or half-yearly depending on the nature of the phenomenon.

  A study of the seasonal variations is extremely useful to businessmen, producers and consumers. Policy decisions can be formulated taking into account the nature of seasonal variations. In scheduling production and inventory, knowledgeof seasonal variations is a must. In fact, in such areas it is seasonal variations alone which constitute the main plank of decision-making.

- **Cyclical Variations:** The cyclical variations in a series are the recurrent variations whose duration is more than one year. Though cyclical movements, by and large are regular, they are not necessarily uniformly periodic. A cycle may not always complete itself with a fixed duration of time. In the field of economics and business, cyclical variations are the results of business cycles.

  A Study of cyclical variations is important for the same reason as the study of seasonal variations. A businessman, if he has knowledge of cyclical variations, can prepare himself for facing a period of recession or depression, by taking appropriate decisions in advance.

- **Irregular Variations:** Irregular variations are the effect of random factors. These generally mixed up with seasonal and cyclical variations and are caused by irregular and accidental factors like floods, famines, wars, strikes, lockout, etc. There is no regular period or time of their occurrence and that is why they are called random or chance fluctuations.

Q7. What do you mean by Decomposition of Time series?

Or

What do you understand by the term decomposition of the time series?

Or

Explain briefly the additive and multiplicative models of time series.

Ans. Decomposition and analysis of a time series is one and the same thing. The original data or observed data 'O' is the result of the effects generated by the long-term and short-term causes, namely, (1) Trend = T, (2) cyclical = C, (3) seasonal = S, (4) Irregular = I. Finding out the values for each of the components is called decomposition of a time series. Decomposition is done either by the Additive model or the Multiplicative model of analysis.

Additive Model: It is based on the assumption that the four components are independent of one another. Under this assumption, the pattern of occurrence and the magnitude of movements in any particular component are not affected by the other components. In this model, the values of the four components are expressed in the original units of measurement. Thus, the original data or observed data, 'Y' is the total of the four component values, that is, Y = T+S+C+I. Where, T, S, C and I represent the trend variations, seasonal variations cyclical variations, and erratic variations, respectively.

This model treats all the constituents as residuals, on the basis of which, by deducting trend from the original data, short-term fluctuation can be determined. Similarly, cyclical variations and irregular variation can be determined by deducting seasonal variation from short-term variations. On the basis of additive model, the analysis of various components is illustrated as follows:

$$Y - T = S + C + I$$

$$Y - T - S = C + I$$

$$Y - T - S - C = I$$

Multiplicative Model: It is based on the assumption that the causes giving rise to the four components are interdependent. Thus, the original data or observed date 'Y' is the product of four component values, that is: Y = T×S×C×I. In this model, the values of all the components, except trend values, are expressed as percentages.

Whatever the component is to be separated, works as a divisor with respect to original data. Analysis of different components on the basis of multiplicative model can be expressed in the following forms:

$$\frac{Y}{T} = SCI \text{ or } \frac{Y}{T \times S} = CI \text{ or } \frac{Y}{T \times S \times I} = C$$

In business research normally, the multiplicative model is more suited and used more frequently for the purpose of analysis of time series. Because, the data related to business and economic time series is the result if interaction of a number of factors which individually cannot be held responsible for generating any specific type of a variations.

Q8. What do you mean by smoothing techniques? List the two basic techniques of smoothing.

Ans. Smoothing techniques are the type of time-series forecasting model that assumes a repetitive underlying pattern can be found in the historical values of the variable being forecast. It is assumed that these historical observations represent not only the underlying pattern but also random variations. By taking some form of an average of past observations, smoothing techniques attempt to eliminate the distortions arising from random variation in the series and to base the forecast on a smoothed average of several past observations.

In general, smoothing techniques work best when a data series tends to change slowly from one period to the next with few turning points. Housing price forecasts would be a good application for smoothing techniques. Gasoline price forecasts would not. Smoothing techniques are cheap to develop and inexpensive to operate.

The simple average and exponential smoothing are commonly used smoothing techniques.

Moving Averages

Moving averages are one of the simplest of the smoothing techniques. If a data series possesses a large random factor, a trend analysis will tend to generate forecasts having large errors from period to period. In an effort to minimise the effects of this randomness, a series of recent observations can be averaged to arrive at a forecast. In this moving average method, a number of observed values are chosen. The average of these values is computed and serves as a forecast for the next period. In general, a moving average may be defined as

$$\hat{Y}_{t-1} = \frac{Y_t + Y_{t-1} + \ldots + Y_{t-N+1}}{N} \quad \ldots(i)$$

where $\hat{Y}_{t-1}$ = forecast value of Y for one period in the future Y_t, Y_{t-1}, Y_{t-N+1} = observed values of Y in periods $t, t-1, \ldots, t-N+1$, respectively

N = number of observation in the moving average

The greater the number of observation N used in the moving average, the greater the smoothing effect because each new observation receives less weight (1/N) as N increases. Hence, generally, the greater the randomness in the data series and the slower the turning point events in the data, the more preferable it is to use a relatively large number of past observations in developing the forecast.

Exponential Smoothing

Exponential smoothing uses a weighted average of past time series values as the forecast: it is a special case of the weighted moving averages method in which we select only one weight—the weight for the most recent observation. The weights for the other data values are computed automatically and become smaller as the observations move farther into the past. The basic exponential smoothing model follows.

$$F_{t+1} = \alpha Yt + (1-\alpha)F_t \quad \text{...(i)}$$

where

F_{t+1} = forecast of the time series for period t+1

Y_t = actual value of the time series in period t

F_t = forecast of the time series for period t

α = smoothing constant $(0 \le \alpha \le 1)$

Equation (i) shows that the forecast for period t + 1 is a weighted average of the actual value in period t and the forecast for period t; note in particular that the weight given to the actual value in period t is α and that weight given to the forecast in period t is $t-\alpha$.

Q9. How can you linearlise an exponential function?

Ans. If the time series is increasing or decreasing by a constant percentage rather than constant absolute amount, the fitting of exponential trend is considered appropriate. Such tendency is found in many economic and business data.

The equation of the exponential data is

$$Y = ab^{Xt}$$

where a is Y-intercept, b the slope of curve at the origin of X, and t for time.

The above equation can be linearlised as

$$\log Y = \log a + (X \log b)t$$

where b is the logarithm base, which is usually either e (natural) or 10 (common).

For common base log b is 1 and for e, 0.4343. Writing Y' for log Y and α for log a and β for x log b, the above equation could be written as

$$Y' = \alpha + \beta t$$

Power function $Y = at^{\beta}$ can also be linearised as below:

$$\log Y = \alpha + \beta \log t$$

Curves like modified exponential, Gompartz, Makeham and logistic, cannot be linearlised, yet are widely used in many specialised fields, like actuary and insurance. Three equi-distant points, which are well apart to cover the data range, are used to estimate these curves.

Fitting of trend curves helps in tracing the future course of trend, which may be a dominant component of the series. When there is no particular reason and two curves may be fitting quite appropriately, choose the simpler one.

Q10. What do you mean by deseasonalisation of a time series? Explain the moving average method of deseasonalisation.

[June-2012, Q.No-10]

Ans. The process of eliminating seasonal fluctuations from the time series data is termed as deseasonalisation. If the original values in the time series are divided by the corresponding seasonal index numbers, the resulting data, expressed in percentages are said to be deseasonalised or adjusted for seasonal variations. Obviously, after deseasonalisation, the time series will consist of trend (T), cyclical (C) and irregular (I) components which in model form can be expressed as:

- $\frac{Y}{S}\times 100 = \frac{T\times S\times C\times I}{S}\times 100 = (T\times C\times I)\times 100$; in multiplicative model.
- $Y - S = (T + S + C + I) - (S) = T + C + I$; in additive model.

Ratio-to-moving average or percentage moving average method consists of expressing the original time series data as percentages of moving averages instead of percentages of trend values as in 'ratio-to-trend method', while rest of the steps are essentially the same. The procedure in this method consists of the following steps:

- Find the centred 12-monthly-moving averages (if monthly data are given) from the given time series data.
- Express the original time series values as the percentage of the corresponding centred moving average values.
- Average these percentages according to year and months and find averages over the year for all the 12 months.
- Find the overall average of these 12 monthly averages. If the overall average is 100, the 12 monthly averages will be taken as seasonal indices, otherwise the monthly averages expressed as percentages of the overall average will be the required seasonal indices for the 12 months.

Symbolically, the logic behind the process may be explained as under:

The 12 monthly moving averages will eliminate the seasonal and irregular components and give us an estimate of the remaining two components namely trend (T) and cyclic (C). In multiplicative model we thus get an estimate of Then the second step results in:

$$\frac{Y}{T\times C}\times 100 = \frac{T\times C\times S\times I}{T\times C}\times 100 = (S\times I)\times 100$$

Now on averaging over in the third step, we are able to eliminate the irregular components with a possible bias. The final step given us the adjusted seasonal indices.

Q11. What do you understand by the index number? Explain its characteristics.

Ans. Index numbers are meant to study the change in the effects of such factors, which cannot be measured directly. **According to Bowley,** "Index numbers are used to measure the changes in some quantity which we cannot observe directly". For example, changes in business activity in a country are not capable of direct measurement but it is possible to study relative changes in business activity by studying the variations in the values of some such factors which affect business activity, and which are capable of direct measurement.

Index numbers are commonly used statistical device for measuring the combined fluctuations in a group related variables. If we wish to compare the price level of consumer items today with that prevalent ten years ago, we are not interested in comparing the prices of only one item, but in comparing some sort of average price levels. We may wish to compare the present agricultural production or industrial production with that at the time of independence. Another important feature of index number is that the changes in magnitude of a group are expressed in terms of percentages. This facilitates the comparison of two or more index numbers in different situation.

Characteristics of Index Numbers

- It measures the relative percentage change of differences from time to time or place to place.
- It is special type of average.
- It measures the effect of some factors which cannot be measured directly.
- Index numbers are expressed in percentage.

Q12. State various formulae, which can be used for making price index numbers.

Ans. In price index number, our main concern is the aggregation of the prices of a number of commodities for obtaining a summary measure of the relative change in the price level

(1) Simple Aggregative Method

This is the simplest method of constructing index numbers. When this method is used to construct a price index, the total of current year prices for the various commodities is divided by the total of base year prices and the quotient is multiplied by 100. Symbolically:

$$P_{01} = \frac{\sum P_1}{\sum P_0} \times 100$$

$\sum p_1$ = total of current year prices for various commodities.

$\sum p_0$ = total of base year prices for various commodities.

Limitations:

- The units used in the price or quantity quotations can exert a big influence on the value of the index.
- No consideration is given to the relative importance of the commodities.

(2) Laspeyre's Method

The Laspeyres Price Index is a weighted aggregate **rice index, where the weights are determined by quantities in the base** period. The formula for constructing the index is:

$$P_{01} = \frac{\sum p_1 q_0}{\sum p_0 q_0} \times 100$$

Limitations:

It does not take into consideration the consumption pattern. The Laspeyres index has an upward bias. When prices increase, there is a tendency to reduce the consumption of higher priced items. Hence, by using base year weights, too much weight will be given to those items, which have increased in price the most. Similarly, when prices decline, consumers shift their purchases to those items, which decline most. By using base period weights, too little weight is given to those items, which decrease most in price again overstating the index.

(3) Paasche's Method

The Paasche's price index is a weighted aggregate price index, in which the weights are determined by quantities in the given year,

The formula for constructing the index is:

$$P_{01} = \frac{\sum p_1 q_1}{\sum p_0 q_1} \times 100$$

Limitations:

The main drawback in Paasche's Method is that every time an index number is constructed weights have to be determined. This is a tedious and expensive task.

(4) Marshall and Edgeworth

In order to correct for over and under estimation, several approaches have been proposed. One suggested by **Alfred Marshall and advocated by EY. Edgeworth** is to use weighted arithmetic average of quantities actually purchased in the two periods. This will yield the following index.

$$P_{01} = \left[\frac{\sum p_1q_0 + p_1q_1}{\sum p_0q_0 + p_0q_1}\right] \times 100$$

(5) C.M.Walsh (1921)

C.M. Walsh (1921) suggested use of weighted geometric mean of quantities actually purchased in the two periods. This yields:

$$P_W = \frac{\sum\left(\sqrt{Q_0Q_1}\right)P_0}{\sum\left(\sqrt{Q_0Q_1}\right)P_1}$$

(6) Fisher's Ideal Index

The Fisher's Ideal Index is given by the formula:

$$P_{01} = \sqrt{\frac{\sum p_1q_0}{\sum p_0q_0} \times \frac{\sum p_1q_1}{\sum p_0q_1}} \times 100 = \sqrt{L \times P}$$

where L = Laspeyre's Method and P = Paasche's Method.

Limitations:

This index number, though theoretically, better than the other index numbers because it is excessively labourious. The data, particularly for the Paasche segment of the index, are not readily available.

Q13. Explain the tests recommended for a good index number.

Ans. In order to judge the efficiency of an index number formula as a measure of the level of a phenomenon from one period to another, the noted economist Irving Fisher suggested certain tests. The three most important tests of index numbers are (1) Time Reversal test, (2) Factor Reversal test, and (3) Circular test. These tests are based on the analogy that what is true for an individual item should also hold for a group of items.

(1) Time Reversal Test

According to this test, a good index number formula should work both ways, forward and backward, with respect to time. In other words, we should get the same picture of change between two points of time, no matter which of the two is taken as base. Consequently, the index number $\left(I_{0n}\right)$ for period n with base period 0 should be the reciprocal of the index number $\left(I_{n0}\right)$ for period 0 with base period n (omitting the factor 100 from each index). Symbolically,

$$\left(I_{0n}\right) \times \left(I_{n0}\right) = 1$$

An index number formula which obeys this relation is said to satisfy the time reversal test. Time reversal test is satisfied by simple aggregative formula. Marshall-Edgeworth's formula. Fisher's ideal index formula, and simple geometric mean of relatives formula. Weighted aggregative formula and weighted geometric mean of relatives formula also satisfy this test, if constant weights are used which do not depend upon the base or current period.

Time reversal test is based on the following analogy: If the price of a commodity changes from ₹4 per unit in 1999 to ₹8 in 2012, the price in 2012 is 200 per cent of (i.e. 2 times) the price in 1999, and the price in 1999 is 50 per cent of (i.e. 0.50 times) the price in 2012. The product of the two price ratios is This is true for each commodity and time reversal test ensures that the same principle holds for an index number, which embraces a group of commodities.

(2) Factor Reversal Test

An index number formula is said to satisfy the factor reversal test, if the product of Price Index $\left(P_{0n}\right)$ and Quantity Index $\left(Q_{0n}\right)$ gives the true Value Ratio (omitting the factor 100 from each index). In other words, a good index number formula should be such that the price ratio multiplied by the quantity ratio between two points of time gives the ratio of total values. Symbolically,

$$P_{0n} \times Q_{0n} = \frac{\sum p_n q_n}{\sum p_0 q_0}$$

Fisher's ideal index is the only formula which satisfies this test.

Factor reversal test is based on the following analogy: If the price per unit of a commodity changes from ₹4 in 1999 to ₹8 in 2012, and the quantity of consumption changes from 60 units to 90 units during the same period, then the price and quantity in 2012 are 200 per cent and 150 per cent respectively of the corresponding factors in 1999. The values of consumption were ₹240 in 1999 and ₹720 in 2012, so that the value ratio is 720/240 = 3. Thus, we find that the product of price ratio and quantity ratio equals the value ratio: Factor reversal test ensures that the principle which holds for a single commodity should apply to the index number as a whole.

(3) Circular Test

This is an extension of time reversal test. An index number formula is said to satisfy the circular test, if the time reversal test is satisfied through a number of intermediate years. Symbolically,

$$I_{01} \times I_{12} \times I_{23} \times \ldots \times I_{(n-1).n} \times I_{n0} = 1$$

This means that the relation is satisfied in a circular fashion through several years, 0 to 1, 1 to 2, 2 to 3,..., (n-1) to n, and finally from n back to 0, Simple aggregative formula and the simple geometric mean to relatives formula satisfy this test. Weighted aggregative formula and weighted geometric mean of relatives formula satisfy this test, it constant weights are used for all time periods.

Q14. Identify the steps involved in construction of price index numbers. Which problems are encountered in conducting price index numbers? [Dec-2012, Q.No.-9]

Or

What are the problems in construction of index numbers?

Or

Discuss the various steps and problems involved in the construction of index numbers.

Or

How do you construct Index numbers? Discuss.

Ans. The steps in the construction of index numbers are as follows:

(1) Definition of Purpose and Scope: Before going to construct an index number, a clear statement as to the purpose and its scope is necessary. All index numbers do not serve the same purpose and there is no all-purpose index. The selection of items, etc. will depend upon the purpose of construction and the people for whom it is intended. For example, in constructing an index number of wholesale prices, the prices from retailers are unnecessary, just as for a cost of living index number, quotations of cloth price ex-mill or prices of cotton yarn are useless. One must be sure of what the index number is going to measure.

(2) Selection of Items: For reasons of economy and ease of calculation, t is not possible to include all commodities in the construction of an index number. For a price index number, only a few selected items are, therefore, included whose price movements appear to be representative for the whole group of commodities. On the other hand, inclusion of too few items would make the index unrepresentative of the general level. With the passage of time, some items lose importance while some other new items appear to be more useful. The less important items should then be deleted from the list of commodities and replaced by new ones in conformity with their relative importance.

(3) Selection of Sources and Collection of Data: For a regular source of index number, a systematic collection of prices and quantities should be made at regular intervals of time from prominent business firms or standard retail stores located at different important centres. The selected shops should be those which are visited by a large majority of customers. Due care must also be taken in selecting the enumerators, who are entrusted with the collection of data; because, upon their honesty and intelligence will depend the quality and reliability of index numbers.

(4) Choice of Base: The base period should be chosen with much care and be such a one when abnormal increase or decrease in price was noticed. It is desirable to select a base period of recent past. The base should not be too long or too short a period. Generally, a year is taken as base, preferably a year of some economic importance for the country. e.g. the year 1951, being the first year of India's Five-year Plans. Sometimes a month, or a group of years, is also taken as base.

(5) System of Weighing: All the commodities includes in the construction of an index number are not of equal importance, in the sense that a change in the price of an item does not affect the price level to the same extent as does the same amount of change in another item. The system of weighting and particularly the allocation of weights to the different items is, therefore, of utmost importance. Price relatives are weighted by value, prices by quantities and quantities by prices. The prices or quantities used as weights may relate either to the base period or to the current period. In Laspeyres' price index formula the base period quantities are used as weights, while in Paasche's price index formula the weight used are the current period quantities. Edgeworth-Marshall's price index formula uses the average of base and current period quantities. In the relative method (e.g. in constructing Cost of Living Index), the weights used for combining group index are the money value devoted to each group, but expressed as percentage of total value.

(6) Form of Average of Use: Price index number is sometimes computed by averaging the percentage positions in price of the commodities. For the purpose of averaging, arithmetic mean or geometric mean is generally employed. In certain cases, median is also used. The arithmetic mean, due to the simplicity in calculation, is used in a great majority of cases; but since it is highly affected by even a few very large or small values, the geometric mean is preferred in many cases.

Q15. Write a short note on the price index number.

Ans. In Economics, most index numbers can be categorised as price index numbers and quantum index numbers. They are a kind of twins, whether it relates to production, consumption or trade. Trade may itself be wholesale trade, retail trade, foreign trade or trade of stocks. Cost of living index numbers are price indices. Yet, it is pertinent to note that there is some conflict between quantity and price indices. Some of the most popular price indices in India are:

- Index Numbers of Wholesale Prices.
- Consumer Price Index Numbers for Industrial Workers.
- Consumer Price Index Numbers for Agricultural Laboueres.
- Consumer Price Index Numbers for Urban Non-Manual Employees.
- Index Number of Harvest Prices.
- Index Number of Mineral Prices.
- Unit Value of Imports.
- Unit Value exports.
- Index Number of Contract Prices.
- Index Number of Security Prices.

Some of us would point out that these indices belong to two categories: bulk transaction prices and small transaction prices. Index related to wholesale, harvest, exports and imports are bulk transaction type while consumer price index numbers are essentially retail or small transaction type.

Q16. Discuss the concept of consumer price index in India.

Ans. The consumer price index is the index number, which measures the average change in prices paid by the specific class of consumers for goods and services consumed by them in the current year in comparison with base year. Change in the price level affects the cost of living of the concerned class of consumers. Accordingly, consumer price indices are also called cost of living indices.

In India, the consumer price indices are mainly constructed for the following consumer groups:

- Industrial Workers (IW),
- Urban-Non Manual Employees (UNME) and
- Agricultural Labourers (AL).

Consumer Price Index Numbers for Industrial Workers (Base Year 2001 = 100)

Labour Bureau of the Ministry of Labour and employment has inter-alia, been entrusted with the responsibility of compilation and maintenance of the Consumer Price Index Number for Industrial Workers (CPI-IW). The CPI-IW purports to measure the temporal change in the retail prices of fixed basket of goods and services being consumed by the target group i.e. an average working class family and thus, is an important indicator of the retail price situation in the country. The CPI-IW is mainly used for the determination of dearness allowance being paid to millions of Central/State Government employees as also to the workers in the industrial sector besides fixation and revision of minimum wages in scheduled employments.

Consumer Price Index of Agricultural Labourers

The Labour Bureau compiles this index number for the state and for all India on a monthly basis with a view to measure overall changes in the retail prices of goods and services consumed by the agricultural labourers. The first series of index number was started in September 1956 with the year 1950-51 as base and continued upto August 1964. The data for weighing figure and base price were obtained through agriculture labour enquiries (1959-51) conducted by the Ministry of Labour. A revised series with agriculture year 1956-57 as weighting base and 1960-61 as comparison base was issued for, 15 states on all India level. This series have been prepared on the basis of second Agriculture Labour Enquiries conducted by NSS. The items included in this index are divided in to four groups (i) Food, (ii) fuel, (iii) clothing, bedding and footwear, and (vi) miscellaneous.

CPI for Urban Non-Manual Employees (UNME)

The central statistical Orgnisation has been preparing consumer price index for urban non-manual employees since 1961. A middle class family living survey was organised in 1958-59 in selected 45 urban centers covering 36000 households of urban non-manual employees across the country. The base adopted was 1960.

The NSSO collects retail prices from 1022 markets on items varying from centre to centre-from 145 in Imphal to 345 in Delhi. Various items of goods and services are classified in five groups, viz. (i) food, beverages and tobacco, (ii) fuel and light, (iii) housing, (iv) clothing, bedding and footwear, and (v) miscellaneous.

In construction of these index numbers, Laspeyres formula (though base and weight years are different) is applied. For each centre, first at sub-group level then at group level and thereafter at general level, price index is complied by using price relatives and weighting diagram of commodities at each level. All-India Index is derived by weighting centre indices, weights being shares of centers' families consumption expenditures to total consumption expenditure of all families surveyed.

Q17. Discuss in detail about the concept of wholesale price index in India.

Ans. The Wholesale Price Index (WPI) measures the relative changes in the prices of commodities traded in the wholesale markets. In India, the wholesale price index numbers are constructed on weekly basis.

In India, the new Wholesale Price Index (WPI) series with base 1993-94 = 100 became effective from April 1, 2000 shifting from the earlier base of 1981-82. Presently, 1999-2000 is being used as the base year.

Commodity group and weightage of Wholesale price index

In India, all the commodities have been classified in the following three groups:

Table 4.2

Commodity Group	Name of Commodities	Weightage
(1) Primary Articles	These include 98 commodities like rice, Fruits, Pulses, Vegetables and non-food articles like Cotton, Jute, metals.	22.02
(2) Fuel Power, Light and Lubricants	These include 19 items like Coal, Petroleum Products, Electricity, LPG.	14.23
(3) Manufacturing	It includes 318 items like textiles, Sugar, Paper, Machinery, Chemicals, Fertilizers, Leather, etc.	63.75

Q18. Identify some of the uses to which price index numbers are put.

Ans. In present times, the importance of index numbers is increasing. Nowadays, they are being used in economics and business fields. To quote Simpson and Kafka, "Index Numbers are economic barometers". The main uses of index numbers are the followings:

- **Index Numbers as Economic Barometers:** Index numbers are indispensable tools for the management personnel of any government organisation or individual business concern and in business planning and formulation of executive decisions. The indices of prices (wholesale and retail), output (volume of trade, import and export, industrial and agricultural production) and bank deposits, foreign exchange and reserves, etc. throw light on the nature of, and variation in the general economic and business activity of the country.

- **Index Numbers Help in Studying trends and Tendencies:** An index number is defined as a relative measures describing the average change in the level of phenomenon between the current period and a base period. This property of the index number can be used to reflect typical patterns of change in the level of a phenomenon. For example, by examining the index number of industrial production, agricultural production, imports, exports, and wholesale and retail prices for the last 8-10 years, we can draw the trend of the phenomenon under study and also draw conclusions as to how much change has taken place due to the various factors.
- **Index Numbers Helps in Formulating Decisions and Policies:** Index numbers of the data relating to prices, production, profits, imports and exports, personnel and financial matters are indispensable for any organisation in efficient planning and formulation of executive decisions. For example, the cost of living index numbers are used by the government and the industrial and business concerns for the regulation of dearness allowance (D.A.) of grant of bonus to the workers so as to enable them to meet the increased cost of living from time to time.
- **Helps in deflating various values:** Index numbers are very helpful in deflating national income on the basis of constant prices, to enable us to find out whether there is any change in the real income of the people. Figures of national at current prices very often give misleading notices about the income level of the people and unless they are deflated the effects of inflationary or deflating polices cannot be understood. Similarly, the nominal sales can be deflated to give an idea about the real sales, and nominal wages can deflated to give an idea about the real wages.
- **Price Indices Measures the Purchasing Power of Money:** The cost of living index numbers determine whether the real wages are rising or falling, money wages remaining unchanged. In other words, they help us in computing the real wages which are obtained on dividing the money wages by the

corresponding price index and multiplying by 100. Real wages help us in determining the purchasing power of money.

- **Useful to Politicians:** The analysis of index number helps politicians to know about the actual economic condition of the country. Accordingly, they offer constructive criticism to the government and make useful suggestions for improvement.
- **Useful in Contract Escalation:** The study of index numbers (*i.e.* past behaviour or trends) helps in adjusting price in contracts extending over long periods of time.

For excellent score, read only GPH Book

❑❑❑

5 Qualitative Methods

An Overview

Qualitative research is a type of scientific research. It seeks to understand a given research problem or topic from the perspectives of the local population it involves. Qualitative research is especially effective in obtaining culturally specific information about the values, opinions, behaviours, and social contexts of particular populations.

The strength of qualitative research is its ability to provide complex textual descriptions of how people experience a given research issue. It provides information about the "human" side of an issue – that is, the often contradictory behaviours, beliefs, opinions, emotions, and relationships of individuals. Qualitative methods are also effective in identifying intangible factors, such as social norms, socioeconomic status, gender roles, ethnicity, and religion, whose role in the research issue may not be readily apparent. When used along with quantitative methods, qualitative research can help us to interpret and better understand the complex reality of a given situation and the implications of quantitative data. Although findings from qualitative data can often be extended to people with characteristics similar to those in the study population, gaining a rich and complex understanding of a specific social context or phenomenon typically takes precedence over eliciting data that can be generalized to other geographical areas or populations.

Q1. State the meaning and characteristics of qualitative research.

Ans. Qualitative research is concerned with phenomena relating to or involving kind/quality. Motivation research is an important type of quality research.

It can be referred to as an umbrella term covering an array of multiple interpretative techniques and practices which aim to show an insight or judgment on how human beings understand, experience, interpret and produce the social world (ibid, 1996). It basically depends on watching people on their settings and interacting with them under their conditions. The qualitative research characterise the following:

- It is carried out through the use of language, historical narratives, photographs, life histories, auto biographical materials, communications, etc.
- It concentrates on specific concrete problems which arise in specific situations rather than concentrative on abstract, universal questions.
- It studies systems and knowledge, practices and experiences in their local context instead of assuming and attempting to test their universal validity.
- It locates problems and identifies solutions in their historical context.
- Qualitative research adheres to a diverse array of orientations to and strategies for maximising the validity or trustworthiness of study procedures and results.

Thus, qualitative research is naturalistic, ethnographic and participatory in its approach. It discerns the perspectives of the people, or what is often referred to as the actor's point of view.

Q2. Identify the type of theoretical formulation under constructive paradigm.

Ans. All qualitative researchers are philosophers in that "universal sense in which all human beings.... are guided by highly abstract principles". These principles combine beliefs about ontology (What kind of being is the human being? What is the nature of reality?), epistemology (What is the relationship between the inquirer and the known?), and methodology (How do we know the world, or gain knowledge of it?). These beliefs shape how the qualitative researcher sees the world and acts in it. The researcher is "bound within a net of epistemological and ontological premises which-regardless of ultimate truth or falsity-become partially self - validating".

The net that contains the researcher's epistemological, ontological, and methodological premises may be termed a paradigm, or an interpretive framework, a "basic set of beliefs that guides action". All research is interpretive; it is guided by a set of beliefs and feelings about the world and how it should be understood and studied. Some beliefs may be taken for granted, invisible, only assumed, whereas others are highly problematic and controversial. Each interpretive paradigm makes particular demands on the researcher, including the questions he or she asks and the interpretations the researcher brings to them.

At the most general level, four major interpretive paradigms structure qualitative research: positivist and postpositivist, constructivist-interpretive, critical (Marxist, emancipatory), and feminist-post-structural.

Table 5.1 presents these paradigms and their assumptions, including their criteria for evaluating research, and the typical form of theory.

Table 5.1: Interpretive Paradigms

Paradigm /Theory	Criteria	Form of Theory	Type of Narration
Positivist/ Postpositivist	internal, external validity	logical-deductive, grounded	scientific report
Constructivist	trustworthiness, credibility, transferability, confirmability	substantive-formal	interpretive case studies, ethnographic fiction
Feminist	Afrocentric, lived experience, dialogue, caring, accountability, race, class, gender, reflexivity, praxis, emotion, concrete grounding	critical, standpoint	essays, stories, experimental writing
Ethnic	Afrocentric, lived experience, dialogue, caring, accountability, race, class, gender	standpoint, critical, historical	essays, fables, dramas
Marxist	emancipatory theory, falsifiable, dialogical, race, class, gender	critical, historical, economic	historical, economic, sociocultural analyses
Cultural studies	cultural practices, praxis, social texts, subjectivities	social criticism	cultural theory as criticism

Contd....

Queer theory	reflexivity, deconstruction	social criticism, historical analysis	theory as criticism, autobiography

Q3. What do you understand by the PRA and RRA? Explain its features.

Ans. PRA can be defined as a semi-structured process of learning from, with any by rural people about rural conditions. It shares much with its parent, PRA, but is distinguished from it in practice. In RRA information is more elicited and extracted by outsiders whereas in PRA is is more shared and owned by the local people. RRA leads to learning by outsiders in a cost effective way. PRA, on the other hand enables rural people to unravel and analyse their own situation in ways they do not normally do, and in optimal cases to plan and act on their own premises. In short, PRA characterise the following:

- The roles of teacher and learner is reversed. They teach us. Rural people own more of the process and output. Investigation, presentation and analysis are done more by the people themselves, including visual sharing of information in maps, models, and diagrams. Quantification is made and presented by them. Most of the activities that we thought necessary-interviewing, transects, mapping, measuring, analysis, planning-are done jointly with villagers or by them on their own. The appraisal and learning are not just by us from them, but with them and by them.
- Rapport with villagers is primary. To achieve good rapport often requires the reorientation and relaxation of outsiders, and critical self-awareness. Rural people's suppressed incapacity and ignorance have often been an artifact of our ineptitude. With few exceptions, we – the outsider professional community – have not known how to help them to express, share and enhance their knowledge. The ignorance of rural people has been a self – sustaining myth, created and maintained by our confident and overweening clumsiness. By wagging the finger, holding the sick, sitting on the chair behind the table; dominating and overwhelming thought and speech; being rushed and impatient; demanding information and answers; believing that we know and they are ignorant, they are the problem and we are the solution; by failing to sit down with respect and interest and listen and learn – in these ways, we have impeded expression of knowledge and creative analysis by rural people.

Q4. What are the strengths of RRA approach?

Ans. In the RRA/PRA approach, knowledge and capability of the villagers is accorded priority. Its visual methods and participatory approaches provide chances for expression to the general, silent and weaker sections also. Information gathered retains its contextual cord, which enhances reliability.

- **Visual Methods:** Visual sharing, diagrams, maps or quantification are presented physically by rural people in a manner they readily understand, since they have created it, and that can be cross checked and amended. Successive approximation is thus built into the process.
- **Ranking and scoring, rather than measuring:** Of course, measurements and estimates can also be sought. But especially for sensitive information like income or wealth, people are often willing to present relative values when they would conceal or distort absolute values. In seasonal analysis, for example, people readily use seeds or other counters to show relative amounts or income and expenditure by month. Similarly, with changes and trends over time, relative values can be given. Ranking items by people's own criteria, and scoring different items out of ten, five or three, have also proved feasible and popular.
- **Reliable:** Combinations and sequences of methods have proved powerful and practical. Participatory mapping and modelling, where villagers make their own map or model on the ground or on paper, lead easily and naturally to other activities, such as discussing routes for walking transects and to household listings and wealth ranking, to identify types of people in a community, and marking other details.
- **Interesting:** The approach and methods are popular and empowering. Questionnaires are often a bore for all concerned. PRA methods are often enjoyed. We have had to learn not to interview and not to interrupt when people are being creative with a map or model, when they are thinking, and reflecting on estimates. People are no longer "respondents". They are players, performers, presenters, and own their play, performance and presentation. And the word "fun" comes into the development vocabulary.

Q5. What is difference between PRA and RRA approach of qualitative research?

Ans. The tabulated difference between PRA and RRA as follows:

Table 5.2: Differences between RRA and PRA

RRA	PRA
Responding to needs of development workers and agencies	Responding to needs of communities and target groups
More emphasis on efficient use of time and achievement of objectives	More emphasis on flexibility to adapt to time frame of community
Communication and learning tools used to help outsiders analyse conditions and understand local people	Communication and learning tools used to help local people analyse their own conditions and communicate with outsiders
Focus of RRA decided by outsiders	Focus of PRA decided by communities
End product mainly used by development agencies and outsiders	End product mainly used by community
Enables development agencies and institutions to be more "participatory"	Enables (empowers) communities to make demands on development agencies and institutions
Can be used purely for "research" purposes without necessarily linking to subsequent action or intervention	Closely linked to action or intervention and requiring immediate availability of support for decisions and conclusions reached by communities as a result of the PRA

Q6. Name the various tools that are used for collection of qualitative data.

Or

Explain the different strategies, tools and techniques of qualitative data collection.

Ans. Following tools are identified and often used for data collection:

Social Mapping of the Village

The exercise on social mapping generates basic data on the layout of the village with location of different groups/communities, i.e. the number of houses as well as households and their location. A lot of information regarding the name of the households head, agricultural land, animals, and other physical assets owned, family size, status indicator, possession of LPG, TV, Motorbike, etc. can be gathered depending upon the requirement of the research. Such data for each household emerges from the consensus among villagers. Participating in the mapping exercise is recorded by one of the participants on small coloured cards numbered in accordance with the household's location in the map drawn on the floor/ground using coloured rangoli powders by the villagers.

Resource mapping/Transect walk

The resource map/transect walks are useful for providing basic understanding on types of trees dotting the village boundary, fuel wood situation, and availability of other relevant indicators, like cropping pattern, fuels, etc. The involvement of team members in these exercises reassures the villagers about the stated research objectives as well as the teams, interest in their lifestyles and environment. In a proverbial sense, these exercises broke the ice and appear to encourage the participation of the villagers in the qualitative research activities.

Wealth ranking of the households

For ranking of well being of households, persons from different groups/communities are independently asked to sort the cards made while doing social mapping. The criterion for wealth ranking/well being of households is chosen by them. The criteria may include: (a) quantum of crop land and number of milk animals owned, (b) household size, (c) type of house, (d) tractor/pumpset ownership, (e) motorcycle/scooter, TV/Fridge possession, (f) marriage alliance struck for boys/girls, and (g) membership of village panchayat/cooperatives, etc. It is interesting to note that annual income from all sources hardly figure in the ranking of well being done by the villagers. The procedure outline in the qualitative literature for collecting the data on ranking of well–being is followed to arrive at the total score for final ranking from which households are picked randomly for the semi–structured interviewing.

Preference Ranking

The exercise on preference ranking provides insights into usage patterns which may be a valuable guide for related programmes/schemes.

Semi–structured interview, Group Discussion and Experiments on consumption pattern

Semi–structured interviews with individual households provides household level (micro) variation in the usage pattern and their perceptions where group discussions revealed their perceptions at the aggregate levels. The focus group in both types of discussions is on issues related to the programme.

Apart from the above issues, the team members are obliged to give a patient hearing to issues unrelated to the programme because some of the issues agitate the minds of the rural folk.

For example, the issue of not handling over the community hall built for SC's, from Jawahar Rozgar Yojna Funds and its use for running a school in the village is a bone of contention between the persons belonging to SCs and other people. One group reported it as misuse of a facility and discrimination against the socially disadvantaged community while the other emphasised its use for a noble purpose of educating children of all communities till a separate building is constructed. In another village, a lot of land was purchased by the film personalities. Many fenced estates sprang up restricting access to villagers for grazing their animals, collection of fuel wood, etc. Some elders lament their inability to go for morning walks/rituals in the changed situation. Though land prices have skyrocketed bringing them more monetary value, many villagers dread the prospect of becoming landless and homeless. In another village, the villagers regret their decision to donate land for a noble cause i.e. setting up a leprosy cure centre. In their perception over the years, the influx of ashram inmates has begun affecting their life and environment. Now, they want ashram to be shifted elsewhere and the land to be handed over back of the villagers. In another village, setting up of a sugar cooperative was initially welcomed as it provided easy access for their sugarcane output, generated some employment and rise in the income levels. But now, the villagers perceive the factory as the main pollutant of their drinking water sources thereby affecting their lives. Considerable resentment is noticed among the villagers on this account.

Participatory mapping: people, health, nutrition

Participatory mapping is an important method for PRA/PLA-type exercises and can help in highlighting different aspects of community life such as social aspects, resources, livelihood, health, wealth, literacy, census, livestock, harvest, economic activities, social stratification, etc. Such mapping can portray the image of dwellings in a community, of huts, houses, natural resources, open spaces, farms and fields, water collections, forests, soils and of many other aspects depending on the topic under consideration. In participatory mapping and model-building, local communities prepare the map/model of their locality with chalks, colour powders and other materials such as stones, leaves, flowers, etc. either on ground or on paper.

Participatory mapping involves spatial drawing of any area, drawn on ground, paper or on other medium by the local people to show and explain their locality and other related areas, such as residential areas, forests, fields, etc. Participatory mapping can include a range of items like households, school, office, infrastructure, crops, livestock, farm size, water bodies, fields, forest, trees, roads, facilities, common property resources, literacy, diseases, etc. depending on the theme/themes under discussion. Such mapping can be theme-specific such as a resource map indicating natural resources of the locality; social map showing households and other buildings in the area; health map showing health status; literacy map showing literate/illiterate/semi-literate, etc.

Seasonal analysis

Villagers in India have shown ability to estimate and rank conditions that vary seasonally. Festivals, major seasons, months, or kartiks (fortnightly periods distinguished and named especially during the monsoon) are used to define times of year and intervals. Most commonly months have been used, represented by 12 stones. Villagers use seeds other counters or sticks to estimate and rank conditions as numbers of days of rain, amount of rain, soil moisture, numbers of days (or proportion out of 10) of agricultural labour in each month, income, expenditure, debts taken, food availability, and so on. When presented as a histogram this information points clearly to the months of greatest difficulty and vulnerability.

Ranking of wealth and well being

Wealth ranking is an ingenious and simple method of eliciting relative wealth or well–being in a community. Knowledgeable informants are presented with slips of paper, one for each household, and asked to place them in piles according to their wealth or poverty, or according to their well–being or ill being, depending on local criteria. The piles, usually three to six in number, are then checked. The criteria used can be elicited by asking, for example, why each household in the worst–off pile, was placed there. Four to five different criteria (far more subtle and realistic than a crude poverty line) usually emerge for the rankings, and respondents weigh these mentally in making their allocations to wealth or well–being groups.

Matrix ranking and scoring

Matrix ranking and scoring method is used for assessing entities in a class, such as fodder trees, varieties of a crop, types of firewood, domestic animals, or even political parties and political leaders. The entities are selected, their good and bad qualities listed to elicit criteria, and then ranked or scored for each criterion. This method generates insight into other people's criteria and preferences. Rural women, for example, readily indicate their preference for different fuel woods on the basis of availability, ease of collection, and quality and quantity of smoke in the kitchen.

Although, matrix ranking and scoring has not been used much directly in health and nutrition, but there are potential applications of this method for assessing different foods, methods of cooking, fuel types, treatments for diseases, and sources of treatments for diseases.

Time lines and trends

Time lines establish well known past events and provide a framework for discussing changes that have taken place. As example, changes in the composition of diets can be quantified using counters. In one case, an old woman showed with small stones the main staples she ate as a girl, and those she eats now, using 12 stones for her staples as a girl, when she ate more, and only eight for now, when she eats less. Trends can be shown and estimated in various ways. Presumably, such health and nutrition–related aspects of life as changes in diet, the prevalence of diseases, treatments, costs of treatment, and ways of raising resources for treatment, could be analysed. Indeed, at many places, these have already been made standard questions in health and nutrition appraisal.

Q7. What are the methods of collecting primary data?

Ans. For collection of primary data, the investigator may choose any one or a combination of the following methods:

(1) Direct Personal Observation: Under this method, the investigator collects data by having direct contact with the units of investigation. The accuracy of collected data depends, to a large extent, upon the training and attitude of the investigator and the supporting attitude of the respondents.

This method is suitable for an intensive type of investigation where (a) the scope of investigation is narrow, (b) the process of investigation is so complex that it requires personal attention of the investigator, (c) the investigation is confidential, and (d) more emphasis is to be given to the accuracy of the data.

(2) Indirect Oral Interview: This method is used when the area of investigation is very large or the respondents are reluctant to part with the information due to various reasons. Under this method, the investigator collects data from a third party or witness or head of an institution, etc. who is supposed to be in touch with the respondents. This method is generally adopted by the police department for the collection of information regarding bad elements of a locality. When the field of investigation is very large, the information about a large number of respondents can indirectly be obtained from one person who may be head (or pradhan) of that community.

(3) Information through Local Agencies or Correspondents: Under this method, local agents or correspondents are appointed in different parts of the area under investigation. These agents send the desired information at regular intervals of time. This method is often adopted by newspapers.

(4) Questionnaire Method: This is a very commonly used method of collecting primary data. Here, information is collected through a set of questionnaire. A questionnaire is a document prepared by the investigator containing a set of questions. These questions relate to the problem of inquiry directly or indirectly. Here, first the questionnaires are mailed to the informants with a formal request to answer the question and send them back. For better response the investigator should bear the postal charges. The questionnaire should carry a polite note explaining the aims and objective of the inquiry, definition of various terms and concepts used there. Besides this, the investigator should ensure the secrecy of the information as well as the name of the informants, if required.

Q8. Discuss the various sources of secondary data.

Ans. The secondary sources can be classified into following categories:

(1) Published Sources: There are various national and international institutions, semi-official reports of various committees and commissions and private publications which collect and publish statistical data relating to industry, trade, commerce, and health, etc. These publications of various organisations are useful sources of secondary data. These are as follows:

- **Government Publications:** Central and State Governments publish current information along with statistical data on various subjects, quarterly and annually. For example, Monthly Statistical Abstract, National Income Statistics, Economic Survey, Reports of National Council of Applied Economic Research (NCAER), Federation of Indian Chambers of Commerce and Industry (FICCI), Indian Council of Agricultural Research (ICAR), Central Statistical Organisation (CSO), etc.
- **International Publications:** The United Nations Organisation (UNO), International Labour Organisation (ILO), International Monetary Fund (IMF), World Bank, Asian Development Bank (ADB), etc. also publish relevant data and reports.
- **Semi-official Publications:** Semi-official organisations like Corporations, District Boards, Panchayat, etc. publish reports.
- **Committees and Commissions:** Several committees and commissions appointed by State and Central Governments

provide useful secondary data, e.g. the report of the 10th Financial Commission or Fifth Pay Commissions, etc.

- **Private Publications:** Newspapers and journals publish the data on different fields of Economics, Commerce and Trade. For example, Economic Times, Financial Express, etc. and Journals like Economist, Economic and Political Weekly, Indian Journal of Commerce, Journal of Industry and Trade, Business Today, etc. Some of the research and financial institutions also publish their reports annually like Indian Institute of Finance. In addition, to this, reports prepared by research scholars, universities, etc. also provide secondary source of information.

(2) Unpublished Sources: It is not necessary that all the information/data maintained by the institutions or individuals are available in published form. Certain research institutions, trade associations, universities, research scholars, private firms, business institutions, etc. do collect data but they normally do not publish it. We can get this information from their registers, files, etc.

(3) Electronic Sources: The secondary data is also available through electronic media (through Internet). We can download data from such sources by entering websites like google.com, yahoo.com, msn.com, etc. and typing the subject for which the information is needed.

Q9. List the steps involved in compilation of qualitative data.

Ans. Compilation of qualitative data is not an easy task. First of all, there should not be any biasness in the compilation. It means that whether the scheduled caste respondent or the highest caste respondent provides the information, it has to be treated at par. This will not only strengthen our database but also provide appropriate direction to our policy-making through qualitative approach of data collection.

The different steps involved in the compilation of qualitative data are described below:

(1) Description

The first step in qualitative analysis is to develop comprehensive descriptions of the phenomenon under study. Information about context i.e. situations and actions within the social, cultural and historical backdrop against which it takes place is recorded. In qualitative analysis strong emphasis is laid on understanding the subjective meaning. The idea of process is then linked to the change.

(2) Classification

It involves sorting out mass of data into classes bases on certain characteristics, which enable us in the development of a conceptual framework. Data are carefully put together so that the resultant picture may give an accurate representation of the social reality. Organising the data into groups based on certain characteristics is essentially the process of categorisation.

(3) Making Connections

Description and classification of data are not ends in themselves but serve a more important purpose i.e. to produce an account of the analysis. The concepts need to be connected together with the idea. We have to establish associations between various variables and try to see the patterns within the data, so that we can discern regularities, variations, and exceptions.

(4) Theoretical Coding

In order to analyse our data, we have to read it in an interactive way, and constantly ask the questions "Who"? "What"? "When"? "Where"? and "Why"? This will open up our data for us and help us to think about it in a creative way. The processing of field material, once it has been gathered invariably implies hard work for researchers who are inexperienced in handling field data.

The key function of this exercise is to convert the material on the schedules into suitable code form. Coding is considered a tedious and demanding job. Further, this is an area where methods of analysis of quantitative and qualitative data complement and supplement each other.

Coding represents the operations by which data are broken down, conceptualised and put back together in new ways. A grounded theory is, "a rich, tightly woven, explanatory theory that closely approximated the reality it represents" (Strauss and Corbin). Analysis in grounded theory comprises three major kinds of coding, viz. Open coding; Axial coding; and Selective coding

- **Open Coding:** Open coding refers to close examination of the data so that phenomena may be named and categorised. An observation, a sentence, a paragraph from an interview transcript is taken apart and given a name, which stands for or represents the phenomenon. We ask question, like "What is this?" "What does it represent?" On the way, we make comparisons so that similar phenomena may be given the same name.

  There are various ways of doing open coding. Strauss and Corbin recommend analysing the first interview, line-by-line, so that concepts and categories are freely generated. Subsequently, this can be done paragraph-wise or in terms of an entire document or case. It is important not to lose touch with the aims of coding, namely, breaking down and understanding a text in order to generate categories, which can be used for comparing. The result of open coding should be a list of codes and categories written alongside the text itself, along with "code notes" that explain the content of the codes. "Memos" which contain observations on the material and your thoughts about it also go a long way in developing grounded theory.

- **Axial Coding:** The next step is to refine and differentiate the categories generated in open coding. Those categorises are selected which hold out promise for further development. Strauss and Corbin suggest a coding paradigm, which is given in the figure below:

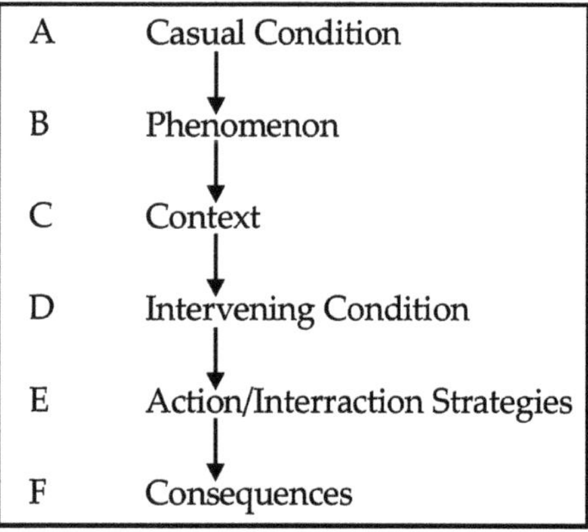

Fig. 5.1: Axial Coding

In axial coding, categories are developed in terms of the causal conditions that give rise to the phenomenon, location of the phenomenon in terms of its properties, the context, the action/interactional strategies used to handle, manage and respond to the phenomenon with regard to the context and the consequences of any action/interaction that is taken.

- **Selective Coding:** The third step, selective coding, continues the axial coding at a higher level of abstraction. It aims at laying bare the core category around which the other categories can be arranged. In other words, it reveals the: story of the case". The story of the case is to be set down briefly, before developing the story line. From studying the content and meaning of the text, the researcher uses his/her interpretative abilities to formulate code and categories, takes them to a higher level of abstraction and then constructs a story or an account, which is applicable to the whole data. The researcher is able to say, "under these conditions, this is what occurs".

(5) Qualitative Content Analysis

Content analysis is one of the classical procedures for analysing textual material, be it interviews or media products. It differs from coding in the sense that rather than generating categories from the data themselves, it uses categories brought from the outside and "fits" the empirical material against them, of course, modifying the categories wherever necessary. The aim of qualitative content analysis is to reduce the material so as to make it manageable.

- **Summarising Content Analysis:** Here, the material is paraphrased, that is, omitting less relevant passages or those having the same meaning reduces it (first reduction). Similar paraphrases are summarised together (second reduction). Thus, the material becomes more coherent, economical and manageable. It is a kind of editing of the material in order to draw out its essence.
- **Explicative Content Analysis:** this works in the opposite way. Here, statements which are puzzling contradictory or unclear, are explained or clarified by keeping in mind their context, or by looking for clues in other parts of the text that would help make their meaning clear.
- **Structuring Content Analysis:** Here, the researcher looks for types or formal structures in the material by applying categories that emerged at the stage of formulating the research question itself, and organising the material accordingly. Thus, qualitative content analysis helps the researcher to reduce to manageable level large masses of text, using a uniform scheme of categories, which also helps in the comparison of different cases to which it is applied throughout.

Q10. What do you understand by the term 'Focus Group Discussion'? Under what situation, it is used as a tool for conducting qualitative research. [June-2011, Q.No.-10]

Ans. The focus group discussion is a technique for eliciting information from specific population subgroups. Issues addressed may be little known or relatively well known to the researcher. The method is most effectively used when the objective of the investigation is to elicit points or view of client or consumer groups, which may differ from those of the providers.

The focus group is a qualitative research method for eliciting descriptive data from population sub groups. Usually, a group of eight to twelve persons are gathered together for a group discussion on a focussed topic. It may be used to elicit opinions on known topics in order to develop an understanding of client or user perspectives on the given topic. The recommendation itself can be tested with a focus group in an attempt to validate its appropriations to a particular population.

In focus group research, i.e. in qualitative methods, reasoning proceeds from observation of a series of particular facts to a general statement or hypothesis. The strength of qualitative methods are that they generate rich, detailed, valid data process that usually leave participant's perspectives intact. Owing to the reason, focus group discussions have been defended as a valid tool in Social Science research (Stycos 1981; Morgan and Spanish 1984; Basch 1987).

The focus group discussion should examine a narrowly focussed topic. The topic should be of interest to both the investigators and the respondents. The emphasis should be placed on the interactions between or among group members.

Q11. Describe the various workshop and field methods that are used to facilitate the processing of qualitative data through triangulation.

Ans. Various workshop and field methods are used to facilitate this process:

(1) Team Contracts: Team contracts developed by all the team members help to ensure good group dynamics and may include agreements to hold evening discussions and morning brainstorming sessions. One person may be elected to monitor team interactions to provide feedback. The monitor can make a note of each member's location and record interactions by drawing a circle around individuals' names when they speak or an arrow from talker to person being talked to with duration of speech recorded in seconds. The results are used simply for showing team members how the discussion developed. It then becomes clear who had dominated and who is quiet.

(2) The Night Halt: Rapport between outsiders and villager is facilitated by staying in the village. Many have made this an essential part of participatory analysis and planning. It provokes change in outsiders' attitudes: they sleep and eat as villagers do; it allows for early morning and evening discussions when people are less busy; and it is an explicit commitment by outsiders to village life.

(3) Work Sharing: When outsiders are taught something by villagers, roles are reversed. Professional soon learn how much skill is required, say to plough a furrow, transplant rice, weed, lop tree fodder, cut firewood, dig compost, and wash clothes. Such activities prompt changes in attitude and help to build rapport.

(4) Rapid Report Writing with Self-correcting Notes: It is essential to record, as a team, the key findings before members disperse to their own organisations. Report writing is made easier by writing a brief summary of how diagrams are constructed of the key findings. Individuals can be encouraged to keep a private diary or series of notes to focus on things they would like to improve the next time.

(5) Shared Presentations: The key findings should always be presented to villagers and outsider. This is an important opportunity for cross-checking and feedback. Professional presents the report and invites comment and criticism. This is a fundamental reversal of roles and is crucial for establishing the trustworthiness of the findings.

(6) Transect Walks and Direct Observation: These are systematic walks with key informants through the area of interest, observing, asking listening, looking, and seeking problems and solutions. The findings can be mapped on a transect diagram. Most transect walks result in the outsider discovering surprising local practices such as indigenous conservation practices, multiple uses of plants, and a great variety of crops. It has been instructive for many professional to realise how much they do not see or do not think to ask about.

(7) Wealth Rankings and social Maps: Wealth ranking is used to classify households according to relative wealth or well-being. Informants sort cards, each with one household name on it, into piles. The wealthiest are put at one end, the poorest at the other, and as many piles as desired are made.

Wealth rankings are useful for (i) leading into other discussions on livelihoods and vulnerability, (ii) producing a baseline against which future intervention/impact can be measured, (iii) providing a sample frame to cross-check the relative wealth of informants who have been or will be interviewed, and (iv) producing local indicators of welfare.

(8) Semi-Structured Interviews (SSI): This is guided interview in which some of the questions and topics are predetermined. (i) Other questions arise during the course of the interview. The interviews appear informal and conversational, but are actually carefully controlled and structured. Using a guide or checklist, the multidisciplinary team poses open-ended questions and probes topics as they arise. New avenues of questioning are pursued as the interview develops. SSIs are a central part of all participatory methods

(9) Types, Sequencing, and Chains of Interviews: Many types of interviews may be combined in sequences and chains. These include key informant interviews, by asking who the experts are and then putting together a series of interviews (e.g., men on ploughing, women on transplanting and weeding, shopkeepers for credit and inputs); and group interviews which may be groups convened to discuss a particular topic (focussed or specialist groups), groups comprising a mix of people whose different perceptions illuminate an issue (structured groups), casual groups, and community groups.

The fourth element is the emphasis on diagramming and visual construction. In formal surveys, interviewers, who transform what people say into their own language, take information.

(10) Participatory Mapping and modelling: This involves constructing, on the ground or on paper, maps or models, using materials such as sticks, stones, grasses, wood, cigarette packets, tree leaves, coloured sands and soils, rangoli powders, coloured chalk, pens and paper. Great play is made of the issue of who holds the stick or pen. The person who holds the stick talks about what is most important to him or her. As maps take shape, more people become involved, and so want to contribute and make sequential changes. There are many types of maps: resource maps of catchments, villages, forests, fields, farms, home gardens, social maps of residential areas of a village, wealth rankings and household assets surveys on social maps, health maps, where the health status of each family member is shown on each house, using coloured stickers or other markers (categories might include cases of malnutrition, ear infection, jaundice, and the like); topical maps such as aquifer maps drawn by the water diviner or soils maps by soils experts; impact monitoring maps, where villages record or map pest incidence, input usage, weed distribution, soil quality, and so forth. Some of the most illuminating maps combine historical views with those of the present.

(11) Seasonal Calendars and Activity Profiles: Seasonal constraints and opportunities can be diagrammed month by month throughout the year. Ceremonies can be used as a cross-check so that names of months are agreed upon. People use pieces of stick, draw histograms in the dust or with chalk, or make piles of stones, seeds, or powders to represent relative quantities and patterns of rainfall, soil moisture, crops, labour, food consumption, illnesses, prices, animal fodder, fuel, migration, pests, income, expenditure, debt, children's games, and so on. Seasonal calendars can be drawn in linear fashion with twelve months to show a typical year or eighteen months to illustrate changes between years, or they can be drawn in a circle. Daily patterns of activity can be similarly explored by charting typical activities for each hour of the day, amount of effort, time taken, and location of work. These can be compared for men, women, the old, the young, and others.

(12) Time Lines and Local Histories: Historical analyses have been found to be a good icebreaker for field exercises and include detailed accounts of the past, of how things have changed, particularly focussing on relationships and trends. These include technology histories and review, crop histories and biographies, livestock breed histories, labour availability, trees and forest histories, education change, and population change. Folklore and songs are valuable resources for history.

(13) Venn and Network Diagrams: Venn diagrams involve the use of circles of paper or card to represent people, groups, and institutions. These are arranged to represent real linkages and distance between individuals and institutions. Overlap indicates flows of information, and distance on the diagram represents lack of contact.

(14) Matrix Scoring and Pair wise Ranking: These methods are for learning about local people's categories, criteria, and priorities. For pair wise ranking, the items of interest are compared pair by pair; informants are asked which of the two they prefer, and why. Matrix scoring takes criteria for the rows in a matrix and items for columns, and people complete the boxes row by row. The items may be ordered for each of the criteria (e.g. for six trees, indicate from best to worst for fuel wood, fodder, erosion control, and fruit supply); or participants may put stones, seeds, or berries into piles for relative scoring.

Q12. Write a short note on Participatory Learning Method (Palm).

Ans. Palm approach was developed by MYRADA in Bangalore, India around 1989 (a nongovernmental organisation that has been active in rural development since 1968 in some 2000 villages in Southern India).

Areas in which it has been successfully applied are participatory planning of natural resource development at the village level and in urban neighborhoods; participatory project management and integrated rural development programmes dealing with healthcare, poverty alleviation and the situation of women and children; rural credit management; customs and coping with local conflicts; participatory impact monitoring and assessment of development programmes.

Special features

PALM uses the key RRA concepts, but emphasises participation by village residents and the function of the externals as catalysts and partners for self-determined development. The aim of PALM is to go beyond "appraisal" and arrive at participatory analysis and a common understanding of rural conditions. The focus is on learning from and with local people.

Tools/techniques

Geographical and historical transects, participatory mapping; seasonality diagramming, ranking and scoring, as well as the other well-known RRA/PRA techniques.

Assessment

With 25-30 externals, the PALM village studies involve a relatively large team. In this form, PLAM is tailored to conditions in India. The number of aspects dealt with and the depth of the studies, which are conducted within a short space of time, mean that the externals must be familiar with local conditions and sociocultural structures.

Q13. By applying which criteria, you would like to test the trustworthiness of qualitative data.

Ans. Some writers have suggested that qualitative studies should be judged or evaluated according to quite different criteria from those used by quantitative researchers. Lincoln and Guba (1985) and Guba and Lincoln (1994) propose that is is necessary to specify terms and ways of establishing and assessing the quality of qualitative research that provide an alternative to reliability and validity. They propose two primary criteria for assessing a qualitative study: trustworthiness and authenticity.

Trust worthiness is made up of four criteria, each of which has an equivalent criterion in quantitative research:

- credibility, which parallels internal validity;
- transferability, which parallels external validity;
- dependability, which parallels reliability;
- confirmability, which parallels objectivity.

A major reason for Guba and Lincoln's unease about the simple application of reliability and validity standards to qualitative research is that the criteria presuppose that a single absolute account of social reality is feasible. In other words, they are critical of the view that there are absolute truths about the social world that it is the job of the social scientist to reveal. Instead, they argue that there can be more than one and possibly several accounts.

Q14. Which are the two basic approaches to analyse the qualitative data?

Ans. The analysis of qualitative information requires judgement and skill. It is in this aspect that qualitative research differs most from the quantitative research. The two basic approaches of analysis are **systematic coding using content analysis**, and **ethnographic summarisation.**

The narratives provided by each group of participants can be summarised numerically. However, the rich context in which the words of the respondents are embedded offers a unique opportunity to search the text, and the context, for adding meaning.

The first step in the analysis of the qualitative information/data is the transcription of the individual, pre-labelled tapes. If the discussion has been recorded in a language different from the language in which the analysis will take place, then the transcription must also be translated. Standard rules of translation are to be followed. While describing the interviews as 'contextualised data', it is invaluable to be able to include the more descriptive indicators on addition to more straightforward reporting of contents.

The analysis can be conducted manually or by computer using word processing programme, which are developed to assist in qualitative analysis. While computer programmes enforce consistency, there is nothing that cannot be done by hand. Conversely, computer analysis poses a risk of performing an oversimplified analysis through too-early identification of core text as the key to answer. Excessive reliance on computer may yield results that are flat and oversimplified. It is shortsighted to assume that computers are capable of gleaning the meaning embedded in the narrative data.

Investigators usually conduct a content analysis of the responses and construct representative tables to organise and display/present the data. Next, they develop an ethnographic summary of the data using direct quotes with narrative explanations. The balance between these analytical approaches depends upon the research question and the nature of the audience for whom the research has been conducted. If the research question is exploratory, then the analysis should focus on the developing alternative possibilities. If the research question tests a hypothesis, the analysis should try to determine the best answer to the problem.

If we are addressing an audience, which are accustomed to viewing tables and graphs in order to interpret the data, it is wise to start with the data tables showing percentages. Having established a foundation for discussion, the investigator can move to present the patterns of narrative demonstrating the identification of themes important to the analysis. If, on the other hand, one is prepared to hold a follow-up meeting with village head, the preferable format is to present a shot set of straightforward graphs using number and percentages, which illustrates the two or three points of most interest to them.

Q15. Identify the methods of content analysis.

Ans. The two common methods in content analysis are identification of themes and incidence density.

(1) In the theme identification, the researcher looks for particular patterns, themes, concerns or responses, which are posed repeatedly by the respondents. The group is the unit of analysis.

While constructing tables to classify data or identify themes, a variable is listed in the table if it is mentioned by a group. However, it is listed only once, no matter how many times respondents in a particular group mention it. The number of groups, not the number of individuals, is used as the denominator. The results of such an analysis of themes, with the number of groups constituting the denominator for each area separately and the two areas can be displayed together. The results can be presented as numbers or percentages.

Using the group as the unit of analysis is the most common method of data analysis. Simple statistical frequencies are most effective in depicting the more important characteristics of the problem being investigated.

The data can be represented in pie charts to provide a visual representation of the relative importance of different indicators. A graphic representation is particularly appropriate if the findings are being interpreted for community members themselves, who may be more accustomed to thinking visually then numerically. Graphs can also be used effectively to compare responses of the two groups. More complex statistical analyses are not feasible because of the limited and primarily qualitative nature of the data.

The ethnographic summary is developed through repeated reading of the narratives for their underlying meaning – something bigger, more abstract, and more elusive than a count or words. When the investigator has a clear sense of what the respondents are trying to convey, quotations illustrative of key points are selected from the transcript and woven together with accompanying narrative explanations.

(2) Another method of analysis is **incidence density,** which is defined as the number of times a theme is mentioned within each group. To establish incidence density, the transcribed narrative text is coded using the

procedures for identification and emergent themes. In recording incidence/density of data, it is more effective to choose to be counted a particular reaction to theme rather than simply counting repetitions of the occurrences of the theme itself.

Q16. State the strengths and limitation of RRA/PRA approaches.

Ans. From the available literature, discussions with researchers, and personal experiences with RRA as a methodological tool, there is a consensus of opinion that RRA is a very useful methodological tool, whether used independently or in conjunction with other conventional methods, for development-oriented research. Among the strengths identified are:

Findings are Multi-Disciplinary

There is general belief that the adoption of a multi-disciplined approach is one of the strongest advantages of RRA. Multidisciplinarity brings different perspectives into problem identification, planning, evaluation and monitoring and enriches the final outcome. Multi-disciplinarity acknowledges the complexities of social phenomena and underscores the need to look at the systemic nature of social problems and to pool disciplinary expertise.

Triangulation

It is argued that, since RRA aims at capturing the breadth, diversity and complexity of a given situation, it pursues the use of different sources and methods for getting information. Each aspect of an issue is investigated in a variety of ways using multiple sources, multiple techniques and multiple approaches. Triangulation technique is employed in selecting methods, sites, teams, and respondents such that usually a minimum of three methods are used. The aim is to obtain a holistic knowledge of a given situation through the rapid build-up of diverse information.

The Adoption of the "Emic Perspective"

Emic perspective envisages looking at problems from the point of view of the user/informant/beneficiary. This is one strength of RRA that has won the admiration of many of its users. In underscoring the power of the emic perspective, it has been argued that most development strategies have failed to significantly improve the lives of the target population because these strategies have often approached the issues from an outsider's point of view. Chambers has pointed out that successful rural development projects have been those responsive to beneficiary needs and those that focus on rural people rather than on the planners. It is further stressed by the practitioner of RRA that strategies that allow more direct dialogue between researchers and rural inhabitants yield more fruitful results than do conventional socio-economic surveys. The emphasis of this emerging development paradigm is on the participation between rural people and development professionals. While it is acknowledged that this approach is beneficial, especially in the diffusion and receptivity of research results by end-users, it is noted that it does not advocate the total rejection of the "ethic" perspective, that is, expert inputs or Western science and innovation. Rather, it seeks for an appropriate blend of local and outside help.

RRA is also acclaimed for its ability to extract information that is otherwise difficult to attain. Through the use of such techniques as wealth ranking or drama, researchers are able to gather sensitive and otherwise difficult-to-gather data quickly and easily.

Another frequently mentioned advantage of RRA is rapidity in the writing of RRA reports. While conventional research reports take three to four months to write, RRA reports are either finished in the field or very shortly thereafter. This rapidity allows for timely intervention.

More can be said about the usefulness of RRA, but as with many new paradigms, there are real and potential limitations that must be recognised and alleviated in order to push the frontiers of this methodology.

Limitations of Findings

The limitations of RRA could be considered from two points of views: those inherent in the methodology itself, and those that result from its application.

(1) Inherent Limitations and Suggestions

It is argued that the word "rural" in the title of the methodology is misleading since it can be applied to urban settings as well. A change or modification in the title may be desirable.

It has been pointed out that sometimes adherents of RRA portray is as a panacea for all research problems. However, in spite of the numerous advantages in this methodology, it must be seen as only a means to an end and not an end in itself. It should complement or be supplemented by other conventional methods as and when appropriate.

One methodological impediment to the success of RRA field work can be the problem of language. In many situations in Africa, researchers may not be well versed in the local dialect of the target group because many dialects exist in the region. In such situations, researcher cannot adequately translate some technical terms into local languages; for example, engineering terms. This, certainly, affects the research results adversably.

(2) Limitations Resulting from Application

There are three critical pre-requisites that will be needed for application of RRA. In case of non-fulfilment of these pre-requisites, RRA approach may not work. These are given below:

- **Leadership:** An important prerequisite for the success of RRA field work is competent, and experienced leadership. A competent leader will be able to determine the optimum size of a group for an effective RRA. It is generally held that a minimum of three researchers and a maximum of seven is desirable to allow for effective triangulation and for optimum derivation of benefits from the multi-disciplinarity of the experts.
- **Team Selection:** Selecting a poor team can introduce bias into RRA fieldwork and nullify its result. The criteria for selection should b e strictly guided by the topic or issue under study and the experience of prospective members. The members of the team should be selected according to the relevance of their disciplines to the issue under study. It is also suggested that for an inquiry on any gender-sensitive issue, both male and female members should be on the team.
- **Administration of Semi-structural Questionnaire:** In situations where a team of researchers is not well versed or trained sufficiently in the administration of a semi-structured questionnaire, wrong results wrong results will be collected and wrong conclusions may be drawn. This methodological weakness can render an entire RRA project useless. Because the semi-structured questionnaire is at the heart of RRA, it is suggested that researchers develop the skill of administering such instruments. The team leader should ensure this an also insist that the questions asked are probing in nature. The six important questions are: What? When? Where? Who? Why? How? The leader must ensure that team members avoid questions that are leading and questions are asked in a logical manner.
- **The Issues of "Rapidity" and Cost:** RRA techniques may be rapid, but the process of development is not. Therefore, practitioners must take into consideration the long preparation period needed for

effective mastery of these techniques. Recognising associated cost, it is argued that RRA may not be cheap as proponents care to believe. An example is a situation where costing does not include the time and inputs necessary to take high level professional into the field for several days. It is suggested that all elements need to be specified to enable practitioners to have a complete picture of cost and avoid any unrealistic illusion of cheapness.

Q17. Describe the process of presentation of findings of qualitative research.

Or

Write a short note on Group Discussion. [Dec-2010, Q.No-11(d)]

Ans. The key findings should always be presented to the villagers and outsiders. This is an important opportunity for cross-checking and feedback. Professional present and invite comment and criticism. This is a fundamental reversal of roles and is crucial for establishing the trustworthiness of the findings.

Village Level Data Set

In the qualitative approach, village level data set emerges from various tools used for the purpose. For example, the social/village maps generate information on number of households, size of households, socio-economic status, asset holding, user and non-user of any scheme/programme, etc. Data pertaining to the social mapping is presented in terms of univariate tables and original maps.

The focus group discussions, individual interviews, preference ranking exercises, etc. bring out overall viewpoints and concerns of villagers on different aspects of the schemes and its impact on their life styles/environment. This is presented in the form of ratios and visual charts.

In RRA/PRA approach, social/village mapping is parallel to the listing in the sample survey approach. The participatory character of social mapping exercises and involvement of several villagers in RRAs/PRAs provide a reliable basis for building up the village level data set. Such a data set is used further for detailed probes by employing other tools. This points to the possibility of using social/resource mapping as a substitute to village schedule and the listing of households in the studies requiring data/information on a variables.

After having generated data set from both these approaches, it is necessary to identify a third source of data on the same parameter for triangulation purposes.

Qualitative Data on Preference Ranking

The preference ranking exercises in RRAs generate highly reliable information. These exercises are taken up with small groups/number of villages (including some women groups) from different social/community groups. Efforts are made to involve nearly all social/community groups in these exercises. Preference ranking is usually done at least with two sub-groups in each social/community grouping. The final group ranking is developed by averaging the scores given by the sub-groups. Village level composite ranks of any indicator are developed by assigning weights to each social group in proportion to its household count emerging from the social/resource maps. Final village level ranks to various indicators are assigned in accordance with the aggregated weighted scores.

For the purpose of ranking of any indicator, villagers are asked to list the characteristics (qualities) of the indicator from their usage point of view and assign scores to different indicators on a ten point scale with reference to the listed characteristics of indicator used by majority of the households belonging to their group. The closeness of the qualitative data with that of the quantitative data of household parameters point to the dependability of preference ranking exercises in the qualitative studies. Triangulation (verification) of the data confirms the accuracy of the RRA/PRA results.

State Level Data

It is quite clear that qualitative approach provides fairly reliable estimates of the village level database of physical entities and resources. Besides this, it also provides in-depth information and insights into contextual linkages, socio-economic behavioural patterns, opinions/perceptions, etc. However, collection of data from a larger geographical spread (beyond village level) is crucial for imparting representative character to the data set and for quantitative estimation (generation of parameters). The efficacy of qualitative method of data collection for an extended geographical spread continues to its limitation.

In qualitative approach, information/data on a variable is obtained through social/village mapping exercises. After mapping the village, each household is identified with a coloured card on which household information is filled and it is numbered in accordance with its location on the map. Since reliability of household income can be ascertained through personal interviews with each of the households, it is not feasible to collect such data on cards during mapping of the villages. However, the wealth (well-being) ranking tool, a basis for stratification of the households into 'not so poor', better off' 'medium' and 'high income' categories of households is fairly well. For the purposes of qualitative research, households are distributed in low, medium and high-income groups based on the composite well being rank of each household. Participating groups in well being ranking exercises are asked to indicate the level of income at or below which the households in poor and better off categories operate. The dominant opinion, emerging from all the groups participating in well being ranking exercise across the villages, present the final picture and decide the poor and better off households.

Other Qualitative Information

Socio-economic impact of any programme on rural life can be evaluated by seeking opinion on the beneficiaries on various aspects. Most of the results presented on qualitative information give percentages of households responding positively or negatively to the perceived benefits/defects and so on. The qualitative data set is then converted into quantitative ratio-estimates designed to suggest beneficiary agreement/disagreement with the suggested benefits/gains derived from the scheme.

In the qualitative approach, information on various aspects emerges largely through **group discussions** and semi-structured interviews with selected beneficiaries. The mode of eliciting opinions on qualitative aspect of the beneficiaries is vastly different as well as time consuming. **Group discussions** are arranged with as many sub-groups (small number of participants from different strata, women, etc.) as possible for the purpose. Care is taken to initiate and guide the discussion on standardised list of benefits/gains so that opinions are expressed by all groups on the issues listed similar to those asked in the quantitative approach. The participants thus, have an opportunity to agree or disagree with the views expressed during the course of discussion and explain the reasons for each one of them. Ultimately, a dominant viewpoint emerges in these discussions, which are more or less taken as the consensus and a range of opinions are also noted. Team members make notes as well record conversations on audio-cassettes. Finally, all groups are brought together and the range of opinions expressed by them is presented by replaying the audio-cassettes to them. This enables them to re-discuss the issues in larger gathering to arrive at the village level dominant view or consensus. It is noteworthy that the emerging consensus has the basis of participants' personal experiences.

The results thrown by the qualitative approach is qualitatively different from that of quantitative approach. In the qualitative approach, the findings emerge from the group discussion and the figures are put forward frequently across all the villagers. The qualitative data set provides direct estimates, which in statistical terminology are referred to as mode. The qualitative results appear firm and direct rather than being indirect as in the case of the sample survey approach.

Thus, the approach in the qualitative framework is entirely different. The participants in the group discussion are are made aware of the disadvantage of the schemes in the perception of the villagers. Thus, the attention of the group is focussed on the causal factors and the problems faced by the beneficiaries. This helps in bringing out an informed responses from the villagers. Secondly, it also helps the villagers to leave out the problems arising other than the schemes. The responses of individuals are recorded in the semi-structured interviews, which are further related, with the response in the group discussions.

Q18. How PRA/RRA approach is superior to sampling survey approach?

Or

Explain the relative advantages of Rapid Rural Appraisal over sampling survey approach in conducting a research study.

[Dec-2010, Q.No.-8]

Ans. PRA/RRA approach is superior to sampling survey approach by the followings points:

- Basically the cost includes expenses on travel, salaries, per diem allowances, material aids, expenses on training and trainers, etc. some of the costs incurred in sample surveys such as cost on printing the questionnaires, stationery items, data entry, data validation/checks, etc. are too high in the sample surveys. However, expenditures incurred during the post-data validation phase of tabulation, analysis and drafting of reports, viz. computer costs, secretarial services and salaries of staff working during this phase are not amenable to prorate allocation because works in these phases are planned and executed for national or regional tabulation and analysis in the sample surveys.
- The costs of training of fieldworkers and collection/validation of data are higher in sample survey based studies by 55 per cent as compared to that of the RRA/PRA based studies. On the other hand, the per village data collection cost in RRAs/PRAs is 7 times more than the sample survey approaches.

- The comparison of time taken for completion of the two studies also needs to be restricted to fieldwork and training components only. In the sample survey approach, one has to wait for all data to get ready for tabulation for overall analysis.
- As regards duration of training time, RRA/PRA methods require only 50 per cent of training time as compared to the training duration of the survey approach. However, RRA/PRA training sessions are designed to cover all aspects in five to six days even when the trainee number ranges from 20 to 25. The fieldwork for RRA/PRA approaches takes a maximum of 30 days as against 80 days in the sample survey for the same sample size. The scale of coverage beings so different in the two approaches, it may not be in order to make observations on time tradeoffs at this stage.

The main aim of GPH book is to provide knowledge as well as good marks in exams.

❑❑❑

6 Data Base of Indian Economy

An Overview

All researchers work with data and/or datasets. For undertaking meaningful research in terms of situational assessment, testing of models, development of theory, evolving policy, assessing the impact of such policy etc, data is crucial.

Data on different variables is thus and essential input for assessment and analysis of economic situations. The availability of data determines the scope of analysis. The reliability of the conclusions arrived at also depends on the availability and veracity of data. Hence researcher's knowledge about the availability of data is important for conducting a meaningful research.

The best statistical source for data on the Indian economy is the Handbook of Statistics on Indian Economy published by the Reserve Bank of India. It is available online at www.rbi.org.in under the "Annual publications" section. The handbook provides not only data compiled and published by RBI, for example on money and banking and balance of payments, but also data produced by other specialised government agencies. RBI's quarterly publication, Macroeconomic and monetary developments, available from the website provide a detailed and up-to-date analysis of the economy.

Q1. Discuss the characteristics of present Indian Statistical System. Explain the various approaches followed by the Indian Statistical System in generating data on various economic and social phenomena. [June-2010, Q.No.-4]

Ans. The Indian Statistical System presently functions within the overall administrative framework of the country. The Indian federal structure has influenced the organisation of the statistical system as well. The division of administrative functions between the Government of India and the State Governments is on the basis of the subject classifications under the Union, State and Concurrent Lists as detailed in the Constitution of India. At the Centre, the responsibilities are further divided amongst the various ministries and departments, according to the Allocation of Business Rules, 1961 that are amended from time to time. The collection of statistics on any subject generally vests in the authority (Central Ministry or Department or State Government Department) that is responsible for that subject according to its status in the Union, State or Concurrent Lists. By and large, the flow of statistical information emanates from the States to the Centre except in cases where the State-level operations are an integral part of Centrally-sponsored schemes or data are collected through national sample surveys.

The main features of the Indian Statistical System can be thus summarised as follows:

- The Administrative Statistics System is its major component;
- It is laterally and vertically decentralised;
- In it, not only data collection but also compilation, processing and preparation of results are carried out by the States for most of the sectors; and
- It is the State-wise results, which flow to the Centre, and statistics at the all-India level are obtained as the aggregates of State-level statistics.

Approaches followed by the Indian Statistical System

The Indian Statistical System generates data on a variety of economic and social phenomena, essentially through seven approaches.

- Acts like the Census Act and the Collection of Statistics Act enable it to conduct large-scale enquiries for collection of data at regular intervals.

- Statutory returns prescribed under several other Acts like the Factories Act and the Reserve Bank of India Act and the implementation of these Acts generate data on matters covered by such legislation.
- Large-scale sample surveys like those conducted by the National Sample Surveys Organisation (NSSO), throw up data on various aspects of the specific subject areas covered by these surveys.
- Data collected by individual Ministries, Departments and organisations of the Central and State Governments as part of their specific functions reflect the emerging situation in different sectors and sub-sectors of the economy and administrative divisions of the country.
- The administrative reports of these organisations supplement such data.
- Information derived from the ***data flows mentioned above***, like the National Accounts Statistics and indices of prices and production provide readily usable inputs for research and policy as well as for monitoring the impact of policies.

Q2. State the major functions of CSO.

Ans. Central government established central statistical organisation, under cabinet secretariat with the objective of creating coordination of large variety of statistical information, collected at the centre and state level. It performs many more functions as listed below:

- Coordination of statistical activities at the centre and the state
- Advisory work concerning the statistical matter, particularly standardisation of concepts and definitions to maintain uniformity, throughout the country
- Collection of statistical data related to planning
- Training of statistical personnel
- Compilation of national income estimates
- To provide statistical data of the nation to the United Nations statistical offices and other international institutions
- To plan and coordinate the conduct of the annual survey of industries and publish the results
- To attend to the work of International Statistical Institutes (conferences) held in India and abroad

- The display of charts and graphs pertaining to the national data which are of administrative interest
- Circulation of regular publications

This organisation does many other things concerning statistical matter, needed from time to time. Each of the above mentioned functions is looked after by a separate division with its head quarters in Delhi, except the Industrial Statistics wing at Kolkata.

Q3. Which precautions should be taken care of while using data assembled from various sources?

Ans. A word of caution is necessary while using data assembled from sources other than one's own. Data extracted from printed publications or websites have to be checked for printing errors/errors that occur while data are being posted on the websites. A check of the row and column totals of the tables and other identity relations relevant to the data under reference in the tables should take care of such errors. More importantly, you should also look into aspects of the data like their coverage, quality (concepts, definitions and methodology adopted by the source-agency for collecting and compiling the data and the methods used for collecting data, reliability and so on), periodicity and timeliness in the availability of data, integrity (confidentiality, etc.) and access of the data to public. This is essential so that conclusions based on the data are firmly moored to what the data are actually supposed to reflect. These aspects are collectively referred to as "metadata". All these details are generally available in the publication containing the data or in a related publication of the agency publishing the data or in the relevant website of the agency.

Q4. What do you understand by the term Special Data Dissemination Standard?

Ans. The Special Data Dissemination Standard (SDDS) was established by the International Monetary Fund (IMF) to guide members that have, or that might seek, access to international capital markets in the provision of their economic and financial data to the public. Subscription to the SDDS was opened in early April 1996.

The SDDS identifies four dimensions of data dissemination:

- The data: coverage, periodicity, and timeliness;
- Access by the public;
- Integrity of the disseminated data; and
- Quality of the disseminated data.

The SDDS prescribes that subscribing members provide a summary description of methodology for each data category, including statements of major differences from international guidelines. The term "methodology" is used in the SDDS in a broad sense to cover the aspects of analytical framework, concepts, definitions, classifications, accounting conventions, sources of data, and compilation practices.

Q5. What type of data will you need to assess the performance of Indian economy? Explain the various sources of such data.

[June- 2011, Q.No-4]

Ans. To assess the performance of an economy we may be able to look at the trend in the production of rice or wheat to be able to say something about the performance of paddy or wheat crop. We can make a similar assessment about the production of steel. If we want to say something on agricultural production, where we find that some crops have done well and others have not, we think of making an overall assessment of agricultural performance by constructing an index of agricultural production for the purpose we might similarly construct an index of industrial production to review the performance of industrial production. But we should like to go beyond levels of output or production and look at performance in terms of incomes flowing from output in the form of rent, wages, interest and profit to those participating in the creation of the output, namely, the factors of production – land, labour, capital and entrepreneurship. Alternatively, we would like to base our judgement of performance on value addition made by the production system, namely, value of output net of the (intermediate) costs incurred in creating the output. It is (i) this overall value addition computed for all sectors/activities of the economy, that is referred to as the National Product, (ii) macro-aggregates related to it, and (iii) trends in (i) and (ii), that can help us in analysing the performance of an economy.

National Income (NI) is the Net National Product (NNP). It is also used to refer to the group of macroeconomic aggregates like Gross National Product (GNP), Gross Domestic Product (GDP) and Net Domestic Product (NDP). All these of course refer to the total value of the good and services produced during a period of time, the only differences between these aggregates being depreciation and/or net factor income from abroad. There are other macroeconomic aggregates related to these that are of importance in relation to an economy. What data would you, as an analyst, like to have about the heath of an economy? Besides a measure of the National Product every year or at smaller intervals of time, you would like to know how fast it is growing over time. What are the shares of the national product that flow to labour and other factors of production? How much of the national income goes to current consumption, how much to saving and how much to building up the capital needed to facilitate future economic growth? What is the role of the different sectors and economic activities – in the public and private sectors or in the organised and unorganised activities or the households in the processes that lead to economic growth? How does the level and pattern of economic growth affect or benefit different sections of society? How much money remains in the hands of the households for consumption and saving after they have paid their taxes, (Personal Disposable Income) – an important indicator of the economic health of households? What is the contribution of different institutions to saving? How is capital formation financed? Such a list of requirements of data for analysing trends in the magnitude and quality of, and also the prospects of, efforts for economic expansion being mounted by a nation can be very long. Such data, that is, estimates of national income and related macroeconomic aggregated form part of a system of National Accounts that gives a comprehensive view of the internal and external transactions of an economy over a period, say, a financial year and the interrelationships among the macroeconomic aggregates. National Accounts thus constitute an important tool of analysis for judging the performance of an economy vis-à-vis the aims of economic and development policy.

Below are given some sources of economic data for Indian economy:

Table 6.1: Important sources of Economic Data for India

Organisation	Publication	Type of Data
GOI-MOSPI-CSO (Government of India Ministry of Statistics and Programme Implementation-Central Statistical Organisation (http:// mospi.nic.in/cso_test1.htm)	National Income Accounts	Macro-economic data.
	National Income Accounts: Sources and Methods	Gives the methodology of compiling macro-economic data.
	Input Output Tables	Industry-and commodity-wise total input consumption and output.
RBI (Reserve Bank of India) (http://www.rbi.org.in/)	RBI Bulletin	Monthly data on various financial indicators.
	Report on Currency and Finance	Yearly account of changes in the financial indicators.
	Trend and Progress of Banking in India	Review of the policies for and performance of the financial sector.

Contd....

	Macro-economic and Monetary Developments	Provides an analytical overview of macro-economic and monetary developments during the year under review.
	Handbook of Statistics on Indian Economy	Provides time-series data (annual/quarterly/monthly/fortnightly/daily) pertaining to a broad spectrum of economic variables, including data on national income, output, prices, money, banking, financial markets, public finance, trade and balance of payments,.
	Flow of Funds Accounts of the Indian Economy	Uses and sources of financial flows.
GOI-MCI-DGCIS (Government of India ministry of Commerce and Industry-Director General of Commercial Intelligence and Statistics (http://dgciskol.gov.in/Dgcis.htm)	Foreign Trade Statistics of India, Monthly Monthly Statistics Foreign Trade of India	Commodity-and country-wise data on import and exports. Monthly data on imports and exports.
GGOI-MOF (Ministry of Finance) (http://finmin.nic.in/)	Economic Survey	Provides detailed account of the changes in the economic conditions during the year.

Q6. Why do we need to make estimates of National Income and related macro aggregates at current and constant prices? Explain the various components of the system of national accounts of India.

[Dec-2012, Q.No.-4] [June-2012, Q.No.-4]

Ans. The Central Statistical Organisation (CSO) in the Ministry of Statistics and Programme Implementation (MoSPI), Government of India compile and publish National Accounts, which include estimates of National Income and related macroeconomic aggregates like NNP, GNP, GDP & NDP, consumption expenditure, saving capital formation and so on for the country and for the public sector for every financial year. Quarterly estimates of GDP are also made. Estimates prepared for any year at the prices prevailing in that year are called estimates at current prices. Estimates of national income and other aggregates over time of national do not help in analysing changes in the magnitude of these aggregates over time. Suppose we need to compare the performance of the economy in terms of national income or other macroeconomic aggregates, over a period of time, say, five years. A comparison of estimates of, say, national income at current prices in the opening year and the final year of the five-year period will give us the increase or decrease, as the case may be, in national income at current prices. We can easily note that the quantum of change observed in national income is the composite measure of the change in national income and the changes in the prices of goods and services between the two points of time. How then to get at the actual change, or the change in real terms in national income (or any other macroeconomic aggregate) over the period? This is done by removing the effect of changes in prices while comparing the aggregate in question at different points of time. Estimates of the aggregate for different years are, therefore, prepared at the prices of a selected year, called the base year, called the base year. Estimates so prepared are called estimates of the aggregate at constant (base year) prices. The comparison of estimates of the aggregate at constant (base year) prices at different points of time is comparison of the magnitude of the aggregate in real terms and measures the real change over time in the magnitude of the aggregate.

CSO releases, every January, Quick Estimates of GDP, National Income, per capita National Income, Consumption Expenditure, Saving and Capital Formation by broad economic sectors for the financial year that ended in March of the preceding year. Quick Estimates for any financial year are thus available with a time lag of ten months. It also releases, along with Quick Estimates for any financial year, revised estimates of national accounts aggregates for earlier financial years. Further, CSO brings out Advance Estimates of GDP, GNP, NNP and per capita NNP at factor cost for the current financial year in February – two months before the close of the financial year. These advance estimates are revised thereafter and the updated advance estimates are released by the end of June, three months after the close of the financial year. Meanwhile, by the end of March, Quarterly Estimates of GDP for the quarter ending December of the preceding year are also released. Thus, by the end of March every year, that is, by the end of every financial year, advance estimates of national income for the financial year that just ended, quick estimates of national income for the preceding financial year and the quarterly estimates of national income up to the preceding quarter that ended in December of the financial year, just ended would have become available.

Components

The presentation of national accounts data may vary by country (commonly, aggregate measures are given greatest prominence), however the main national accounts include the following accounts for the economy as a whole and its main economic actors.

Current accounts:

- Production accounts which record the value of domestic output and the goods and services used up in producing that output. The balancing item of the accounts is value added, which is equal to GDP when expressed for the whole economy at market prices and in gross terms;
- Income accounts, which show primary and secondary income flows - both the income generated in production (e.g. wages and salaries) and distributive income flows (predominantly the redistributive effects of government taxes and social benefit payments). The balancing item of the accounts is disposable income ("National Income" when measured for the whole economy);
- Expenditure accounts, which show how disposable income is either consumed or saved. The balancing item of these accounts is saving.

Capital accounts

Capital accounts record the net accumulation, as the result of transactions, of non-financial assets; and the financing, by way of saving and capital transfers, of the accumulation. Net lending/borrowing is the balancing item for these accounts

Financial accounts

Financial accounts show the net acquisition of financial assets and the net incurrence of liabilities. The balance on these accounts is the net change in financial position.

Balance sheets

Balance sheets record the stock of assets, both financial and non-financial, and liabilities at a particular point in time. Net worth is the balance from the balance sheets.

Q7. What are the relationships depicted in Input-Output Tables? How are these tables useful in research work?

Ans. Input-output table is an important technique of input-output analysis. This table shows (i) how each output is distributed between other sectors or industries of the economy and (ii) what inputs are available to each industry from other industries or sectors. In the words of **Leontief,** "An input-output table describes the flow of goods and services between the individual sectors of a national economy over a stated period of time, say, a year". The statistics of input-out table express the flow of goods and services within the economy. In the words of **Todaro,** "Input-output table provides a convenient framework for measuring and tracing the inter-industry flows for current inputs and outputs among the various sectors of the economy.

Input-output table is shown in the form of a matrix. A matrix is a rectangle having equal number of rows and columns. Under this method, a matrix with rows and columns equal to the number of the sectors is made. Rows represent outputs and columns represent inputs. Input-output table is explained with the help of an illustration. Let us suppose that there are three sectors, namely agriculture, industry and household sector, in an economy. Agriculture and industry are inter-industry sector and household is final demand or final goods sector. The following input-output table shows the inter-dependence of the above three sectors.

Table 6.2: Input-output Table

Using Sector Inputs ↓ / Producing Sector →	Column (1) Agriculture	Column (2) Industry	Column (3) Final Demand	Column (4) Total Output
Row (1) Agriculture	100	80	220	400
Row (2) Industry	140	60	300	500
Row (3) Final Demand	160	360	80	600
(4) Total Inputs	**400**	**500**	**600**	**1,500**

Rows in the above table show how the output of each sector is distributed among other sectors. Columns show how each sector obtains its inputs from other sectors. For example, Row (1) shows that the total value of output of Agriculture sector is ₹400 crore. Of it, output of the value of ₹100 crore is used by the agriculture sector itself in the form of seeds, etc. or it constitutes the input of agriculture sector. Agriculture output worth ₹80 crore serves as input in the industrial sector and output worth ₹220 crore serves as input in final demand sector i.e. consumers, government, investors, etc. Similarly, Row (2) shows that the total value of output of Industrial sector is ₹500 crore. Of it, output of the value of ₹140 crore serves as input in agricultural sector. Output worth ₹60 crore is used by the industrial sector itself as input (raw material, etc.). Output worth ₹300 crore is used as input by the final demand sector.

Study of col. 1 of the above table shows that agricultural output worth ₹400 crore could be produced with the help of agricultural inputs worth ₹100 crore, industrial inputs worth ₹140 crore and household inputs, i.e., factor services like services of labour, managers, etc. worth ₹160 crore. Col. 2 shows that for producing industrial output worth ₹500 crore, agricultural inputs worth ₹80 crore, industrial inputs worth ₹60 crore and factor services worth ₹360 crore are needed. Col. 3 shows that to produce output of final demand worth ₹600 crore, agricultural inputs worth ₹220 crore, industrial inputs worth ₹300 crore and factor services (final demand sector) inputs worth ₹80 crore are needed. Input-output table thus shows the inter-relationship found in the inputs and outputs of different sectors.

It is prepared by CSO from time to time. It gives, besides the complete table, the methodology adopted, the database made use of, analysis of the results and the supplementary tables derived from the I-OTT giving the input structure and the commodity composition of the output. The Planning Commission updates and recalibrates the I-OTT and prepares an Input-Output table for the base period of a Five Year Plan being formulated and another Input-Output table for the terminal year of the Five Year Plan. The detailed results of this exercise, carried out in the Planning Commission for the formulation of any Five Year Plan, are published by the Planning Commission as the **Technical Note to the Five Year Plan.** The Technical Note contains the relevant Input-Output Table, the methodology adopted and related material. The latest available in this series is the **Technical Note to the Tenth Five Year Plan.** The I-OTT of CSO and the Input-Output Table of the Planning Commission would be useful to researchers interested in exploiting the power of the input output technique in economic and econometric analysis in their research work.

Q8. Write short note on 'Capital formation'.

Ans. Capital is an essential means of economic development. Its basic characteristic is that it is man-made. It accumulated with the efforts of man. In the terminology of Economic, capita is that part of income, which is used for further production. That part of income which is not spent on consumptions is called saving. If we spend our savings on capital goods, such as, machines, instruments, factories, or on increasing the stock of raw material or finished goods, this expenditure is called investment. Investment results in the production of capital goods, or in the increase in capital stock. The increase in capital stock is called capital formation.

In the words of **Colin Clark,** "Capital formation refers to the net addition made to the existing stock of capital in a given period of time".

Q9. Which major efforts have been made to collect data on different aspects of agriculture? **[Dec-2010, Q.No-9]**

Or

What type of data is available on agriculture? Identify the agencies involved in compilation of agricultural data.

Ans. The Directorate of Economics and Statistics (DESMOA) in the Department of Agriculture and Cooperation and the Animal Husbandry Statistics Division (AHSD) of the Department of Animal Husbandry, Dairy and Fisheries in the Ministry of Agriculture are the major sources of data on agriculture and allied activities. The major effort to collect data on different aspects of agricultural sector are as follows:

- The quinquennial agricultural census and the input survey
- The cost of cultivation studies
- Annual estimates of crop production
- The quinquennial livestock census
- Integrated sample survey to estimate the production of major livestock products.

DESMOA releases statistics on agriculture and allied activities flowing from its work and also collected from other divisions (like the **Agriculture Census Division**) and Departments of the Ministry of Agriculture and other Ministries and agencies in their comprehensive annual publication **Agricultural Statistics at a Glance (ASG).** Other publications include, **"Cost of Cultivation in India"**, the monthly bulletin **"Agricultural Situation In India". AHSD** publishes the data flowing from its activities [which include the activities mentioned at (iv) and (v) above] and those collected from divisions of the Department of Animal Husbandry, Dairy and Fisheries and other agencies in its biennial publication **Basic Animal Husbandry Statistics (BAHS).**

Agricultural Census

This was started in 1970-71. The seventh of these censuses relates to 2001. The census is carried out in three phases. The first is the preparation of a list of all holdings with data on primary characteristic like area, the gender and the social group of the holder and the location (code) of the holding. The second phase collects detailed data on the irrigation status and tenancy particulars of the holding, the cropping pattern of the holding and the number of crops cultivated by the holding. The third phase, which is better known as the Input Survey and conducted in the year following the census year, relates to collection of data on the pattern of input-use across crops, regions and size-groups of holdings. The inputs covered are availability of infrastructural facilities and use of chemical fertilizers, organic manures, pesticides, agricultural implements and machinery, livestock, agricultural credit and seeds. The results of the **2001 Agricultural Census** are being processed. The results of the **1995-96 Agricultural Census** are available with the Agricultural Census Division of the Ministry of Agriculture. Those of the **Agricultural Census and the Input Survey** have been computerised. The results are presented from the level of tehsil upwards. The data are also available in CD ROM and the CD ROM contains an information retrieval system for use at micro and macro levels for decision-making. Further, selective information is available on the internet for easy access to the public. This is a query-based facility and can provide data on operational holdings at the national, State, district and tehsil levels by type, characteristics and size class/group.

Studies on Cost of Cultivation

DESMOA implements a comprehensive scheme for studying the cost of cultivation of principal crops in India and this results in the collection and compilation of field data on the cost of cultivation and production in respect of 29 principal crops leading to estimates of crop-wise and State-wise costs of cultivation and also computation of the index of the terms of trade between agriculture and non-agricultural sectors. The scheme covers 16 States and foodgrain crops, oil seeds and commercial crops and selected vegetables.

The **Commission for Agricultural Costs and Prices (CACP)** makes use of the estimates of cost of cultivation and production and the structure of cost of cultivation flowing from these studies, along with an analysis of a wide spectrum of data on variables like market prices, productivity of the crops concerned, domestic and global inter-crop price parity, the terms of trade between the agricultural and the non-agricultural sectors and the supply-demand situation in arriving at their recommendations to government on Minimum support Prices (MSP). The **CACP Reports** thus contain not only the data thrown up by the cost of cultivation studies but also those assembled by it from various sources for its work.

Annual Estimates of Crop Production

DESMOA makes and releases annual estimated of area, production and yield in respect of principal crops of foodgrains, oil seeds sugarcane, fibres and important commercial and horticulture crops. These crops account for about 87 per cent of the total agricultural output. Estimates of area and yield form the basis of estimates of agricultural production. While estimates of area are based on a reporting system that is a mix of complete coverage and coverage by a sample, those of yield are based on a **system of crop cutting experiments** and **General Crop Estimation surveys.** The preparation of these estimates takes time. Estimates of crop production are, however, needed earlier and in fact even before the crops are harvested, for policy purposes. Advance estimates of crop production are, therefore, made. The first assessment of the kharif crop is made in the middle of September, that is, when the South-West Monsoon is about to be over. The second advance estimate – a second assessment of the earlier estimate of the kharif crop and the first assessment of the rabi crop – is made in January. The third advance is made at the end of March or the beginning of April and the fourth in June. The methodology for estimating area and yield of crops and for making advance estimates are given in **ASG.**

Livestock Census

The last quinquennial livestock census, the seventeenth in the series, was conducted in 2003. The census has collected information, district-wise on livestock, poultry, fishery and also agricultural implements. Livestock covers cattle buffaloes, sheep, goats, pigs, horses and ponies, mules, donkeys, camels, yak, mithun and pigs, dogs and rabbits. These are classified by age (appropriate for the species), sex, breed, function ('breeding', 'work', 'both' and 'others' for males and 'in milk' or 'dry' in the case of females). Poultry covers cock, hen, duck, and drake, which are classified as desi and 'improved' varieties. Fishery covers fishing activity (inland capture, inland culture, marine capture and marine culture), members involved in fishing (male, female and child), persons engaged in fishing (part time male, full time male, part time female and full time female) craft/gear, namely, trawlers, gill-netters, liners, seiners, motorised canoe/maran, non-motorised canoe/maran, and miscellaneous gears like trawler-net, gill netter-net, cast-net, drag-net, hook lines, set barriers and others. Each of these classes except the last one is further classified into size (length) and horsepower. Agricultural cover annually operated implements, animal operated implements, plan protection equipment, water lifting devices, tractor and power operated implements, equipment for livestock and poultry and horticulture tools. Each group provides further data on four or five specific equipments like for example, thresher under the first group, ST Plough under the second, TPO Spray under the third, diesel, under the fourth, Crawler tractor under the fifth, incubator under the sixth and power operated tools under the sixth group.

The provisional results of the 2003 census are available on the **website of the Department of Animal Husbandry** on a query-based format.

Data on Production of Major Livestock Products

AHSD is responsible for collection of statistics on animal husbandry, dairy and fisheries.

Q10. Discuss in detail about the ASG.

Ans. The total geographical area of the country is made up of land and water bodies like rivers and lakes. Land in turn consists of forests, barren and uncultivable land, land used for non-agricultural purposes, pastures, fallows, cultivable land and so on.

Land utilisation statistics are available in **ASG.** As for inputs and access of individual operational holdings to such inputs, **ASG** provides data on:

(1) Land: Size-distribution of operational holding and area operated by these holdings and average size of operational holdings in each size group – marginal (size less than one HA area), small (1 to 2 HA), semi-medium (2 to 4 HA), Medium (4 to 10 HA) and large (more than 10 HA) and the position in different States:

(2) Intensity of land use or cropping intensity: gross area sown and net area sown for principal crops; gross and net sown area in different size classes of operational holdings;

(3) Water:

(a) the status of important reservoirs in the country;

(b) rainfall (distribution of the 36 meteorological divisions into which the country is divided by those with excess rainfall, normal rainfall and deficient/scanty rainfall:

(c) area under irrigation – gross area irrigated and net area irrigated for different crops;

(4) Seeds: production of breeder seeds and foundation seeds; and crop-wise distribution of certified/quality seeds;

(5) Soil conservation: area covered by soil different conservation measures;

(6) Fertilizers and Pesticides:

(a) consumption of fertilizers in terms of nutrients (N–nitrogenous, P–phosphatic and K–potassic fertilizers) and farmyard manure as also pesticides in different agricultural crops, in States and over the years;

(b) consumption per hectare in different States and selected countries.

(7) Inputs – Overall: Production and use of agricultural input in India:

(8) Power: consumption of electricity for agricultural purposes vis-à-vis total consumption in different States;

(9) Flow of Institutional credit: (I) flow of (a) production (short-term) credit; and (b) medium term credit to agriculture from (i) cooperative banks (ii) regional rural banks (RRBs) and (iii) commercial banks. (II) Kisan Credit Cards issued by cooperative banks, RRB and commercial banks in different States; and

(10) Institutional Credit availed of: estimated amount of credit (in the form of inputs and loans taken for agricultural purposes by operational holdings of different size classes from different institutions.

ASG provides a time series of the amount of subsidy given to agriculture with its break-up into subsidy for (i) fertilizers, (ii) electricity, and (iii) irrigation, (iv) other subsides given to marginal farmers and Farmers' Cooperative Societies in the form of seeds, development of oil seeds, pulses, etc. one can easily derive the size of the total subsidy relative to GDP in current prices.

ASG also presents the share of agricultural subsidies in selected OECD countries – it presents two figures, one a "Producers support Estimate" (PSE) and another " per cent PSE". PSE is an indicator of the annual monetary value of gross transfers from consumers add taxpayers to agricultural producers, measured at the farm gate level, arising from policy measures that support agriculture, regardless of their nature, objective, impacts on farm production or income. " per centPSE" is support expressed as a percentage of gross farm receipts, and shows the amount of support to farmers, irrespective of the sectoral structure of a given country.

Other kinds of data on the agricultural sector presented in **ASG** are:

(1) Procurement of rice, wheat, cotton, raw jute, oil seeds, pulses, and onion by public agencies;

(2) Minimum Support Prices (MSP) for different agricultural commodities;

(3) Marketed Surplus Ratios of (a) important agricultural commodities in different States, and (b) different crops – national level;

(4) Per capita availability of important articles of consumption and percentage share of Monthly Per capita Consumption Expenditure (MPCE) on cereals and non-cereals in total food items;

(5) Stocks of cereals by type held by Central and State agencies;

(6) Imports and exports of agricultural commodities;

(7) Livestock population;

(8) Production of milk, egg, fish and wool in different States;

(9) Conversion factors between primary and secondary agricultural commodities in respect of important agricultural commodities; and

(10) GDP from the agricultural sector – national and for States and its sub-sectors and ICOR for different sectors.

Q11. Discuss the sources covering the entire industrial sector.

Or

Indicate the major sources of data on levels of industrial employment.

Ans. There are three sources that cover the whole spectrum of economic activity or non-agricultural activities and, therefore, the entire industrial sector. However, these sources give data only on levels of industrial employment:

(1) The first source is **the decennial Population Census.** This provides data on the levels of employment in various economic activities across the economic spectrum, and, therefore, the industrial sector, down to the NIC 1987 three-digit code levels. It also provides (i) employment levels in each of the three-digit NIC code classified by Occupational Divisions [the first digit of the National Classification of Occupation 1968 (NCO 1968)], (ii) industrial employment in broad industrial sectors (first digit of NIC 1987 code) classified by broad age groups, and (iii) industrial employment in broad sectors (first digit of NIC 1987) by levels of education. Such details are available up to district levels. These data, however, become available after a large time lag.

(2) The second source consists of the quinquennial sample survey relating to employment and unemployment conducted by the National Sample Surveys Organisation (NSSO). These surveys also provide similar type of data on industrial employment, down to State levels. Data by the NSS regions can also be obtained as the primary data collected (unit record data) can be obtained on floppies from NSSO. Key results from the NSSO surveys are available after about a year, while the final report becomes available two years after the surveys are completed.

(3) The third source is the Economic Census, which has been conducted in 1977, 1980, 1990, 1998, and 2005. The Economic Census covers all economic enterprises in the country except those engaged in crop production and plantation and provides data on employment in these enterprises. This provides a frame for the conduct of more detailed follow up (enterprise) surveys covering different segments of the unorganised non-agricultural sectors, which in turn throw up data on production and employment in these segments, useful for an analytical study of these segments and in the compilation of national accounts.

(4) The fourth source is the Employment Market Information (EMI) programme of the Directorate General of Employment & Training (DGE&T), Union Ministry of Labour & Employment and the Directorates of Employment under the State Governments. This is based on the statutory quarterly employment returns furnished by non-agricultural establishments in the private sector employing 10 or more persons and all public sector establishments. This source of industrial employment provides data at quarterly intervals down to district levels. The quarterly data are available with a time lag of about a year.

Q12. Describe the agencies, which generate the data on small scale industries.

Ans. The Office of Development Commissioner (Small Scale Industries) also known as Small Industries Development Organisation (SIDO) functions as the nodal Development Agency for small industries. SIDO functions under the Ministry of SSI (Ministry of Small Scale Industries). The organisation was set up with a mission of imparting greater vitality and growth impetus to the small, tiny and village enterprises in terms of output, employment and exports and instilling a competitive culture based on heightened technology awareness.

The Development Commissioner for Small Scale Industries (DCSSI) has conducted a Census of SSI – 2001-02 released by the Ministry of Small Scale Industries. Broad details of the performance of small-scale industries are available in the Annual Reports of the Ministry of Small Scale Industries. Time series data on employment, production, labour productivity in small-scale industries (SSI) and value of exports of the products of small-scale industry are also available in the RBI Handbook. Data on some part of Khadi and Village Industries Commission (KVIC), handlooms and handicrafts do get included in ASI but data relating exclusive to these sub-sectors are available in the Annual Reports of these organisations or in the Annual Reports of the Ministries under which these Boards/Commissions function.

Surveys of unorganised manufacturing conducted once in five or six years contribute to the strengthening of the database of the unorganised sector.

Q13. Write a short on the data of industrial credit and finance.

Ans. The RBI Handbook on Statistics of the Indian Economy provides time series data on the sectoral deployment of non-food gross bank credit provided by Scheduled Commercial Banks to different sectors of the economy, which enables us to study trends in the flow of bank credit to small-scale industry, medium and large industries, wholesale trade other than food production and export credit. This would enable us to evaluate the implementation of the policy regarding allocation of bank and institutional credit to the priority sector, which includes small-scale industries. It also provides time series data on deployment of bank credit to some 25 industrial categories and power. In addition, it presents time series data on the health of SSI and non-SSI units: (a) the number of SSI units that are sick, (b) the number that are weak, (c) the number of non-SSI units that are sick, and (d) the amounts outstanding (loans) from each of these categories of units.

Data on assistance sanctioned and disbursed by financial institutions like Industrial Development Bank of India (IDBI), Industrial Credit and Investment Corporation of India (ICICI), Small Industrial Development Bank of India (SIDBI) and Life Insurance Corporation (LIC) of India can also be obtained from the **Handbook.** Similarly, some data on the financing of project costs of companies are available in the **Handbook.** All these data of course relate to companies, which may include non-industrial ventures too. The primary source of such data is the Ministry of Company Affairs. The publication of the Securities Exchange Board of India (SEBI) **"Handbook of Statistic on the Indian Securities Market – 2004"** provides annual and monthly time series data on industry-wise classification of capital raised through the securities market – the industrial sector activities by which the classification is made being, cement and construction, chemical, electronics, engineering, entertainment, finance, food processing, healthcare, information technology, leather, metal, mining, packaging, paper and pulp, petrochemical, plastic, power, printing, and rubber.

Q14. Describe the kind of data available in India in the area of trade.

Or

State the various source of data on trade.

Ans. Trade is the means of building up an enduring relationship between countries and the means available to any country for accessing goods and services not available locally for various reasons like the lack of technical know-how. The different sources of data on trade are as follows:

(1) Merchandise Trade

The Directorate General of Commercial Intelligence and Statistics (DGCI&S) collects and compiles statistics on imports and exports. It releases these data at regular intervals through their **publications** and through **CDs.** It prepares **"Quick Estimates"** on aggregate data of export and imports and principal commodities within two weeks of the reference month and releases these in the monthly press release. It publishes:

- A monthly brochure *Foreign Trade Statistics of India (Principal Commodities and Countries)* containing provisional data issued to meet the urgent needs of the Ministry of Commerce, other government organisations, Commodity Boards (CBs), Export Promotion Councils (EPCs) and research organisations. It contains commodity-wise, country-wise and port-wise foreign trade information.
- *Monthly Statistics of Foreign Trade of India, Volume I (Exports) & Volume II (Imports)* containing detailed data on foreign trade at the 8-digit level codes of the ITS (HTS).
- Foreign Trade Statistics of India (Principal Commodities and Countries)
- Inland and Coastal Trade Statistics and Shipping and Air Cargo Statistics
- The **DGCI&S website (www.dgciskol.nic.in)** has two parts, one consists of static pages and other the dynamic pages. The first contains the history and the activities of DGCI&S and summary data on principal commodities, and countries and is updated regularly. The dynamic pages are mainly for on-line data dissemination and provide access on free and payment basis. This contains at least 24 months final foreign trade data at 8-digit commodity and principal commodity level and updated regularly; and
- *The Priced Information Service System (PISS)* provides information to private parties, EPCs, CBs, Foreign Embassies etc. on payment basis @ ₹1/- per unit record of information. It does not give the whole baskets of 8-digit commodity-country data for any particular period for reasons of 'copyright' provision of the DGCI&S. It however, provides aggregate and

detailed data to Centre for Monitoring Indian Economy (CMIE), Mumbai for an efficient trade intelligence service.

Foreign trade data published by DGCI&S relates to merchandise trade through all recognised seaports, land customs stations and inland container depots located all over India. Data on exports include re-exports and relate to the free on board (values and imports relate to cost, insurance and freight (C.I.F) values. Exports and imports are based on a general system of recording. According to this, exports relate to Indian merchandise and re-export relates to foreign merchandise previously imported into India. Imports relate to foreign merchandise, whether these are intended for consumption in India, bonding or re-exportation.

Kinds of data on foreign Trade

Time series on the following data (DGCI&S data) are published in the RBI Handbook of Statistics of the Indian Economy 2005.

- Value (in US dollar and Indian Rupees) of exports and imports and trade balance is given, the last being defined as the excess of exports over imports. Each of these three groups is split into three classes – first relating to oil, the second to non-oil commodities and the last to all commodities. Trade balance likewise gets split into three categories—oil trade balance, non-oil trade balance and (overall) trade balance;
- Value (in US dollar and Indian Rupees) of exports of principal commodities;
- Value (in US dollar and Indian Rupees) of imports of principal commodities;
- Value (in US dollar and Indian Rupees) of exports of selected commodities to principal countries;
- Direction of Foreign trade (in US dollar and Indian Rupees) showing exports and imports for each year by trade areas, group so countries and countries; and within each group of countries or trade area, data are presented only for selected countries;
- Year-wise indices, both UVI (Unit Value Index) and QI (Quantity Index). For imports and exports (base 1979-80 = 100) and the three terms of trade measures; GTT (Gross Terms of Trade), NTT(Net Terms of Trade) and ITT(Income Terms of Trade);
- QI and UVI for exports for each product under the classification used up to 1987-88 for the years 1980-81 to 2003-04; and
- Similar type of data on imports.

(2) Service Trade

Besides export and import of merchandise, a number of service, like transportation service, travel service, software, Information Technology-Enabled Services (ITES), business services and professional services are exported and imported. These are captured by "non-factor services" included in the entry "Invisibles" in the Tables on Indian's Overall BoP and the Key Components of India's BoP in the RBI handbook. It names the item "non-factor services" in the BoP table in the RBI Handbook referred to above as "services" and gives (i) figures for 'credit', 'debit' and 'net' against each of the items in the BoP table, and (ii)separate figures for "software services" included in the category "miscellaneous".

Q15. What is the existing base year of constructing unit value Index and quantum index by DGCI&S?

Ans. It is important to analyse the growth in foreign trade both in terms of value and volume, since both are subject to changes over time. Exports and imports are made up of a large number of commodities and fluctuations in the export and imports of individual commodities contribute to overall fluctuations in the volume and value of exports and imports. We, therefore, need a **composite indicator of the** trends in trade. The index number of foreign trade of a country is a useful indicator of the temporal fluctuations in exports and imports of the country in terms of **value, quantum and unit price and** so on. Similarly, measures of the terms of trade could be derived from such indices relating to imports and exports.

The index number of foreign trade is computed and presented as Unit Value Index (UVI) and Quantum Index (QI). These are defined as follows:

$$UVI=\left[\sum P_t Q_t\right]/\left[\sum P_0 Q_t\right] \text{ ....(1)}$$

$$QI=\left[\sum P_0 Q_t\right]/\left[\sum P_0 Q_0\right] \text{ ....(2)}$$

Where P_t is the unit value of an item in the current period and Q_t is the quantity of the same item in the current period, P_0 and Q_0 are the unit value and the quantity respectively of the same item during the base period and Σ is the summation over all commodities. These indices have been computed with 1979-80 as the base year.

Three types of Terms of Trade are computed from these indices:

(1) Gross Terms of Trade (GTT) = 100 x [(QI of imports)/(QI of exports)]

(2) Net Terms of Trade (NTT) = 100 x [UVI of exports)/(UVI of imports)]

(3) Income Terms of Trade (ITT) = [NTT x QI of exports]/100

= [UVI (exports)xQI(exports)]/[UVI (imports)].

The existing index numbers have the base year 1979-80. Changes in the ITC since April, 1987 and the recasting of the basket of commodities to suit the new classification system, the base year 1979-80 has become too old to serve the purpose of temporal comparability and the new ITC adopted in April, 1987. The DGCI&S, therefore, decided to construct new index number with the **base year 1998-99.** It also decided to bring out global monthly indices and for selected countries.

Q16. Explain the reasons for divergence between merchandise trade deficit/surplus data provided by DG (I and S) and RBI's BOP data.

Ans. Data on merchandise imports and exports or trade data are also available from the Reserve Bank of India (RBI) organisation (which are also presented in the RBI Handbook); the Balance of Payments (BoP) data reported by RBI show the value of merchandise imports on the debit side and that of exports on the credit side. It also shows trade balance – a trade surplus – depending upon whether the difference 'export – imports' is negative or positive. These are all shown in the balance payment format as part of current account, which also shows another entity 'invisibles'. However, there is a divergence in trade deficit/surplus in merchandise trade shown by **DGCI&S data** and that shown by **RBI's BoP data**. This discrepancy between the two sources also affects data on current account deficit (CAD)or surplus (CDS), since current account deficit/surplus is the total of trade deficit/surplus and net invisibles (inflow of invisibles net of outflow in the category 'invisibles'). For example, the **Economic advisory Council to the Prime Minister noted, in its Report on Balance of Payment (BoP)** submitted to the prime Minister recently, that the divergence between the two sources of data on trade was growing. It noted that trade deficit is projected for the year 2005-06 at 5.2 per cent of GDP on the basis of trade data from DGCI&S, while it is 7.7 per cent according to RBI's BoP data — a difference of the size of 2.5 per cent of GDP. CAD based on trade data of DGCI&S is only 0.3 per cent of GDP while it is 2.9 per cent of GDP if the estimate of CAD is based on trade data from BoP. The reasons for the divergence in the data between the two sources are, as noted by the Council 1:

- DGCI&S tracks physical imports and exports while BoP data tracks payment transaction relating to merchandise trade;

- DGCI&S data fail to capture Government imports, which are exempted from customs duty. Defence imports fall into this category; and
- DGCI&S data do not capture imports that do not cross customs boundary (for example, oil rigs and some aircrafts) while they are still paid for and get captured in BoP data.

Q17. List the type of data on the following compiled by SEBI and RBI:

(a) Public finance

Ans. The **RBI Handbook 2005** presents the following time series data in respect of public finances:

(1) Central Govt. Finances

- Major components of Central Govt. Receipts – direct and indirect taxes and their components, non-tax revenue and one of its important components, interest receipts and capital receipts;
- Major heads of capita receipts of the Central Government – market borrowings, small savings, provident fund special deposits, recoveries of loans, disinvestments receipts, external loans (net);
- Major heads of Central Govt. expenditure – revenue expenditure and its important components (defence, interest and subsidies), capital expenditure including loans and advances and defence expenditure; Also the breakup of expenditure into developmental and non-developmental heads and the shares of economic services in development expenditure;
- Public sector Plan, its sectoral profile and the manner which it is financed – from sources like own resources, domestic market borrowings and net capital inflow from abroad;
- Key deficit indicators- gross Fiscal Deficit (GFD), Net Fiscal Deficit (NFD), Gross Primary Deficit (GPD), Net Primary Deficit (NPD), Revenue Deficit (RD), Primary Revenue Deficit (PRD), Budgetary Deficit (BD), Net RBI Credit;
- Financing of Central Govt.'s GFD – through external financing and internal financing (market borrowing, other borrowings, and draw down of cash balances);
- Outstanding liabilities of the Central Govt;

- Small savings schemes – total receipts during the year and amount outstanding at the end of the year;
- Pattern of receipts of Govt. of India loans by category (maturity period) of loans;

(2) Finances of the State Govts.

- Revenue receipts – tax receipts (like sales tax and State excise duties), the share of Central taxes like income tax and union excise duties; and capital receipts like interest receipts, loans and grants from the Centre, recovery of loans and advances, market loans, provident fund and small savings;
- Expenditure pattern-revenue and capital expenditure; developmental outlay and the shares of economic services and the shares of interest payments administrative services and pension and miscellaneous general services;
- Key deficit indicators of State Govts. – GFD, GPD, RD, PRD, Overall Deficit and Net RBI Credit and financing of GFD;
- Outstanding liabilities of the State Govts.

(3) Combined Finances of Central and State Govts.

- Receipts and Disbursements;
- Direct and Indirect tax revenues;
- Developmental and non-developmental expenditure;
- Market borrowings;
- Outstanding liabilities;
- Range and weighted averages of Central and State Govt. dated securities;
- Holders of Central and State Govt. Securities – 9 categories like RBI, commercial banks, LIC, Employees Provident Fund and primary dealers;

(4) Transaction with rest of the world

The RBI handbook 2005 gives time series data (which are often in US dollar as well as in Indian Rupees) on a number of these parameters:

- India's overall BoP showing current account and capital account and key components of these like trade balance, invisibles, types of foreign investment, net external assistance, net commercial borrowing, rupee debt service and net NRI deposits. It also shows monetary movements in terms of increase/decrease in forex reserves. IMF and SDR allocation;

- Exchange rates for Indian Rupee vis a vis the SDR, US$, £, DM/Euro and Japanese Yen;
- Indices of Real Effective Exchange Rate (REER) and Nominal Effective Exchange Rate (NEER) of the Indian Rupee – based on 36 country bilateral weights. Figures for REER and NEER are given for both export based weights and trade based weights – base 1985 = 100;
- External Assistance showing loans and grants authorised and extent of utilisation, debt service payments by amortisation and interest payments and the net inflow of assistance.
- Various types of NRI deposits and outflows and inflows from and to these deposits;
- Inflow of foreign investment consisting of foreign direct investment (FDI) and portfolio investment; (see paragraph below for more details);
- Foreign exchange reserves in terms of SDRs, gold and foreign currency assets; and
- India's external debt, short-term debt and long-term debt grouped in to seven categories— multilateral, bilateral, IMF, commercial borrowing, NRI and FC (B&O) DEPOSITS AND Rupee debt; further details under each of these categories like govt./non-govt. borrowing, concessional/non-concessional, donor agency, beneficiary organisation, trade credit (buyers' or suppliers' credit, export credit) are available, also given are ratios of concessional debt and short-term debt to total debt and debt indicators– debt stock to GDP ratio and debt-service ratio.

FDI data collected by RBI now cover (a) equity capital, (b) reinvested earnings, and (c) other capital. **The RBI Handbook 2005 and the SEBI handbook** presents time series data on the breakup of FDI flows by

(i) The three categories (a), (b) and (c) mentioned above; and

(ii) Further breakup of equity capital by (the route/manner of flow)

(1) Government (through Secretariat for Industrial Approvals – SIA + Foreign Investments Promotion Board-FIPB);

(2) RBI;

(3) NRI;

(4) Acquisition of shares and

(5) Equity capital of unincorporated bodies.

It also gives the breakdown of portfolio investments by

(i) Amounts raised by Indian Corporates through Global Depository Receipts (GDR) and American Depository Receipts (ADR);

(ii) Inflow of funds (net of outflow) by Foreign Institutional Investors (FIIs); and

(iii) Off Shore Funds and others.

(b) Currency, Coinage, Money, and Banking

Ans. The RBI Handbook 2005 presents time series data on

- Notes and coins of different denominations issued by the RBI;
- Liabilities and assets of the Issue and Banking Departments of the RBI, which are generally in terms of items like, notes in circulation, gold coins and bullion rupee coins, Govt. of India Rupee securities, loans and advances to Central and State Govts., banks and other agencies and bills purchased and discounted;
- Components of money stock, namely, Reserve Money (M_0) made up of currency in circulation, other deposits with RBI and banks' deposits with RBI, Narrow Money (M_1) consisting of currency with the public, other deposits with RBI and demand deposits and Broad Money (M_3) comprising Narrow Money and time deposits;
- Sources of change in the money stock consisting of net bank (RBI and banks) credit to the commercial sector, net forex assets of the banking RBI and banks) sector Govt's currency liabilities to the public, net non-monetary liabilities of the banking (RBI and Banks) sector and RBI's gross claims on banks;
- Monthly data series on the detailed composition of each of the components of the money stock (the "C" components) and the composition of individual sources of change in the money stock; also defining new monetary aggregates NM_2 and NM_3, these being respectively equal to "M_1 short-term time deposits" and "[NM_2 + long-term deposits +call/term funding from Financial Institutions (FIs)]= [domestic credit + Govt.'s currency

liability to the public + net forex assets of the banking sector – capital account – other items (net)];

- Monthly data series on Liquidity aggregates, namely, $L_1 = NM_3 + \text{Postal deposits}$; $L_2 = L_1 + \text{liabilities of FIs}$;

  $L_3 = L_2 + \text{Public Deposits with NBFCs}$ (L_3 is compiled on a quarterly basis);
- Monthly series of WPI (base year 1993-94=100), CPI-IW (base year, 2001 = 100), (b) CPI-UNME (base year 1984-85=100), and (c) CPI-AL (base year 1986-87 = 100).
- Monthly average price of gold and silver in domestic (Mumbai) and foreign markets;
- Major monetary policy measures – Bank Rate, Cash Reserve Ratio (CRR) and Statutory Liquidity Ratio (SLR) over the years;
- Selected Aggregates of Scheduled Commercial Banks (SCBs) like outstanding demand and time deposits, investment in Govt. and other securities, bank credit (food and non-food), cash in hand and balance with the RBI.
- Deployment of non-food credit to priority sector and its sub-sectors (like agriculture, small-scale industries), industry and its groups, wholesale trade and export credit; and short and long-term direct and indirect institutional credit to agriculture and allied activities and to farmers by size of holdings;
- Consolidated balance sheets of SCBs; Gross and net Non-Performing Assets (NPAs) of SCBs by bank groups Distribution and SCBs and different sub-groups of SCBs by Capital to Risk-weighted Assets Ratio(CRAR); and
- Important banking indicators of Regional Rural Banks (RRBs) State Cooperative Banks, Primary Agricultural Coop. Societies (PACS), State Coop. Agricultural and Rural Development Banks and Primary Coop. (A&RD) Banks.

(c) Financial Markets

Ans. The RBI handbook of Statistics of the Indian Economy – 2005 and the Handbook of Statistics on the Indian Securities Market- 2005 published by SEBI contain comprehensive data on the financial market. The two together provide annual time series data on several aspects of the financial market [those available in the SEBI handbook appear with the word "(SEBI)" at the end of the item]:

- The structure of interest rated – call/notice money rates, commercial bank rate, lending institutions like IDBI, dividend and yields of the units of UTI, annual gross redemption yields of Govt. Securities and average annual price and yield rate of Central Govt. Securities (SGL transaction);
- Financial assistance and disbursed and financing of project cost of companies by FIs, loans sanctioned by HDFC and NABARD, and refinancing operations of National Housing Bank (NHB);
- Aggregate deposits of NBFCs and non-banking non-financial companies (NBNFCs);
- Taxable and tax-free bonds issued by public sector undertaking-both public issue of bonds and privately placed bonds;
- Resource mobilisation in the Private placement Market – financial and non – financial institutions in the public and private sector;
- Net resources mobilised by mutual funds (MFs) – MFs sponsored by banks, financial institutions (FIs), UTI anf the private sector;
- New capital issues (number and amount mobilised) by non-govt. public Ltd. Companies;
- Absorption of private capital issues – the no. of issuing companies, the number of shares and amount subscribed by promoters, etc. and Govt., FIs, etc. and the number of shares and amount subscribed by public other than underwriters and other groups;
- Investments of LIC by sector and instrument and of UTI by instrument;
- Assets and liabilities of institutions like IDBI, NABARD, EXIM Bank, NHB and SIDBI;
- Annual averages share price indices – BSE SENSEX (base 1978-79 = 100), BSE National (base 1983-84=100) and RBI Index (base 1980-81=100) and Market Capitalisation;
- Market intermediaries like stock exchanges (cash and derivatives market). Brokers, corporate brokers, sub-brokers,

custodians, FIIs depositories, merchant bankers, bankers, to issues and underwriters registered with SEBI; and registered brokers by stock exchanges and by ownership categories proprietory, partnership and corporate; (SEBI)

- Long-term capital raised during 1957-90 (pre-reform period) through shares, debt and loans; (SEBI)
- Annual and monthly data series on resources raised by the corporate sector through (i) equity issue and (ii) debt issues (public issues and private placement) and the share of private placement in total debt and total resource mobilisation and the share of debt in total resource mobilisation; (SEBI)
- Pattern of funding for non-govt. non-financial public limited companies – I. internal sources [(i) reserves and surplus, and (ii) depreciation], and II. External sources [(paid up capital through new issues and premium), borrowings (debentures, from loans and from FIs) and trade dues and other current liabilities]; (SEBI)
- Annual and monthly series on resources mobilised, instrument wise, from the primary market – number and amount mobilised by category of issue (public issue and rights and rights issue); by type of issues [by listed companies and Initial Public Offering (IPOs)]; by equities at par and equities at a premium; cumulative convertible preference shares (CCPS); bonds; and other; (SEBI)
- Annual and monthly series of data on capital raised by (i) industrial (economic activity) classification (banks/FIs), industries like electronics, and engineering, entertainment, finance, etc.); (ii) size of capital raised; (iii) sector (public and private); and (iv) region (north, east, south and west); (SEBI)
- Annual and monthly data series on the number and quantum of Euro Issues; (SEBI)
- Annual and monthly data series on transactions of MFs on the Stock Exchanges – gross purchases and sales and net purchase/sales in (a) equity, and (b) debt; (SEBI)
- Trends on trading on stock exchanges – the number of shares traded and the number and value of shares delivered; (SEBI)

- Indicators of liquidity – Market capitalisation-GDP ratio (BSE), market capitalisation – GDP ratio (NSE), turnover ratio-BSE, traded value ratio – BSE, traded value ratio – NSE; (SEBI)
- Trends in foreign investment flows – direct and portfolio investment; (SEBI)
- Annual and monthly series on trends in FII investment – gross purchases and sales and net investment; (SEBI)
- Comparative evaluation of Indices through Price to Earnings Ratio and Price to Book Ratio (these are monthly averages of closing values) for BSE SENSEX, BSE 100 Index, S&P CNX NIFTY, CNK NIFTY Junior (SEBI); and
- Survey of investor households – a joint effort of SEBI and the National Council of Applied Economic Research – results giving an estimate of investor and non-investor households by type of investment households by type of instruments invested in and so on.

Q18. State the various kinds and sources of data on employment and unemployment.

Ans. Comprehensive data on employment and unemployment covering the entire country at regular intervals are available from two sources, namely, the **Population Census** conducted by the **Registrar General, India** every ten-year and the **quinquennial sample survey on employment and unemployment** conducted by the National Sample Survey Organisation (NSSO). The former is based on a complete enumeration of the population. Workers in the Census are enumerated as main workers and marginal workers.

All other data on employment and unemployment and are available at the district level upwards for rural and urban areas and the urban data by urban agglomerations and size classes of cities and towns. The kind of data on employment and unemployment available from the Census for rural (R) and urban (U) and (R+U) is shown below:

- The distributions of the male and female main workers by economic activity (the first digit level of the NIC code) – ten categories of economic activities[7] and classified further by age groups and educational level (for the all India table) and by educational level for the table on India, States and Union Territories;

- Similar distribution for male and female marginal workers;
- Main workers, marginal workers, non workers, those marginal workers that are available for or are seeking work (unemployed) and those non workers that are available for or are seeking work (unemployed) by sex and educational level;
- Similar distributions for unemployed SC population, ST populations and further classification of the distribution for unemployed general population by religious communities;
- Distributions of (i) main workers, (ii) marginal workers, and (iii) non workers by main activity, educational level, age and sex; and
- Similar distributions for SC population, ST population, further classification of the distribution in item "e" above for the general population by religious communities;
- The number of disabled among main workers, marginal workers and non workers by type of disability, age and sex; and
- As in the last Census, also available are (or will be, shortly) distribution of the male and female workforce by detailed economic activities at the three or four digit levels, distribution by occupations (as per the **National Classification of Occupations – 1968 (NCO 1968),** cross classification of the male and female workforce in each Occupational Division by economic activity and educational profile and the distribution of non workers by their activity status like housewife; pensioner, inmates of institutions and unemployed by age and sex.

The NSSO quinquennial surveys on employment and unemployment constitute the other major source of data on employment and unemployment. The last survey for which results have been published is the 55th Round survey conducted during July, 1999 and June, 2000 and the results of the next survey on the subject conducted during July, 2004 to June, 2005 (61st Round) are awaited. The earlier surveys related to October, 1972 to September, 1973, July 1977 to June, 1978, January – December, 1983, July 1987 to June, 1988 and July, 1993 to June, 1994. These measure employment/unemployment/labour force status on the basis of the Usual Status and Current Status and arrived at four measures of employment/unemployment/labour force, namely, the Usual Principal

Status (UPS), the Usual Principal and Subsidiary Status (UPSS), the Current Weekly Status (CWS) and the Current Daily Status (CDS) employment/unemployment/labour force status.

These surveys provide the per thousand distribution of variables by characteristics along with estimated number of persons and/or the sample number of persons for each column and row characteristic. These can be used to estimate new proportions – like for example the worker participation rate or the unemployment rate among the poor (those below a certain income class) and the non poor – and also estimates of the magnitude of employment or unemployment using the estimated sample proportions and the relevant population projection for the midpoint of the survey period. The surveys provide the following type of data for Rural, (R) Urban (U) and (R+U) at national and State levels:

- Distribution of male and female UPS/UPSS/CWS/CDS workforce by employment status – self-employed, regular wage/salaried employment and casual labour – and by age group, educational level and primary, secondary and tertiary economic activity;
- Distribution of UPS/UPSS male and female workforce by economic activity up to the three-digit code of NIC; and similar distribution by occupation up to the three-digit code of NCO 1968;
- Distribution of male and female UPS/UPSS/CWS/CDS workforce by employment status and by primary, secondary and tertiary economic activity and by MPCE classes;
- Distribution of UPS workers in each employment status by usual subsidiary economic activities;
- Distribution of UPSS employed by place or word (same village/town, another village/town) and by distance of the place or work from the place of residence;
- Proportion of persons who are more or less regularly employed and the distribution of persons who are not regularly employed by duration for which they are available for work; (underemployment)
- Distribution of UPS employed by "CWS employed", "CWS unemployed", "out of the labour force by the CWS criterion", showing underemployment among the UPS employed;

- Similarly, distribution of the CWS "employed", "unemployed," and "out of the labour force" on each half day of the reference week giving the underemployment among the CWS employed;
- Distribution of person-days of employment by (i) principal economic activity of the household, (ii) household type, and (iii) household land cultivated class, [distribution at (iii) only for rural areas];
- Distribution of households and female-headed households by the number of male and female adults (aged 15+) employed under the UPS criterion – households with no adult UPS employed, number with one male adult UPS employed, number with one female adult employed, number with one male adult and one female adult employed and so on;
- UPS/UPSS/CWS/CDS unemployment rates (can be easily estimated from the tables on distribution of 1000 persons by various characteristics, as indicated in the main paragraph) for all groups together and for different groups like gender, age group, educational level, MPCE classes, household type, household land cultivated class and principal household economic activity, etc.
- Average daily salary/wage earning of regular wage/salaried employees aged 15-59 by sex, sector of work and education,; a similar distribution by occupational groups and education; and
- Average daily wage/earnings per day received by casual labour by sex, age group, type of operation, and sub-round.

Data on employment are thus available from several sources. Estimates of employment derived from different sources for the same sector or sub-sector will differ.

Q19. Discuss the adequacy about the employment.

Or

State the different measures of employment/unemployment/labour force used by NSSO in different quinquennial surveys.

Ans. NSSO survey data can be use to analyse the quality and adequacy of employment. Besides underemployment among the employed, other aspects of quality can also be looked at. One is the proportion of the employed by employment status, especially the proportion of the workforce in 'casual employment'. The second is a comparison of the average daily earnings of male and female, regular and casual workers in different sectors and operations with the prevailing statutory minimum wage and the poverty line. The third is a look at the pattern of employment status of the workers belonging to poor households. These will throw light on the quality of employment enjoyed by the workforce, quality in terms of the intermittent nature of work, tenure of employment, employment security and low wages and above all, the prevailing gender differences in these aspects of quality.

The Labour Bureau, Shimla under the Ministry of Labour also publishes data on wage levels in the organised sector and on the welfare of labour. Data on total earnings of factory workers are collected through the statutory returns under the Payment of Wages Act, 1936 from establishments defined as factories under the Factories Act, 1948. The was applicable to employees with earnings up to ₹200. This limit has been increased from time to time to 1600 in 1982.

As for the unregistered sector and the unorganised part of other sectors, the **DE, NDE and OAE survey and other Establishment Surveys of the CSO** in different sectors and the **unorganised sector surveys the NSSO** provide data on average annual earnings for men, women and children in such establishments. **Regular reports like "Wage Rates in Rural India"** (the latest published relates to 2004-2005) and the **Report on the Working of the Minimum Wages Act, 1948** (the latest is for 2003), of **Labour Bureau** enable an analysis of rural/unorganised sector wage levels vis-à-vis statutory minimum wages and poverty line.

The prevalence of child labour, which depicts an exploitative dimension of the economic system, can be seen from the Census and NSSO tables on the distribution of the workforce by age groups and activity, the former down to the district level and the latter up to the State level (technically down to NSS regions due to availability of the unit record data on floppies/CDs). Such data may not fully reflect the ground level realities because surveys may not be able to extract information on employment of children, for various reasons. Further, such data are also dated. These can help only in drawing attention to the areas where child labour is prevalent so that the authorities concerned can initiate further action. It is usually the Non Government Organisations (NGOs) active in the field of the rights of children that succeed in locating establishment employing children and press the Government to take further action.

Q20. Identify the different aspects of labour welfare on which data are compiled.

Ans. The Labour Bureau publishes data on several aspects of labour welfare – data on industrial injuries, injuries in mines, compensation to workers for injuries and death, industrial disputes, health insurance, provident fund and trade unions of employers and workers. Statistics on industrial injuries are collected through statutory returns under the Factories Act, 1948 that provides that industrial accidents due to which the affected persons are prevented from attending to work for at least 48 hours should be reported to the inspector of factories. These depend on returns, and the sizeable non-response in the submission of these mars the quality of this source of data on incidence of fatal and non-fatal injuries in factories. Data on industrial injuries in mines under the Mines Act, 1952, as amended in 1983. Initially, data on the number of serious accidents and the accident rate were classified as 'fatal' and 'serious'. Subsequently, from 1984, accidents and the accident rate (accidents per 100 employees) were classified as 'fatal' 'spot serious' and 'reportable serious'. Statistics on 'compensated injuries' and the amount of compensation paid, both classified as (resulting in) 'death' and (leading to) 'disability' - 'permanent' and 'temporary', are collected under the Workmen's Compensation (WC) Act, 1923 on the basis of annual returns received from the State Governments, Posts and Telegraph Departments and the Railway Board for different Zonal Railways under the Act. Compensation is payable to workers employed in 'scheduled employments' for injuries due to accidents resulting in death or disablement for more than three days, provided that it is not caused through the fault of the worker himself. The number of injuries reported in the returns does not reflect the total number of injuries that occur, as all the injuries are not compensated for. Further, many of the establishments covered by the Act fail to submit returns and, therefore, the information received by the State Governments about the compensated injuries and the amount of compensation paid is incomplete. Compensation for injuries in establishments covered by the Employees State Insurance (ESI) Act, 1948 are paid under the ESI Act and not under WC Act.

Q21. State the various kinds and sources of data on education.

Ans. The Department of School Education and the Department of Higher Education of the Ministry of Human Resources Development (MHRD), the National Council for Educational Research and Training (NCERT) and the University Grants Commission (UGC) collect and publish educational statistics, conduct research studies and surveys in the area of education. The publications **"Selected Educational Statistics" (annual), "Education in India" (annual), "A Handbook of Educational and Allied Statistics" (1996) and "Educational Expenditure in India: 1951-2001" of MHRD "The**

Sixth All India Educational Survey (Sixth AIES) – Selected Statistics" (1998) and the **"Report of the Sixth AIES, Volumes I to VII" of the NCERT are the major sources of data on education.** (IAMR), New Delhi has set up a National Technical Manpower Information System (NTMIS) – a project sponsored by MHRD – that provides data on technical manpower – intake in and output from institutions and the utilisation patterns of such output in detail through Tracer Studies and other studies. These are disseminated through reports released from time to time and also through their **"Manpower Profile of India"** which is published every year by IAMR. **The 52nd, 53rd and 55th Round surveys of NSSO (1995-96, 1998-99 and 1999-00) and the social and cultural tables of the population Census 2001 (RGI)** also provide useful data on literacy and educational composition of the population or stocks of educated manpower of different levels of education and their utilisation patterns – snapshots, at specific points of time, of the impact of the efforts in the area of education.

The kind of data available in these publications and sources are indicated below:

Educational Infrastructure

- Levels of literacy and progress of efforts under literacy campaigns; (MHRD)
- The number of institutions – colleges (including universities, deemed universities and institutions of national importance) and all types of general, technical and professional schools; MHRD & UGC)
- The number of universities, deemed universities and institutions of national importance, the distribution of the number of colleges by categories like those teaching arts, science and commerce, oriental learning and different categories of professional subjects like law, agriculture, engineering and technology and medicine and the distribution of schools in the area of general education (and stages like pre-primary and primary, etc.) and different categories such as those dealing with vocational, professional, special education, etc. (MHRD and UGC);
- Teachers (male and female and those belonging to SC/ST communities), the proportion trained among them, terms and conditions of their employment and attrition of the stock of teachers by cause (Sixth AIES);

- Patterns of management of colleges including professional colleges and deemed universities, recognition by appropriate bodies, availability of teachers and facilities like laboratory and equipment, etc. (UGC);
- Teachers in professional and technical institutions and the number of technical teacher training institutions (MHRD & UGC);
- The number of Industrial Training Institutions (it is) and Advanced Training Institutes and the training capacity for apprenticeship training in industry under the Apprenticeship Act, 1961 for those passing out of it is and the vocational stream of schools (MoLE and MHRD);
- The number of institutions for training instructors for ITIs (MoLE);
- The Number of Vocational Rehabilitation Centres (VRCs) for the Physically Handicapped set up by the DGE&T all over the country for giving adjustment training and placement in suitable employment through the Special Employment Exchanges for this group of people (DGE&T);
- Expenditure on education by programmes like the Sarva Siksha Abhiyan, the Total Literacy Campaign and Adult Education; direct and indirect expenditure on recognised institutions of education (MHRD);

Infrastructure Utilisation and Access to Educational Opportunities

- Literacy rates – overall and age-specific, among SC/ST and adults; (Census – Social & Cultural Tables' NSSO – 52nd and 53rd Rounds, Census 2001 & MHRD);
- The number of students and the number of female students in the institutions specified in item 'b' above;
- The number of students and the number of girl students by courses and stages of education in recognises institutions – from the nursery class to the high/higher secondary level and in schools for vocational and professional education and special education and similar data for rural areas (MHRD);
- The number of male and female workers and marginal workers in the age groups 5-9 and 10-14 – child labour; (Census 2001); a comparison of this with the population in these age groups and data on school enrolment would lead to an assessment of the

number of children who are neither in school nor in the workforce;

- (o)Enrolment and output in institutions specified in items 'g', 'h' and 'i' above;
- Enrolment (and enrolment of female students) in university level general education courses by stages (degree, post graduate degree, diploma/certificate, research) and university level professional and technical education courses by faculty (MHRD & UGC);
- Similar information of the kind mentioned above for scheduled Castes and Tribes (SC/ST) and females belonging to such sections of society (MHRD &UGC);
- Teacher-Pupil ratios at different levels of education (MHRD);
- Intake and output of graduates and postgraduates in different disciplines and faculties (KHRD & UGC);
- Coverage of population in appropriate age groups by different stages of education (MHRD);
- Dropout rates at different stages of education (MHRD);
- Distribution of population attending educational institution by age, sex and type of educational institution for general and SC/ST population;
- Access of the general and SC/ST population to (or availability of) facilities for different levels of education in rural habitations and urban settlements belonging to different population slabs, in terms of distance of the habitation from the facility; similar information regarding non-formal education (NFE) centers (Sixth AIES);

Q22. State the various kinds and sources of data on health.

Ans. One of the important dimensions of quality of life is health. A healthy individual can contribute effectively to production of goods and services. Investment in health is, therefore, an essential instrument of raising the quality of life of people and the productivity of the labour force.

The publication "Health Information of India (HII)" published every year by the Central Bureau of Health Intelligence (CBHI) of the Ministry of Health and Family Welfare, the publications "Sample Registration System (SRS): Statistical Reports", "SRS Compendium of India's Fertility and Mortality Indicators, 1971-1997", Mortality Statistics and Cause of Death" and SRS Bulletin and the Social and Cultural Tables (C Series Tables) of Census 2001 of the Office of the Registrar General of India (RGI), Ministry of Home Affairs and the "Report on the National Family Health Survey (NFHS-2) – 1998-99" of the International Institute of Population Studies and OCR Macro contain a large amount of information on these aspect of health.

Health Infrastructure

Health Information of India (HII) of the Central Bureau of Health Intelligence (CBHI) Provide the following types of data:

- The number of hospitals, dispensaries, beds – State-wise and by ownership (Govt., Local Boards and private and voluntary agencies) in rural and urban areas and population served;
- The number of Public health Centres (PHCs), sub-Centres (PH-SCs) and Community Health Centres (CHCs) – progress in t he setting up of these and the number of PHCs and PHSCs required in tribal areas and the number set up;
- The number of (a) Central Government Health Scheme (CGHS) dispensaries in different cities, (b) Employees State Insurance (ESI) hospitals, annexes, dispensaries and mobile dispensaries and hospital beds in the ESI infrastructure and those reserved in other hospitals, (c) Central hospitals, regional hospitals and dispensaries – ayurvedic and allopathic, mobile medical units and small (medical) community centers under each of the Coal Mines, Mica Mines, Iron Ore, Chromium Ore and Limestone and Dolomite Mines Welfare Funds, (d) hospitals, T.B. hospitals and chest clinics under *Beeri* Workers' Welfare Scheme, and (e) medical and health facilities available in each Railway Zone;
- Facilities for Indian Systems of Medicine (ISM) available under the State Governments and Central Ministries – CGHS, Railways, ESI, Mica Mines, Coal Mines, etc. Welfare Funds;
- Number of institutions intake (gender-wise) and out turn (gender wise) for (a) degree in medicine, post graduates/diploma in different medical disciplines, (form Medical Council of India – MCI (b) degree and post graduate degree in dental science, (from Dental Council of India – DCI) (c) nurses, midwives, auxiliary nurse midwives (ANM) and Lady Health Visitors (LHV), (from Nursing Council of India – NCI) (d) Pharmacists (from Pharmacy

Council of India – PCI), and (e) different paramedical courses – health workers, dais (from CBHE);

Public health, Morbidity and Mortality Indicators

- Progress of the programme for vaccination of children and pregnant women;
- The number of cases detected, treated and discharged in respect of diseases like leprosy and tuberculosis;
- The number of patients treated, discharged and deaths due to (a) different types of cancer in specialised cancer hospitals, (b) different types of mental diseases, and (c) communicable diseases like diphtheria, poliomyelitis, tetanus (neonatal and others), hepatitis and rabies;
- Progress in the National Aids Control Programme and other National Control/Eradication programmes;
- Utilisation by beneficiaries of facilities provided by CGHS, ESI scheme, Mica Mines, etc. Welfare Funds schemes;
- Incidence of morbidity and mortality by causes in zonal Railway hospitals;
- Incidence of morbidity by diseases in the ESI scheme;
- Medical certification of cause of death – distribution of such deaths by age, sex and major cause groups (18 groups of causes) and the extent of coverage of such certification to total death in each of the 18 groups (RGI);
- Birth Rates (BRs) Death Rates (DRs) and natural growth rates and State-wise BRs and DRs (from SRS, RGI);

National Family Health Survey (NFHS)-2

The first National Family Health Survey (NFHS–1) conducted in 1992-93 succeeded in answering this question and also in building up an important demographic and health database in India. This success paved the way for the conduct of the **second National Family Health Survey in 1998-99 (NFHS–2)** to strengthen this database further and facilitate implementation and monitoring of population and health programmes in the country.

NFHS–2 provides — (a) urban and rural estimates for most States, (b) regional estimates for four (Bihar, Madhya Pradesh, Rajasthan and Uttar Pradesh) – States that are at the bottom of whatever chart of social and economic indicators is considered, (c) separate estimates for the three metro cities, (Calcutta, Chennai and Mumbai) and (d) estimates for the slum areas of Mumbai. Besides a national report, reports have been prepared for the States.

The kind of data on health and nutrition status of women and children and estimates of parameters related to these presented by NFHS–2, are indicated in brief below:

- Educational level of the household population, school attendance of boys and girls and reasons for not attending school;
- Age at first marriage of (women) respondents, their exposure to mass media, their employment status and aspects of their empowerment or lack of it, including domestic violence;
- Current fertility, variation in current fertility by various factors, fertility trends, pattern of outcome of pregnancy, median number of children ever born and living to ever married women, patterns of birth order and birth intervals, median age of women at the first birth and the last birth of child, patterns of fertility preference and sex (of the child) preference;
- Estimates of age-specific death rates, crude death rates, infant and child mortality by mother's demographic, economic, social and cultural characteristics, her level of education, birth order and birth size of the child/incant, birth interval, medical care and so on;
- Vaccination of children vitamin A Supplementation for children, prevalence of acute respiratory infection, fever and diarrhoea, treatment of diarrhoea and awareness of treatment like ORS packets;
- Knowledge about AIDS and ways of avoiding it;
- Health problems of pregnancy, antenatal care, assistance during delivery, place of delivery, post-partum care, and care and treatment of reproductive health problems: and
- Couple protection rate.

Q23. Write short note on the followings:

(a) Social consequences of development

Ans. The development experience of the last few decades shows that the cost of development is not shared equally by all sections of society. Often the burden of the cost falls almost entirely on the poor and the voiceless.

The recent example that invited wide attention is the acquisition of the lands of tribals in Orissa for the industries in Kalinganagar in the State. The problem of people ousted from the land submerged by the water filling the reservoirs crested by the dams or, for that matter, people whose lands are acquired by the State for purposes of development (building factories, dams, etc.), called "oustees", has been coming up ever since the first development projects were taken up in 1951. The State promised jobs to the oustees in the industries that came up in their lands in addition to compensation for the land acquired or alternative land to prevent loss of their livelihood.

The DGE&T, the organisation concerned with employment exchanges at the national level. Past data with the DGE&T in the Ministry of Labour might show the proportion of registrants of this category that got placed in a job and the proportion of those who just ceased to be in the register. This source of data, however, would have represented a very small part or whatever rehabilitation was done, because the kind of vacancies that can be filled through employment exchanges is restricted to jobs in Government no filled through competitive examinations, public service commission's and other commissions/recruitment boards and jobs up to a specified salary level in public sector undertakings. The private sector is not obliged to fill its vacancies through the employment exchanges.

A study on development-induced displacement in West Bengal, between 1947 and 2000, conducted by a team led by Walter Fernandes has made estimates of (a) the number of people adversely affected by projects, (b) the number physically displaced, (c) the number resettled by the projects, (d) the rest that had been left to fend for itself following displacement, and (e) the proportion of those in (d) who were dalits and tribals.

This aspect of development projects will cast greater responsibilities on the respective project authorities in these matters and closer monitoring of the implementation of resettlement plans. These will necessarily require the setting up of a reliable and transparent system of collection, compilation and analysis of statistics relating to displacement of people due to the project, their demographic, social, cultural and economic profiles, their resettlement in alternative livelihood, number absorbed in employment in the industrial establishment(s) for which the lands of the oustees were acquired, details relating to the levels of living of the oustees in the area of resettlement in terms of parameters like incomes, access to basic needs of life like water, shelter, education for their children and health and medicare at least until a reasonable number of year after resettlement, the time taken and the expenditure incurred for resettlement and so on. To get success in your studies, read only GPH Book.

(b) Environment

Ans. The process of development adversely affects the environment and through it the quality of life of society. For instance, the excessive use of fertilizers and pesticides rob the soil of its nutrients. Letting sewers and drainage and industrial effluents without prior treatment into rivers and water bodies pollute this water causing destruction of aquatic life and endanger the health of people using such polluted water.

The exhaust fumes containing Carbon Monoxide (CO) and lead (Pb) particles let in to the air we breathe by vehicles using petrol or diesel is an example of air pollution.

The Central and State Pollution Control Boards and the Ministry of Environment and Forests (MOEF) evolve and, monitor implementation of policies to protect the environment. Statistics on environment are collected through this process by the agencies mentioned above and the CSO. The annual reports of the MOEF and the Compendium on Environment Statistics, India 2003 published by the CSO from time to time are excellent sources of data on environment. The latter especially is very comprehensive and includes a very informative write up. The compendium (and the annual report of MOEF) can be accessed in the respective websites of the two organisations. The type of data on environment available from these publications are mentioned below by way of illustration:

- Ambient Air Quality Status [concentration of Sulphur dioxide, Nitrogen dioxide and Solid Particulate Matter (SPM) in air] in major cities of India;
- Percentage of petrol-driven two-wheelers, three-wheelers and four-wheelers meeting CO emission standards; and
- Water quality of Yamuna river (in the Delhi Stretch) in respect of selective physio-chemical parameters between April, 1998 and March, 1999 – dissolved oxygen (milligrams./litre), Biological Oxygen Demand (BOD) (mg./1), faecal coliforms (number/100ml), total coliforms (number/100ml) And ammonical nitrogen (mg/1).

Annexure

Annexure

Chapter-2, Q.No-14, Eq.- (iii)

A–1 Sampling Variance of Sample Mean Based on a SRSWR Sample.

(i) When a Sample of Only One Unit is Selected:

$V(y_1)=E[y_1-E(y_1)]^2=E\left[y_1{}^2-2y_1E(y_1)+\{E(y_1)\}^2\right]=E[(y_1{}^2)-2(y_1)M+(M^2)]$

$=E(y_1{}^2)-2E(y_1)M+E(M^2)=E(y_1{}^2)-2MM+M^2=E(y_1{}^2)-2M^2+M^2$

$=E(y_1{}^2)-M^2$

Thus $V(y_1)=\sigma^2=E(y_1{}^2)-M^2$ ...(a)

Simplifying (a) further, $E(y_1{}^2)-M^2=\sum_i[Y_i^2(1/N)]-M^2,[\sum_i i=1 \text{ to } N]$

$=(1/N)\sum_i Y_i^2-M^2$

Thus $V(y_1)=\sigma^2=(1/N)\sum Y_i^2-M^2$, summation i = 1 to N ...(b)

(ii) When a Sample of 'n' Units is Selected: E.*q.-(iv) – E.q.-(viii)*

$V(m_{srswr})=E[m_{srswr}-E(m_{srswr})]^2=E[1/n\sum y_i-M]^2$, summation being i = 1 to n.

$=E[1/n\sum(y_i-M)]^2=1/n^2E\left[\sum(y_i-M)^2+\sum\sum(y_i-M)(y_k-M)\right]$, [the double summation being over i = 1 to n and k = 1 to n and i ≠ k]

$=1/n^2\sum E(y_i-M)^2+\sum\sum E(y_i-M)(y_k-M)=1/n^2\sum V(y_i)$ ...(c)

[$E(y_i-M)(y_k-M)$ is the covariance of y_i and y_k for i ≠ k and is 0 as the selections in the i–th and k–th draws are independent].

$=1/n^2\sum\sigma^2=(1/n^2)n\sigma^2=(1/n)\sigma^2$;

Thus, $V(m_{srswr})=(1/n)\sigma^2$ ...(d)

Also, from equation (c) above,

$V(m_{srswr})=1/n^2\sum E(y_i-M)^2=1/n^2\sum E(y_i^2-2My_i+M^2)$,

$=1/n^2\sum[E(y_i{}^2)-2ME(y_i)+E(M^2)]=1/n^2\sum[E(y_i{}^2)-2MM+M^2]$

$=1/n^2\sum[E(y_i{}^2)-M^2]$

$=1/n^2[nE(y_i{}^2)-nM^2]=1/n[E(y_i{}^2)-M^2]$

Therefore, $(1/n)\sigma^2=1/n[E(y_i{}^2)-M^2]$, or, $\sigma^2=E(y_i{}^2)-M^2$ ...(e)

Again, $V(m_{srswr})$ is

$$= E[m_{srswr} - M]^2 = E[m_{srswr}{}^2 - 2m_{srswr}M + M^2] = E(m_{srswr}{}^2) - 2ME(m_{srswr}) + E(M^2)$$

$$= E(m_{srswr}{}^2) - 2MM + M^2 = E(m_{srswr}{}^2) - M^2, \text{ or}$$

$$(1/n)\sigma^2 = E(m_{srswr}{}^2) - M^2 \qquad \text{...(f)}$$

Chapter-2, Q.No-14, Eq.-(ix)

A–2 Unbiased Estimate of the Sampling Variance of Sample Mean under SRSWR

Let us find the expected value of s^2 in a sample of size in SRSWR.

$$E(s^2) = E\left[(1/n)\sum(y_i - m_{srswr})^2\right] = E\left[(1/n)\sum(y_i{}^2 - 2y_i m_{srswr} + m^2{}_{srswr})\right]$$

$$E\left[(1/n)\sum y_i{}^2 - 2m_{srswr}(1/n)\sum y_i + (1/n)\sum m^2{}_{srswr}\right] = E\left[(1/n)\sum y_i{}^2 - 2m^2{}_{srswr} + (1/n)n\,m^2{}_{srswr}\right]$$

$$= E\left[(1/n)\sum y_i{}^2 - m^2{}_{srswr}\right] = (1/n)\sum E(y_i{}^2) - E(m^2{}_{srswr})$$

$$= (1/n)\sum(\sigma^2 + M^2) - (\sigma^2/n + M^2)$$

[applying the results (e) and (f)from A-1]

$$= (1/n)(n\sigma^2 + nM^2) - (\sigma^2/n + M^2) = \sigma^2 + M^2 - \sigma^2/n - M^2 = \sigma^2[1 - (1/n)]$$

Thus, $E\left[(1/n)\sum(y_i - m_{srswr})^2\right] = \sigma^2[(n-1)/n]$;

Therefore, $E\left[\{n/(n-1)\}(1/n)\sum(y_i - m_{srswr})^2\right] = \sigma^2$ or

$E\left[\{1/(n-1)\}\sum(y_i - m_{srswr})^2\right] = \sigma^2$ and, since we need an unbiased estimate of $(1/n)\sigma^2$,

$$v(m_{srswr}) = [1/n(n-1)]\left[\sum(y_i - m_{srswr})^2\right] = [1/n(n-1)][ss^2], \left[\sum i = 1 \text{ to } n\right]$$

Chapter-2, Q.No.-15

A–3 $E(m_{srswor}) = M$.

$E(m_{srswor}) = \sum_s$ ['m_s' calculated from a specific samples]x[probability of selection of the sample].

The product is summed over $(\sum_s)$ that is, over all the possible samples. That is, $E\left[(1/n)\sum y_i\right] = \sum_s\left[(1/n)\sum_i y_i\right](1/{}_N C_n)$, where $\sum_s$ is the summation over all the ${}_{N}C_{n}$ possible samples and $\sum_{i}$ is the summation over the units of the sample.

$$=(1/n)(1/{}_{N}C_{n})\sum_{s}\left[\sum_{i}y_{i}\right]$$

To evaluate this sum, we have to find out the number of samples in which a given unit occurs. The sample has n distinct units as we have adopted SRSWOR. A unit of the population can occur in a sample with (n – 1) other units of the sample. These (n – 1) units are to be selected from the remaining (N – 1) units of the population. This is possible in ${}_{N-1}C_{n-1}$ ways. Thus any unit of the population will occur in ${}_{N-1}C_{n-1}$ samples.

$\sum_{s}\left[\sum_{i}y_{i}\right]={}_{N-1}C_{n-1}\left[\sum Y_{i}\right]$, the summation being from 1 to N.

Thus,

$$E\{(1/n)\sum y_{i}\}=(1/n)(1/{}_{N}C_{n})\sum_{s}\left[\sum_{i}y_{i}\right]=(1/n)(1/{}_{N}C_{n})[{}_{N-1}C_{n-1}]\left[\sum Y_{i}\right]$$

As $[{}_{N-1}C_{n-1}]/({}_{N}C_{n})=n/N$,

$E\{(1/n)\sum y_{i}\}=(1/N)\left[\sum Y_{i}\right]$, the summation being from 1 to N, or, $E(m_{srswor})=M$

The sample mean from a SRSWOR sample, m_{srswor}, is thus an unbiased estimator of M.

Chapter-2, Q.No.-15, Eq-(i) and (ii)

A–4 Sampling Variance of the Sample Mean is SRSWOR.

$$V(m_{srswor})=E\left[m_{srswor}-E(m_{srswor})\right]^{2}=E(m_{srswor}-M)^{2}=E\left[m_{srswor}{}^{2}-2Mm_{srswor}+M^{2}\right]$$

$$=E\left[m_{srswor}{}^{2}\right]-2ME(m_{srswor})+E(M^{2})$$

$$=E\left[m_{srswor}{}^{2}\right]-2MM+M^{2}=E\left[m_{srswor}{}^{2}\right]-M^{2},$$

Thus, $V(m_{srswor})=E\left[m_{srswor}{}^{2}\right]-M^{2}$; ...(a)

Denoting m_{srswor} by m for convenience,

$V(m_{srswor})=\sum_{s}(m-M)^{2}(1/{}_{N}C_{n})$, [the summation $\sum_{s}$ being over the ${}_{N}C_{n}$ possible samples]

$=\sum_{s}\left[(1/n)\sum_{i}(y_{i}-M)\right]^{2}(1/{}_{N}C_{n})$, the summation $\sum_{i}$ being over i = 1 to n,

$= \sum_s (1/n^2)\left[\sum_i (y_i - M)^2 + \sum\sum (y_i - M)(y_r - M)\right](1/{}_N C_n)$, $\Sigma\Sigma$ being over i and r, $(i \neq r)$ from 1 to n, ...(b)

Any unit of the population will occur in $[{}_{N-1}C_{n-1}]$ samples and, therefore,

$$\sum_s (1/n^2)\sum_i (y_i - M)^2 = \sum_i (1/n^2)(Y_i - M)^2 {}_{N-1}C_{n-1},$$

the summation being from i = 1 to N

Any two units will occur together in ${}_{(N-2)}C_{(n-2)}$ samples and, therefore,

$$\sum_s (1/n^2)\sum\sum (y_i - M)(y_r - M) = \sum\sum (Y_i - M)(Y_r - M)_{(N-2)}C_{(n-2)},$$

the summation $\Sigma\Sigma$ being over i and r, $(i \neq r)$, from 1 to N

We have

$[{}_{N-1}C_{n-1}]/(1/{}_N C_n) = n/N$ and ${}_{(N-2)}C_{(n-2)}/{}_N C_n = n(n-1)/N(N-1)$.

The expression at (b) above is, therefore, equal to

$$\sum_i (1/n^2)(Y_i - M)^2 {}_{N-1}C_{n-1}(1/{}_N C_n) + \sum\sum (1/n^2)(Y_i - M)(Y_r - M)_{(N-2)}C_{(n-2)}$$

$(1/{}_N C_n)$ the summations being from 1 to N,

$$= \sum_i (1/n^2)(Y_i - M)^2 (n/N) + \sum\sum (1/n^2)(Y_i - M)(Y_r - M)[n(n-1)/N(N-1)]$$

...(c)

Now $\sum_i (Y_i - M)^2 + \sum\sum (Y_i - M)(Y_r - M)$, the summation being from 1 to N is

$= \left[\sum_i (Y_i - M)\right]^2 = 0$, since $\sum (Y_i - M)$ (summation i = 1 to N) being 0 (because this the summation of the deviation of Y_i from their mean)

Therefore, $\sum_i (Y_i - M)^2 + \sum\sum (Y_i - M)(Y_r - M) = 0$, that is,

$$\sum_i (Y_i - M)^2 = (-)\sum\sum (Y_i - M)(Y_r - M) \quad ...(d)$$

Using the equation (c) above, we can rewrite equation (b) above as,

$$\sum_i (1/n^2)(Y_i - M)^2 (n/N) - \sum_i (1/n^2)(Y_i - M)^2 [n(n-1)/N(N-1)]$$

$$= \sum_i (Y_i - M)^2 [(1/nN) - (n-1)/nN(N-1)]$$

$= (1/n)(1/N)\sum_i (Y_i - M)^2 [1 - (n-1)/(N-1)]$. Since

$\left[(1/N)\sum (Y_i - M)^2\right] = \sigma^2$, this is

$=(1/n)\sigma^2[1-(n-1)/(N-1)]$, or $=[(N-n)/(N-1)][\sigma^2/n]$, or

$V(m_{srswor})=[(N-n)/(N-1)][\sigma^2/n]=[(N-n)/(N-1)][1/n]$

$[(1/N)\sum(Y_i-M)^2]$, $\sum 1$ to N. ...(e)

Chapter-2, Q.No.-15, Eq-(vi)

A–5 Unbiased Estimate of the Sampling Variance of m_{srswor}

We have, $V(m_{srswor})=[(N-n)/(N-1)][1/n][(1/N)\sum(Y_i-M)^2]$

$=[(N-n)/(N-1)][1/n][(1/N)\sum Y_i^2-M^2]$ ...(a)

We can attempt an unbiased estimate of $V(m_{srswor})$ by finding an unbiased estimate of (i) $\sum Y_i^2$ and (ii) that of M^2, the two important components of $V(m_{srswor})$ in (a) above.

(i) Unbiased estimate of $\sum Y_i^2$

$E\{(1/n)\sum y_i^2\}=\sum_s[(1/n)\sum_i y_i^2](1/{}_NC_n)$, where $\sum_s$ is the summation over all the ${}_NC_n$ possible samples and $\sum_i$ is the summation over the units of the sample.

$=(1/n)(1/{}_NC_n)\sum_s[\sum_i y_i^2]$

Proceeding in the same way we did in the case of $E\{(1/n)\sum y_i\}$, in section A–3 this is

$=(1/n)(1/{}_NC_n)\sum_s[\sum_i y_i^2]=(1/n)(1/{}_NC_n)[{}_{N-1}C_{n-1}][\sum Y_i^2]$

$=(1/N)[\sum Y_i^2]$, the summation being from 1 to N

Therefore, $(1/n)\sum y_i^2$ [summation i = 1 to n] is an unbiased estimate of $(1/N)[\sum Y_i^2]$, the summation being from 1 to N. ...(b)

(ii) Unbiased estimate of M^2

We have $V(m_{srswor})=E[m_{srswor}^2]-M^2$; or $M^2=E[m_{srswor}^2]-V(m_{srswor})$

Let us unbiased estimate of V(m) be denoted by v(m). An unbiased estimate of M^2 is, therefore, given by $[m_{srswor}^2]-v(m_{srswor})$. ...(c)

(iii) Unbiased estimate of $V(m_{srswor})$

Using (1), (2) and (3) above an unbiased estimate of $V(m_{srswor})$ will be

$$v(m_{srswor})=[(N-n)/(N-1)][1/n][(1/n)\sum y_i^2-\{m_{srswor}^2-v(m_{srswor})\}]$$
$$=[(N-n)/(N-1)][1/n][(1/n)\sum y_i^2-m_{srswor}^2+v(m_{srswor})]$$
$$=[(N-n)/n(N-1)][(1/n)\sum y_i^2-m_{srswor}^2]+[(N-n)/n(N-1)v(m_{srswor})]$$

Collecting terms containing $v(m_{srswor})$ together on the left hand side,

$$v(m_{srswor})[1-(N-n)/n(N-1)]=[(N-n)/n(N-1)][(1/n)\sum y_i^2-m_{srswor}^2] \quad ...(d)$$

Since

$$(1/n)\sum(y_i-m)^2=(1/n)\sum y_i^2-(2m/n)\sum y_i+(1/n)\sum m^2=(1/n)\sum y_i^2-2mm+m^2$$

$=(1/n)\sum y_i^2-m^2$ and simplifying (d) further, (d) becomes

$$v(m_{srswor})[\{(nN-n)-(N-n)\}/n(N-1)]=[(N-n)/n(N-1)]$$
$$[(1/n)\sum(y_i-m_{srswor})^2], \text{ or,}$$
$$v(m_{srswor})[(nN-n-N+n)/n(N-1)]=[(N-n)/n^2(N-1)]$$
$$[\sum(y_i-m_{srswor})^2], \text{ or,}$$
$$v(m_{srswor})[N(n-1)/n(N-1)]=[(N-n)/n^2(N-1)][\sum(y_i-m_{srswor})^2],$$

or,

$$v(m_{srswor})=[n(N-1)/N(n-1)][(N-n)/n^2(N-1)][\sum(y_i-m_{srswor})^2]$$
$$=[(N-n)/Nn(n-1)][\sum(y_i-m_{srswor})^2]$$
$$=[(N-n)/N][1/n][1/(n-1)][\sum y_i-m_{srswor}^2]=[(N-n)/N][1/n]$$
$$[1/(n-1)][SS]^2$$

Thus, $v(m_{srswor})=[(N-n)/N][1/n][1/(n-1)][\sum(y_i-m)^2]$

$=[(N-n)/N][1/n][1/(n-1)][ss]^2$, where Σ from 1 to n. ...(e)

Chapter-2, Q.No.-17, Eq-(i) and (ii)

A–6 Sampling Variance of Sample Mean in Systematic Sampling

Let nk = N. Then m* = m. There are k possible samples each sample with a probability of 1/k. Let the sample mean of the r–th systematic sample be $m_r=(1/n)\sum y_{ir}$, (where y_{ir} is the value of the characteristic under study for the i–th unit in the r–th systematic sample, summation is from i = 1 to n.). Thus the sample mean is a random variable m which assumes values m_r, r = 1,2,............,k each with probability 1/k and, therefore, $E(m_r) = M$. Denoting the mean in systematic sampling as m_{sys}, the sampling variance of the sampling mean in systematic sampling is

$$V(m_{sys}) = E(m_{sys} - M)^2 = (1/k)\sum_r (m_r - M)^2, \left[\sum_r 1 \text{ to } k\right] = \sigma_b^{\ 2}$$

(between–sample variance).

$$V(m_{sys}) = \sigma_b^{\ 2} \text{ (the between–sample variance).} \qquad ...(a)$$

But this does not contain the population variance $V(y) = \sigma^2$.

$$V(y) = (1/nk)\sum_r \sum_i (y_{ir} - M)^2 \text{ where } \sum_i \text{ is } i = 1 \text{ to } n \ \& \ \sum_r \text{ is } r = 1 \text{ to } k$$

$$= (1/kn)\sum_r \sum_i (y_{ir} - M)^2$$

$$= (1/kn)\sum_r \sum_i (y_{ir} - m_r + m_r - M)^2, \text{adding and subtracting } m_r,\ r = 1 \text{ to } k,$$

$$= (1/kn)\sum_r \sum_i \left[(y_{ir} - m_r)^2 + (m_r - M)^2 + 2(y_i - m_r)(m_r - M)\right]$$

$$= (1/kn)\left[\sum_r \sum_i (y_{ir} - m_r)^2 + \sum_r \sum_i (m_r - M)^2 + 2\sum_r \sum_i (y_{ir} - m_r)(m_r - M)\right]$$

$$= (1/kn)\sum_r \sum_i (y_{ir} - m_r)^2 + (1/kn)\sum_r \sum_i (m_r - M)^2 + (2/nk)\sum_r$$

$$\left[(m_r - M)\sum_i (y_{ir} - m_r)\right], \text{ [since } (m_r - M) \text{ is independent of 'i']}$$

$$= (1/kn)\sum_r \sum_i (y_{ir} - m_r)^2 + (1/kn)\sum_r \sum_i (m_r - M)^2 + (2/kn)\sum_r$$

$$(m_r - M) \times 0, \text{ [since } \sum_i (y_{ir} - m_r) = 0 \text{]}$$

$$= (1/kn)\sum_r \sum_i (y_{ir} - m_r)^2 + (1/kn)\sum_r n(m_r - M)^2, \text{[since } \sum_i \text{ is from } i = 1$$

to n]

$$= \sigma_w^{\ 2} + (1/k)\sum_r (m_r - M)^2$$

$$= \sigma_w^{\ 2} + \sigma_b^{\ 2} = \text{ within–sample variance } + V(m_{sys}), \text{ [from (a)], or,}$$

$$V(m_{sys}) = V(y) - \sigma_w^{\ 2} \qquad ...(b)$$

Chapter-2, Q.No.-18, Eq-(iii)

A–7 Sampling Variance of the Sample Total in PPS Sampling (Sample of One Unit)

The variance of $Y^*_{(1)PPS}$ is $V(y_1/p_1) = E\{y_1/p_1 - Y\}^2$

$= E\{Y_i/P_i - Y\}^2 P_i$, the summation being from i = 1 to N

$= E\left[Y_i^2/P_i^2 - 2Y(Y_i/P_i) + Y^2\right]P_i$, [expanding $\{Y_i/P_i - Y\}^2$]

$= \sum\left[(Y_i^2/P_i^2)P_i - 2Y(Y_i/P_i)P_i + Y^2P_i\right]$

$= \sum(Y_i^2/P_i^2)P_i - 2Y\sum(Y_i/P_i)P_i + Y^2\sum P_i$, [since Y and Y^2 are constant with respect to Σ]

$= \sum(Y_i^2/P_i) - 2Y\sum(Y_i) + Y^2$, [since $\sum P_i = 1$, being the sum of all probabilities]

$= \sum(Y_i^2/P_i) - 2YY + Y^2$, [since $\sum(Y_i) = Y$, by definition]

$V\left[Y^*_{(1)PPS}\right] = \sum(Y_i^2/P_i) - Y^2.$

Chapter-2, Q.No.-18, Eq-(vi)

A–8 Sampling Variance of the Sample Total in PPSWR Sampling (Sample Size n)

We have a sample of size n drawn by PPSWR method and, therefore, have n independent unbiased estimates of the population total Y. An unbiased estimator of the population total $Y = \sum Y_i$, Σ from 1 to N is $Y^* = (1/n)\sum(y_i/p_i)$, Σ from 1 to n.

The sampling variance V(Y*) will be $V\left[(1/n)\sum(y_i/p_i)\right]$, [Σ from 1 to n]

$V\left[(1/n)\sum(y_i/p_i)\right] = (1/n^2)\sum\left[V(y_i/p_i) + 2\,\text{Covariance}\,(y_i/p_i)(y_j/p_j)\right]$, the summation being from i < j = 1 to n

$= (1/n^2)\sum\left[V(y_i/p_i) + 0\right]$, [Covariance $(y_i/p_i, y_j/p_j) = 0$, since (y_i/p_i) & (y_j/p_j) are independent]

$= (1/n^2)\sum\left[V(y_i/p_i)\right]$

$= (1/n^2)(n)\left[\sum(Y_r^2/P_r) - Y^2\right]$, the summation being from r = 1 to N. [as each $V(y_i/p_i) = \sum(Y_r^2/P_r) - Y^2$, for every i = 1 to n]

$=(1/n)\left[\sum\left(Y_r^2/P_r\right)-Y^2\right]$, the summation being from r = 1 to N.

$V\left(Y^*_{PPSWR}\right)=(1/n)\left[\sum\left(Y_r^2/P_r\right)-Y^2\right]$, the summation being from r = 1 to N.

Chapter-2, Q.No.-18, Eq.-(viii)

A–9 Unbiased Estimator of the Sampling Variance of Sample Total in PPSWR Sampling

We have a sample of size n drawn by PPSWR method and, therefore, have n independent unbiased estimates of the population total Y. An unbiased estimator of the population total $Y=\sum Y_i$, Σ from 1 to N is $Y^*=(1/n)\sum\left(y_i/p_i\right)$, Σ from 1 to n. An unbiased estimator of the sampling variance of Y* is,

$v\left(Y^*\right)=\left[1/\{n(n-1)\}\right]\left[\sum\left(y_i/p_i-Y^*\right)^2\right]$, the summation being from i = 1 to n.

$=\left[1/\{n(n-1)\}\right]\left[\sum\left(y_i^2/p_i^2\right)-2Y^*\sum y_i/p_i+\sum Y^{*2}\right]$

$=\left[1/\{n(n-1)\}\right]\left[\sum\left(y_i^2/p_i^2\right)-2Y^*nY^*+nY^{*2}\right]$, since $(1/n)\sum y_i/p_i=Y^*$

$=\left[1/\{n(n-1)\}\right]\left[\sum\left(y_i^2/p_i^2\right)-nY^{*2}\right]$,

$v\left(Y^*_{PPSWR}\right)=\left[1/\{n(n-1)\}\right]\left[\sum\left(y_i^2/p_i^2\right)-nY^{*2}\right]$

Chapter-2, Q.No.-19, Eq-(v)

A–10 Optimum Stratum–wise Sample Size in Stratified Sampling

As we have

$V\left(m_{st}\right)=\sum W_s^2V\left(m_s\right)$, Σ for s = 1 to k, ...(a)

If units are selected in each stratum with replacement, $V\left(m_s\right)$ can be expressed as V_s/n_s, where V_s is the variance of the estimator of M_s based on one sample unit and n_s the sample size in the s–th stratum. This can easily be verified by putting n = 1 in equations 4 of q.no-14 for $V\left(m_{srswr}\right)$ in SRSWR and eq-7 of Q.no-18 for $V\left(m_{PPSWR}\right)$ for PPSWR. Thus, (a) becomes

$V\left(m_{st}\right)=\sum W_s^2\left(V_s/n_s\right)$ ...(b)

This has to be minimised subject to the condition that the survey has to be carried within the budget 'F' sanctioned for it. Let us take the cost function to be $F_0 + \sum n_s F_s$, (Σ 1 to k), where F_0, n_s and F_s are respectively the overhead cost, the sample size in stratum 's' and the per unit cost of surveying a unit in stratum 's' (s = 1,2,..........., k) and this cost is to be = F. The Lagrangian function to be minimised is, therefore, $\phi = V(m_{st}) - \lambda(F_0 + \sum n_s F_s - F)$ equating to zero the partial derivatives of

$$\phi = \sum W_s^2 (V_s/n_s) - \lambda(F - F_0 - \sum n_s F_s) \text{ w.r.t } n_s,\ s = 1,2,\ldots\ldots, k, \text{ we have}$$

$$(1/n_s^2)(W_s^2 V_s) = \lambda F_s, \text{ that is, } n_s = c(W_s/\sqrt{\lambda})\sqrt{(V_s/F_s)},\ s = 1,\ldots\ldots,k. \quad \ldots(c)$$

Substituting the values of n_s in the cost function $F - F_0 - \sum n_s F_s = 0$ (the cost constraint),

$$(F - F_0) = \sum F_s (W_s/\sqrt{\lambda})\sqrt{(V_s/F_s)} = (1/\sqrt{\lambda})\sum(W_s)\sqrt{(V_s)}\sqrt{F_s} \text{ or } \sqrt{\lambda}$$

$$= \sum W_s \sqrt{(V_s F_s)} - (F - F_0)$$

substituting for λ in (c), we have

$$n_s = [(F - F_0)][W_s \sqrt{(V_s/F_s)}] / [\sum W_s \sqrt{(V_s F_s)}],\ s = 1,\ldots\ldots\ldots,k. \quad \ldots(d)$$

The stratum sample size should, therefore, be proportional to $W_s \sqrt{(V_s/F_s)}$. The minimum variance with stratum sizes so determined is, form (c) and (d),

$$\text{Min. } V(m_{st}) = \left[\sum W_s \sqrt{(V_s F_s)}\right]^2 [1/(F - F_0)] \quad \ldots(e)$$

The main aim of GPH book is to provide knowledge as well as good marks in exams.

Question Papers

RESEARCH METHODS IN ECONOMICS: MEC-009

December, 2010

Note: Attempt questions from all the sections as per instructions given in each section. Word limit does not apply in case of numerical questions.

SECTION–A

Answer any two of the following questions in about 600 words each.

Q1. What do you understand by the term 'Paradigm'? How does Kuhn explain the growth of knowledge? Explain.

Ans. Refer to Chapter–1, Q.No.–11 and Q.No.–14(a)

Q2. Explain the different models of scientific explanation.

Ans. Refer to Chapter–1, Q.No.–17

Q3. Name the various methods of random sampling. Explain the operational procedure for selecting the sample by Simple Random Sampling with Replacement. Give examples in support of your answer.

Ans. Refer to Chapter–2, Q.No.–13 and Q.No.–14

Q4. What is the distinction between quantitative data and qualitative data? Explain the the various steps involved in compilation of qualitative data. Give illustrations.

Ans. Distinctions between quantitative and qualitative data

S.No.	Quantitative Data	Qualitative Data
(1)	Based on meanings derived from numbers	Based on meanings expressed through words
(2)	Collection results in numerical and standardised data	Collection results in non–standardised data requiring classification into categories
(3)	Analysis conducted through the use of diagrams and statistics	Analysis conducted through the use of conceptualisation

Now, Refer to Chapter–5, Q.No.–9

SECTION–B

Answer any five questions from this section in about 400 words each.

Q5. How does review of literature help a researcher in conducting the research study?

Ans. A beginning researcher may wonder why it is necessary to review the literature. It might seem more effective simply to decide what he want to research and then go and do it. However, reviewing the literature helps him to develop a comprehensive understanding of the topic, making aware of what is known and what questions need to be answered. This can help to decide exactly what to research and how to go about it.

Familiarity with the body of literature on a topic will help him to identify how his proposed study will fit into the body of literature already available. For example, he might discover that the question he wanted to answer has already been researched using a particular theoretical framework.

Reviewing the literature can also help to narrow down the topic of study. In reading the literature, he may see that his topic is too broad and would entail too many areas of investigation. Knowing the literature can help to select a facet of the topic that would be beneficial to study and that can be kept within realistic bounds.

Reviewing the literature can also help him with the design of his study. By exposure to the approach used by previous researchers investigating the area, he can see the nature of the designs chosen, for example, experimental, phenomenological or historical. He would find that homelessness has usually been studied using interview and fieldwork because it is impossible to contact the homeless through survey methods such as postal questionnaires.

Reviewing the literature can also help him with the details of the study's methodology. He will be able to see the specifics of the previous designs, how they related to their theoretical frameworks, how the data were collected and how they were analysed.

He should be aware that in some qualitative approaches, justification is given for not reviewing the literature prior to the study. In some qualitative research approaches, such as grounded theory, it is not appropriate to do more than a superficial reading of the literature in order to identify whether the topic needs to be studied.

Q6. State the assumptions of classical linear regression model.

Ans. Refer to Chapter–3, Q.No.–12

Q7. What is auto-correlation? What are its consequences? Which technique would you apply to detect auto-correlation?

Ans. Refer to Chapter–3, Q.No.–24

Q8. Explain the relative advantages of Rapid Rural Appraisal over sampling survey approach in conducting a research study.

Ans. Refer to Chapter–5, Q.No.–18

Q9. What type of data is available on agriculture? Identify the agencies involved in compilation of agricultural data.

Ans. Refer to Chapter–6, Q.No.–9

Q10. State the computation device of Gini coefficient index.

Ans. Refer to Chapter–4, Q.No.–2

Q11. Explain any three of the following

(a) Non–sampling error

Ans. Refer to Chapter–2, Q.No.–8

(b) Operationalism

Ans. Refer to Chapter–1, Q.No.–23

(c) Goodness of fit

Ans. Refer to Chapter–3, Q.No.–15

(d) Group discussion

Ans. Refer to Chapter–5, Q.No.–17

(e) Triangulation

Ans. Refer to Chapter–5, Q.No.–16

(f) Logical empiricism

Ans. Refer to Chapter–1, Q.No.–21

Q12. You are given the following results:

$\log C = 4.30 - 1.34 \log P + 0.17 \log Y$

se = (0.91) (0.32) (0.20)

$R^{-2} = 0.27$ N = 46

Where

C = cigar consumption, packs per year

P = real price per pack

Y = real disposable income per capita.

What is the elasticity of demand for cigar with respect to price? Is it statistically significant? If so, it is statistically different from 1?

Ans. Refer to Gullybaba.com, "download section".

RESEARCH METHODS IN ECONOMICS: MEC-009

June, 2011

Note: Attempt questions from each section as per instructions given. Word limits will not apply in case of numerical questions.

SECTION–A

Attempt any two questions from this section in about 700 words each.

Q1. What do you understand by the term 'scientific revolution'? Explain the radical implications of Kuhn's position in this regard.

Ans. Refer to Chapter–1, Q.No.–10

Q2. What is logical empiricism? State the contribution made by T. Hutchison in this regard.

Ans. Refer to Chapter–1, Q.No.–21

Q3. What is systematic sampling? Explain the procedure for drawing sample by systematic sampling. How will you estimate the population mean of the sample drawn by systematic sampling?

Ans. Refer to Chapter–2, Q.No.–14

Q4. What type of data will you need to assess the performance of Indian economy? Explain the various sources of such data.

Ans. Refer to Chapter–6, Q.No.–5

SECTION–B

Attempt any five questions from this section in about 400 words each.

Q5. State the various steps involved in planning and organising survey.

Ans. Refer to Chapter–2, Q.No.–7

Q6. What is the difference between disturbance term and intercept? Explain the assumptions of classical regression model.

Ans. Refer to Chapter–3, Q.No.–11 and Q.No.–12

Q7. What is Hetero-scedasticity? What are its consequences? How will you tackle it.

Ans. Refer to Chapter–3, Q.No.–23

Q8. What is gini ratio? How can you compute it?

Ans. Refer to Chapter–4, Q.No.–2

Q9. Explain the various types of price index numbers. What are their uses?

Ans. Refer to Chapter–4, Q.No.–15 and Q.No.–18

Q10. What do you understand by the term Focus group discussion? Under what situation it is used as a tool for conducting qualitative research?

Ans. Refer to Chapter–5, Q.No.–10

Q11. Distinguish between any three of the followings:

(a) Methodological Monism and Methodological Dualism.

Ans. Methodological monism states that there is just one method for all sciences (natural science) and social sciences. Whereas methodological dualism claims that the study of human beings requires a methodology of its own, distinct from that of the natural science. Methodological monism simply means that the method of science and social science are the same whereas methodological dualism talks about science and social sciences having different methods from each other.

Popper adopts methodological monism according to which the social sciences and natural sciences have a common method and their relation, in so far as method is concerned is one of identity. Adorno adopts methodological dualism according to which natural science and social sciences have essentially different methods, and their relation is one of difference. Popper construes willy-nilly that one method in as we have seen positivist terms. Adorno's methodological dualism accepts positivist characterisation of the method of natural sciences. Therefore, what is common to both Popper and Adorno is their construal of the method of natural sciences, irrespective of the gap between Popper's "identity" thesis and Adormo's "difference" thesis.

(b) Research Methodology and Research Methods.

Ans. Refer to Chapter–2, Q.No.–3

(c) Sampling and non-sampling errors.

Ans. Refer to Chapter–2, Q.No.–8

(d) Sample size and Sampling frame.

Ans. Sample size

The sample size plays a crucial role in the sampling process. There are various ways of classifying the techniques used in determining the sample size. A couple those hold primary importance and are worth mentioning are whether the technique deals with fixed or sequential sampling and whether its logic is based on traditional or Bayesian methods. In non-probability sampling procedures, the allocation of budget, thumb rules and number of sub groups to be analysed, importance of the decision, number of variables, nature of analysis, incidence rates, and completion rates play a major role in sample size determination. In the case of probability sampling, however, formulas are used to calculate the sample size after the levels of acceptable error and level of confidence are specified.

Sampling Frame

Once the definition of the population is clear, a researcher should decide on the sampling frame. A sampling frame is the list of elements from which the sample may be drawn. Continuing with the micro oven ex, an ideal sampling frame would be a database that contains all the households that have a monthly income above ₹20,000. However, in practice it is difficult to get an exhaustive sampling frame that exactly fits the requirements of a particular research. In general, researchers use easily available sampling frames like telephone directories and lists of credit card and mobile phone users. Various private players provide databases developed along various demographic and economic variables. Sometimes, maps and aerial pictures are also used as sampling frames. Whatever may be the case, an ideal sampling frame is one that entire population and lists the names of its elements only once.

A sampling frame error pops up when the sampling frame does not accurately represent the total population or when some elements of the population are missing another drawback in the sampling frame is over–representation. A telephone directory can be over represented by names/households that have two or more connections.

(e) Time series data and Cross section data

Ans. Refer to Chapter–3, Q.No.–8

Q12. Given the following regression results:

$\ln Y_t = 0.7774 - 0.2530 \ln X_t$

se = (0.0152) (0.0494)

RSS = .0226 $r^2 = 0.7448$

Y= Consumption of milk per day

X = real retail price of milk.

(a) Interpret the results

(b) Whether the slope coefficient is statistically significant at 1 per cent and 5 per cent level?

Ans. Same as Chapter-3, Q.No.-26

❑❑❑

RESEARCH METHODS IN ECONOMICS: MEC-009

December, 2011

Note: Attempt questions from each section as per the instructions given. In case of numerical questions word limit do not apply.

SECTION–A

Answer any two questions from this section in about 700 words each.

Q1. 'Experience is the source of knowledge'-in the light of this statement, critically examine the central tenets of Positivist Philosophy.

Ans. Refer to Chapter–1, Q.No.–3

Q2. What is instrumentalism? State the contribution made by Milton Friedman in this regard.

Ans. Refer to Chapter–1, Q.No.–22

Q3. What is Simple Random Sampling With Replacement (SRSWR)? Explain the procedure for drawing sample by SRSWR method with the help of example. How will you estimate the population mean and variance of sample drawn by SRSWR method?

Ans. Refer to Chapter–2, Q.No.–14

Q4. State the various sources of data on trade and finance. Explain the reasons for divergence between merchandise trade deficit/surplus data provided by DG (I and S) and RBI's BOP data.

Ans. Refer to Chapter–6, Q.No.–14, Q.No.–16 and Q.No.–17

SECTION–B

Answer any five questions from this section in about 400 words each.

Q5. What is the distinction between quantitative and qualitative research? State the tools used in compilation of qualitative data.

Ans. Refer to Chapter–2, Q.No.–1 and Chapter–5, Q.No.–9

Q6. State with an example the various steps involved in framing a research proposal.

Ans. Steps involved in research proposal:

Step 1: The Title

Naming your research is an important part of the research proposal. It should tell the user (In 25 words or less) what you intend to research and how you intend to do it. The choice is up to you, as long as your title is relevant to the research question.

Step 2: The Abstract

Your research proposal in its entirety may be anywhere between 5,000 to 25,000 words in length. So it is important that you give a summary of the entire document. This summary is known as the abstract, and should demonstrate to the reader the most important parts of each of the sections of the research proposal in around 200 words. It is often useful to write the abstract last, after the rest of the research proposal has been written and fully thought out.

Step 3: Aims and Objectives

In this section you should expand on the title of your research project to articulate in full detail the aims and objectives of your research. You should be able to provide a detailed description of the research question, the purpose of the research, and a description of your approach (methodology and method) to the research.

Included in this section should be discussion around the research problem that you intend to answer or investigate, your hypothesis, the parameters of the research i.e. what you intend to include within the research, and what you intend to leave out.

Step 4: Background

This section should provide detail about the background to the research question. In this section, you will need to demonstrate an understanding of the existing literature and research studies within the area of your proposed research topic. This is to assist the reader to understand the significance of your research, and where it fits within the existing body of knowledge.

The background section is a significant portion of your proposal and therefore should be an extensive review of the literature related to your topic (see literature review). You should be able to discuss what the existing literature is about and highlight any gaps, issues or contentions that arise. You also need to be able to show where your research fits within this literature and enter into discussions on issues that relate to your research question. The point of this background section is to demonstrate to the reader your understanding and knowledge of the research area, as well as the contribution that your research project will make to the existing research and knowledge.

Step 5: Methodology and Method

In this section of the proposal, you will need to demonstrate how you intend to go about investigating the research question. The methodology generally refers to the theory to be used to justify the use of the particular research methods that you are choosing to use. You may use more than one methodology to inform your method of research.

Step 6: Schedule and Timeline

You need to be able to demonstrate that your research is possible within a given timeframe. You may be able to define your own timeframe, or the institution for which you are writing a proposal may have a set timeframe that you will need to work within. Either way, it is important that you are able to plot the intended progress of the project from start to finish. If you intend to produce any outputs, reports, findings then they should be inserted into this schedule.

Step 7: Ethical Approval

Some institutions require that any research involving interaction with human participants get approval from ethical advisory committees or boards. This ethical approval is sought to ensure that the researcher conducts research in a manner that is respectful to the participants and other human beings that may be influenced by the research process. It is important that you seek out what ethical approval is required within your area of research. You may need to seek approval from more than one advisory committee depending on the institutional, financial and disciplinary context. Applications for ethical approval are obtained directly from the ethical committees themselves.

In the 'ethical approval' section, it is important to outline who you intend to seek ethical approval from, and/or when ethical approval was granted and for what period of time.

Step 8: Resources

This section demonstrates to the reader that you are both suitable and capable of carrying out the proposed research. You will need to discuss what resources you have at your disposal that makes it possible for you to carry out this research. For example, physical resources (such as research instruments), personal resources (such as knowledge of the discipline, area or community under study), as well as any other resources that you have as a researcher (or research team) that will enable you to carry out the research from beginning through to completion.

You may also need to highlight what resources you still require in order to complete the research, and also discuss how you intend to go about acquiring these resources (i.e. through funding, through research collaborations,, etc.)

Step 9: Budget

Not all research proposal require a budget (such as thesis proposals for academic institutions), however if you intend to apply for funding for research it is important that you are able to show how much money you require, and justify the amount asked for. The way to justify the amount you are asking for is to provide a detailed budget outlining what expenses you predict you will incur in conducting the research. Exactly where and how money will be spent will differ from project to project, and the size of the budget should reflect the size of the research project. Some of the main expenses that may be included in any budget could be researcher's time, human resources (such as other research assistants, transcribers, advisory board members), technical equipment (Dictaphones, transcribers, computer hardware and software etc), stationary, koha and others.

Q7. What is classical normal regression model? Explain its uses.

Ans. Refer to Chapter–3, Q.No.–17

Q8. Explain Lorenze Curve as a geometrical device to measure inequality. Describe its properties.

Ans. Refer to Chapter–4, Q.No.–3

Q9. What is the distinction between time series analysis and multivariate analysis? Identify the various components of time series.

Ans. Multivariate analysis is based on the statistical principle of multivariate statistics, which involves observation and analysis of more than one statistical outcome variable at a time. In design and analysis, the technique is used to perform trade studies across multiple dimensions while taking into account the effects of all variables on the responses of interest. On the other hand, a time series is a collection of observations of well-defined data items obtained through repeated measurements over time.

Now, Refer to Chapter–4, Q.No.–6

Q10. What do you mean by PRA/RRA approach? Explain under what circumstances PRA/RRA approach is superior to sampling survey approach?

Ans. Refer to Chapter–5, Q.No.–3 and Q.No.–18

Q11. Distinguish between any three of the following:

(a) Estimator and Estimate

Ans. Refer to Chapter–2, Q.No.–10

(b) Statistic and parameter

Ans. Refer to Chapter–2, Q.No.–10

(c) Statistical hypothesis and Research hypothesis.

Ans. A research hypothesis states the relationship one expect to find as a result of the research, and it is called the heart of the study. It may be a statement about the expected relationship or the expected difference between the variables in the study. A hypothesis about children's IQs and anxiety in the classroom could be stated, "There is a positive relationship between IQ and anxiety in elementary schoolchildren" or "Children classified as having high IQs will exhibit more anxiety in the classroom than children classified as having low IQs." Research hypotheses may be stated in a directional or non-directional form. It is impossible to test research hypotheses directly. For reasons founded in statistical theory, it is a statistical hypothesis that we assess in the process of hypothesis testing. The statistical hypothesis is called a null hypothesis (symbolised H_0). One must first state and assess the probability that the null hypothesis is true. It is called a null hypothesis because it states that there is *no* relationship between the variables in the population. A null hypothesis states a negation (not the reverse) of what c the researcher expects or predicts.

(d) Theoretical Research and Applied Research

Ans. Refer to Chapter–2, Q.No.–1

(e) Induction and Deduction

Ans. Induction and deduction are two different reasoning strategies. In other words, they are two different ways to figure out the solution to a problem.

With induction –we start with our own experience and then generalise a rule. For example, the last ten times I touched the hot stove I burned my hand. I bet every time I touch the hot stove my hand will be burned. Another example, the last few times I eat green peppers I got bad gas. I think eating peppers gives me bad gas.

With deduction –we start with a rule and then apply it to new situations. For example, the sign at the amusement park says "Adult Admission- Rs. 10". Therefore, I bet if I, an adult, try to enter I will be charged ten rupees. *Another example:* The law of gravity says that what goes up must come down, so I bet if I throw this ball up it will fall back down.

We use induction and deduction all the time when making decisions or solving problems. For example, because the last few times I cut my hair, it grew back. Inductive reasoning allows me to generalise that after I cut my hair it will always grow back. *Another example:* Since my teacher's grading policy states that he takes 1 point off for each spelling mistake, I can deduce that I will lose 5 points if I make five spelling mistakes.

Q12. Given the following regression results:

$$\hat{Y}_t = 2.6911 - 0.4795 X_t$$

$$\Delta e = (0.1216)\ (0.1140)$$

RSS= 0.1491, r^2 =0.6628

Where

Y = Consumption of cups of milk per day.

X = retail price of milk in India for the year 1970-80.

(a) Interpret the results

(b) Whether the slope coefficient is statistically significant at 5 per cent level.

Ans. Refer to Chapter–3, Q.No.–26

❑❑❑

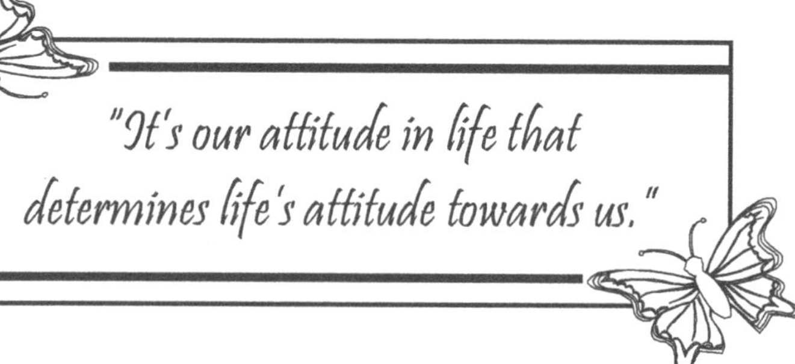

RESEARCH METHODS IN ECONOMICS: MEC-009

June, 2012

Note: Attempt questions from each section as per instructions given below each section.

SECTION–A

Attempt any two questions from this section in about 700 words each.

Q1. What is the distinction between inductivism and hypothesism? Critically examine the control tenets of positivism.

Ans. Refer to Chapter–1, Q.No.–2 and Q.No.–3

Q2. What do you mean by the term 'Scientific explanation'? Explain the characteristics of Hypothetico–Deductive model as model of scientific explanation.

Ans. Refer to Chapter–1, Q.No.–17

Q3. What is Simple Random Sampling With Replacement (SRSWR)? Explain the procedure for drawing sample by SRSWR. How will you estimate the population mean of the sample drawn by SRSWR method?

Ans. Refer to Chapter–2, Q.No.–14

Q4. State the organisational structure of Indian statistical system. Why do we need to make estimates of macro aggregates at current and constant prices?

Ans. The Department of Statistics of the Government of India is the apex body in the official statistical system of the country. This consists of the Central Statistical Organisation (CSO), the National Sample Survey Organisation (NSSO) and Computer Centre (CC). The Directorates of Economics and Statistics function at the level of the State Governments. CSO coordinates the statistical activities in the country, lays down and maintains statistical norms and standards and provides liaison with Central, State and international statistical agencies. There is also a National Advisory Board on Statistics (NABS), which consists of eminent statisticians from research institutions and representatives of Central Ministries and Departments and the State Directorates of Economics and Statistics, to provide (i) guidance for an overall perspective for statistical development in the country, (ii) guidance to Government on policy issues, and (iii) ensure effective coordination of all statistical activities of the Government of India. CSO is the Secretariat of NABS.

Now, Refer to Chapter–6, Q.No.–6

SECTION–B

Attempt any five questions from this section in about 400 words each.

Q5. What is a research design? What type of research design would you like to suggest for descriptive research?

Ans. Refer to Chapter–2, Q.No.–5

Q6. Explain the various functional forms of regression model. For the measurement of growth rate which form of regression model is suitable?

Ans. Refer to Chapter–3, Q.No.–16

Q7. What is multi – colinerity? What are its consequences?

Ans. Refer to Chapter–3, Q.No.–22

Q8. State the relationship between Lorenz curve and Gini coefficient.

Ans. Refer to Chapter–4, Q.No.–2

Q9. State the various steps involved in framing a project proposal.

Ans. Refer to Dec-2011, Q.No.–6

Q10. What do you mean by deseasonalisation of a time series? Explain the moving average method of deseasonalisation.

Ans. Refer to Chapter–4, Q.No.–10

Q11. What is distinction between Participatory Rural Appraisal (PRA) and Rapid Rural Appraisal? Discuss the different tools used for conducting qualitative research.

Ans. Refer to Chapter–5, Q.No.–5 and Q.No.–6

Q12. Distinguish between any three of the following:

(a) Theory and Model

Ans. A model is often used to describe an application of a theory for a particular case. Sometimes it involves a given set of initial and boundary conditions. For example, the behaviour of the Eiffel tower in an earthquake may be modelled by a finite elements computer simulation. The underlying theory employed could be the Prandtl-Meyer's Stress-Strain relationship for elastic-plastic flow in metals and, of course, Newtonian mechanics.

In other cases, the term model is used more generally to mean some abstract representation or approximation to an underlying theory. In this sense, the P–M relationship above can be referred to as a "model" of the behaviour of metals.

(b) Control group and experiment group

Ans. The difference between a control group and an experimental group is one group is exposed to the conditions of the experiment and the other is not.

An experimental group is the group in a scientific experiment where the experimental procedure is performed. This group is exposed to the independent variable being tested and the changes observed and recorded.

A control group is a group separated from the rest of the experiment where the independent variable being tested cannot influence the results. This isolates the independent variable's effects on the experiment and can help rule out alternate explanations of the experimental results.While all experiments have an experimental group, not all experiments require a control group. Controls are extremely useful where the experimental conditions are complex and difficult to isolate. Experiments that use control groups are called controlled experiments. There are two other types of control groups where the conditions the group are subjected to will cause predetermined results. Positive control groups are control groups where the conditions guarantee a positive result. Positive control groups are effective to show the experiment is functioning as planned. Negative control groups are control groups where conditions produce a negative outcome. Negative control groups help identify outside influences, which may be present that were not unaccounted for, such as contaminants.

(c) Statistical hypothesis and Research hypothesis

Ans. Refer to December–2011, Q.No.–11(c)

(d) Parameter and statistic

Ans. Refer to Chapter–2, Q.No.–10

(e) Correlation and Regression

Ans. Refer to Chapter–3, Q.No.–4

❑❑❑

RESEARCH METHODS IN ECONOMICS: MEC-009

December, 2012

Note: Attempt questions from each section as per instructions given.

SECTION–A

Attempt any two questions from this section in about 700 words each.

Q1. What do you mean by the term scientific method? Discuss the fundamental differences between Popper's and positivists' views about the theory of scientific method.

Ans. Refer to Chapter–1, Q.No.–14(c) and Q.No.–6

Q2. Distinguish between realism and instrumentalism. Discuss the contribution made by Milton Friedman towards instrumentalism in Economics.

Ans. Refer to Chapter–1, Q.No.–22

Q3. What is Simple Random Sampling without replacement (SRSWOR)? State the procedure for drawing sample by SRSWOR. How will you estimate the population mean of the sample drawn by SRSWOR ?

Ans. Refer to Chapter–2, Q.No.–14

Q4. Why do we need to make estimates of National Income and related macro aggregates? Explain the various components of the system of national accounts of India

Ans. Refer to Chapter–1, Q.No.–10

SECTION-B

Attempt any five questions from this section in about 400 words each.

Q5. State the various steps involved in carrying out research.

Ans. Refer to Chapter–2, Q.No.–4

Q6. In what way does review of literature help a researcher?

Ans. Refer to Dec–2010, Q.No.–5

Q7. What is goodness of fit? How does coefficient of determination act as a measure of goodness of fit?

Ans. Refer to Chapter–3, Q.No.–15

Q8. What is the distinction between positive measures and relative measures of income in equalities? Enumerate the properties of Lorenz Curve as a measure of income in equality.

Ans. Refer to Chapter–4, Q.No.–3

Q9. Identify the steps involved in construction of price index numbers? Which problems are encountered in conducting price index numbers?

Ans. Refer to Chapter–4, Q.No.–14

Q10. What is Rapid Rural Appraisal (RRA) approach? How is the RRA approach is superior to sampling survey approach?

Ans. Refer to Chapter–5, Q.No.–3 and Q.No.–18

Q11. Distinguish between any three of the followings:

(a) Sampling and non- sampling errors.

Ans. Refer to Chapter–2, Q.No.–8

(b) Induction and deduction.

Ans. Refer to Dec–2011, Q.No.–11(e)

(c) R^2 and adjusted R^2

Ans. R^2 is a statistic that will give some information about the goodness of fit of a model. In regression, the R^2 coefficient of determination is a statistical measure of how well the regression line approximates the real data points. An R^2 of 1.0 indicates that the regression line perfectly fits the data.

Adjusted R^2 is a modification of R^2 that adjusts for the number of explanatory terms in a model. Unlike R^2, the adjusted R^2 increases only if the new term improves the model more than would be expected by chance. The adjusted R^2 can be negative, and will always be less than or equal to R^2.

Adjusted R^2 does not have the same interpretation as R^2. As such, care must be taken in interpreting and reporting this statistic. Adjusted R^2 is particularly useful in the Feature selection stage of model building.

Adjusted R^2 is not always better than R^2: adjusted R^2 will be more useful only if the R^2 is calculated based on a sample, not the entire population. For example, if our unit of analysis is a state, and we have data for all counties, then adjusted R^2 will not yield any more useful information than R^2.

(d) Time series data and cross section data.

Ans. Refer to Chapter–3, Q.No.–8

(e) Variance and co-variance.

Ans. There are following difference between Variance and co-variance:

- Variance is the measure of spread/dispersion in a population while covariance is considered as a measure of variation of two random variables or the strength of the correlation.
- Variance can be considered as a special case of covariance.
- Variance and covariance are dependent on the magnitude of the data values, and cannot be compared; therefore, they are normalised. Covariance is normalised into the correlation coefficient (dividing by the product of the standard deviations of the two random variables) and variance is normalised into the standard deviation (by taking the square root)

(f) Descriptive and explanatory research.

Ans. Refer to Chapter–2, Q.No.–1

Q12. What is Hetero-scedasticity? How can it be detected? What are its consequences?

Ans. Refer to Chapter–3, Q.No.–23

RESEARCH METHODS IN ECONOMICS: MEC-009

June, 2013

Note: Attempt questions from each sections as per instructions given below each section.

SECTION–A

Attempt any two questions from this section in about 700 words each.

Q1. What kind of errors can creep into data collected by you? How would you by to rectify these errors?

Q2. What is scientific revolution? Elaborate the divergent views of Karl Popper and Thomas Kuhn about the essence of science.

Q3. Illustrate hypothesis testing in a regression model. How does assumption of normality play a crucial role for hypothesis testing?

Q4. What do you mean by the term 'scientific explanation? Explain the Hypothetic - Deductive Model as Model of scientific explanation.

SECTION–B

Attempt any five questions from this section in about 400 words each.

Q5. What are the basic approaches to analyse the qualitative data?

Q6. What is autocorrelation? When does it arise? How do you tackle it?

Q7. Describe the various steps involved in the formulation of a research proposal.

Q8. What are the major data sources on employment and unemployment in India? Explain the kind of 'information' available on employment and unemployment.

Q9. Define the terms 'estimator' and 'estimate' with a suitable example.

Q10. What is multi-stage sampling? How is this technique used to estimate agricultural data in India?

Q11. What are the Positive Measures of Inequality? How would you construct Gini Index?

Q12. Differentiate between any three of the following:

(a) Parameters and Statistics

(b) Correlation and Regression

(c) Qualitative and Quantitative research

(d) Time Series and Cross Section Data

(e) Census and Sample Surveys

❑❑❑

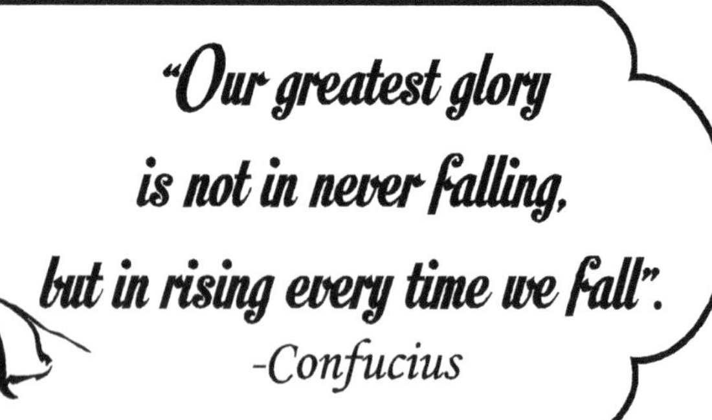

RESEARCH METHODS IN ECONOMICS: MEC-009

December, 2013

Note: Attempt questions from each sections as per instructions given below each section.

SECTION–A

Attempt any two questions from this section in about 700 words each.

Q1. What do you mean by scientism? What are the central tenets of positivist philosophy? Also mention major criticisms of this approach.

Q2. Compare and contrast Karl Popper's and Thomas Kuhn's approaches to scientific methods.

Q3. What do you mean by the term scientific explaination? Explain the Covering-Law model as a model of Scientific Explaination.

Q4. Distinguish between stratified and cluster sampling. When is stratified sampling preferred? How do you measure the sampling efficiency of cluster sampling?

SECTION–B

Attempt any five questions from this section in about 400 words each.

Q5. How is data collected under the systematic sampling approach?

Q6. What is 'goodness of fit'? How is it related to the coefficient of determination?

Q7. What are the assumptions of the Classical Regression Model? Is it necessary to satisfy them all for time series data?

Q8. Distinguish between qualitative data and quantitative data. How do you test the trustworthiness of qualitative data?

Q9. Differentiate between positive and normative measures of enequality. List the various steps invloved in construction of sen's index of enequality.

Q10. What do you mean by smoothing? List the two basic techniques of smoothing.

Q11. How do you find PRA/RRA approach to be superior to sampling survey approach.

Q12. Elaborate on any three of the following:

(a) Focus Group Discussion

(b) Hypothesis Testing

(c) Heteroscedasticity

(d) SRS without replacement

(e) Gini Index

❑❑❑

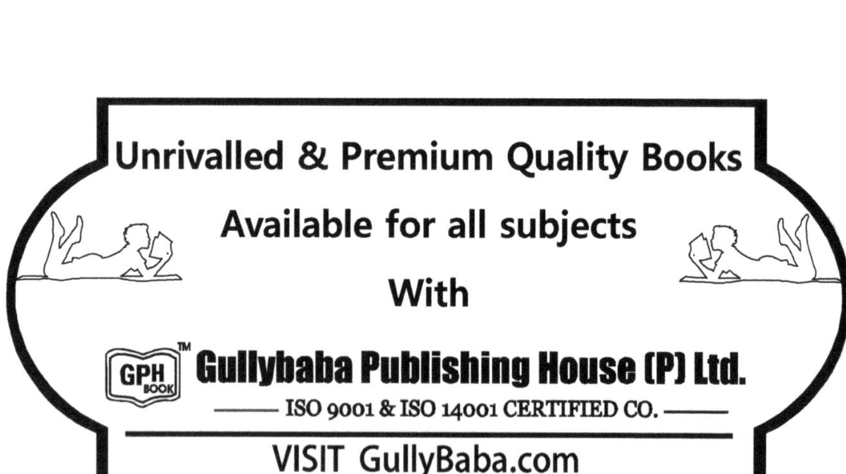

RESEARCH METHODS IN ECONOMICS: MEC-009

June, 2014

Note: Answer questions from each section as directed.

SECTION–I

Answer any two questions from this section.

Q1. What do you understand from the term `precision of estimates'? How will you assess precision of estimates when population variance is unknown?

Q2. What is heteroscedasticity? How will you detect and tackle the problem of heteroscedasticity?

Q3. What do you understand by the term 'scientific explanation'? Explain the Hypothetico-Deductive model of scientific explanation.

Q4. What are the salient features of Indian Statistical System? What type of data are compiled by CSO to assess the performance of the Indian economy?

SECTION–II

Answer any five questions from this section.

Q5. What do you mean by smoothing? How do you smooth time series data?

Q6. What do you mean by normative measures of inequality? Explain Income-Welfare Index proposed by Dalton.

Q7. Explain the properties expected of an Ideal Index Number.

Q8. "Linear in parameter' regression models may have different functional forms." Discuss.

Q9. Explain the various tools used in conducting the research by way of qualitative approach.

Q10. Distinguish between positivism and apriorism in economic analysis.

Q11. What is PRA technique? Explain its use in conducting research with the help of two examples.

Q12. Distinguish between any three of the following:

(a) Focus Group Discussions and Semi-structured Interviews

(b) Exploratory research studies and Experimental research studies

(c) Data collected by NSSO and NFHS

(d) Methodological Dualism and Methodological Monoism

(e) Deduction and Induction

❑❑❑

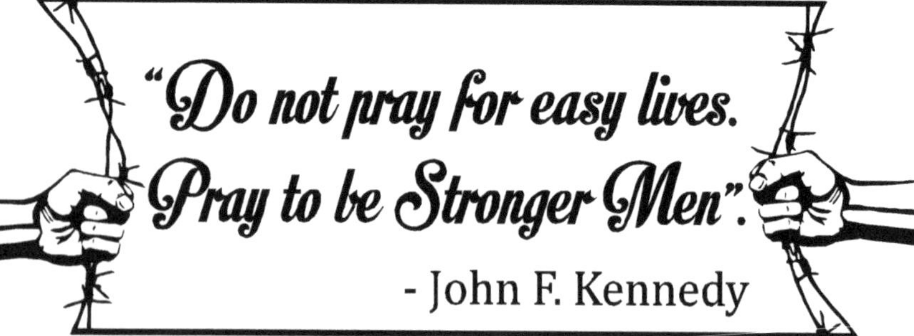

RESEARCH METHODS IN ECONOMICS: MEC-009

December, 2014

Note: Attempt questions from each section as per instructions given below.

SECTION–A

Attempt any two questions from this section.

Q1. Distinguish between inductivism and hypothesism. State the characteristics and process of inductivism.

Q2. What is multiple linear regression? What are advantages of using a linear in logarithm model over simple linear model? Give suitable example.

Q3. Distinguish between qualitative and quantitative research. Explain the various methods used in analysis of quantitative data.

Q4. What do you mean by the social sector of an economy? Explain the kind of data available in this sector in India. Which agencies collect the data on social sector?

SECTION–B

Attempt any five questions from this section.

Q5. What are the different measure of economic inequality? Explain the computations of sen's index of inequality.

Q6. How will you construct a price index number? Identify problems encountered in constructing price index numbers.

Q7. What is multi-collinearity? How does it affect the precision of regression estimates?

Q8. What are the sources of errors in the data? Distinguish between sampling and non-sampling errors.

Q9. What is a sampling design? What its main features?

Q10. Differentiate between realism of instrumentalism. Critically analyse instrumentalism in economics as given by Milton Friedman.

Q11. Explain technique of triangulation in processing of qualitative data.

Q12. Distinguish between any three of the following:

(a) Observation Method and Experimental Method of data collection

(b) Empirical and Theoritical research

(c) Time series data and Cross section data

(d) Data series given by NAS and SAS

(e) Realists and anti-realists

❑❑❑

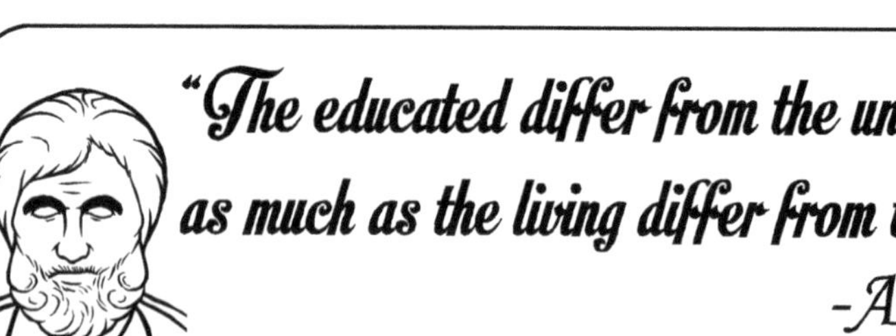

RESEARCH METHODS IN ECONOMICS: MEC-009

June, 2015

Note: Attempt questions from each section as per instructions given.

SECTION–A

Attempt any two questions from this section in about 700 words each.

Q1. Distinguish between inductivism and hypothesism. Critically examine the central tenets of positivism.

Q2. What do you mean by the term 'scientific explanation'? Critically examine the covering law models of scientific explantation.

Q3. What is the difference between random and non-random sampling? How will you determine the appropriate sampling method under various situations?

Q4. What type of variables will you use to assess the performance of Indian economy? Explain the various sources of data for these variables.

SECTION–B

Attempt any five questions from this section in about 400 words each.

Q5. State the various forms of regression models. When will you use a log linear regression model? Give an illustration in support of your answer.

Q6. Which tools are used to collect data under qualitative research? How is group discussion a better tool in relation to semi-structured interview?

Q7. Explain the computation device of Gini coefficient as a measure of income-inequality.

Q8. Briefly discuss the various steps involved in hypothesis testing.

Q9. Make distinctions between any two of the following:

(a) Induction and Deduction

(b) Sampling frame and Sampling size

(c) Labour force and Work force

(d) R^2 and Adjusted R^2

Q10. What is exploratory research? Discuss the various steps involved in carrying out an exploratory research study.

Q11. What are the uses of price index numbers?

❑❑❑

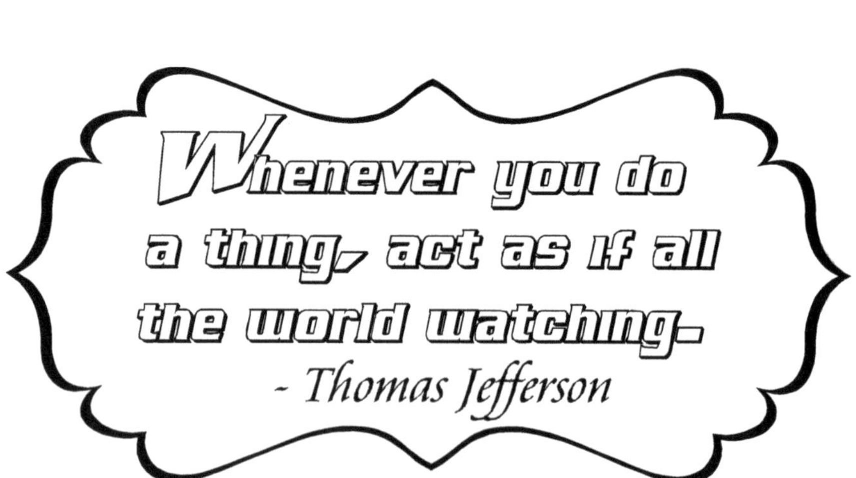

RESEARCH METHODS IN ECONOMICS: MEC-009

December, 2015

Note: Attempt questions from each sections as per instructions given.

SECTION–A

Attempt any two questions from this section in about 700 words each.

Q1. Distinguish between 'Inductivist model' and `Hypothetico-Deductive model'. Discuss the central components of hypothetico-deductive model.

Q2. 'Economics is a science'–In the light of this statement critically examine the methodological position taken by Robbins and T. Hutchison.

Q3. What is systematic sampling? State the procedure of drawing a sample by systematic sampling. How will you estimate the population mean of the sample drawn by systematic sampling?

Q4. What type of data on agriculture is available in India? Explain the different sources of agricultural data and the various agencies involved in their compilation.

SECTION–B

Attempt any five questions from this section in about 400 words each.

Q5. How will you estimate the parameters in two variable regression model? State the various assumptions of classical linear regression model.

Q6. What is content analysis? What are its objectives?

Q7. What is the distinction between positive measures and relative measures of inequality? State how relative quartile range method

is an improvement over relative range method as a measure of inequality.

Q8. What is multi-collinearity? How can it be detected? What are its consequences?

Q9. Distinguish between any two of the following:

(a) Control group and Experimental group

(b) Research methods and Research methodology

(c) Parameter and Statistic

(d) PRA technique and RRA technique

Q10. What do you mean by descriptive research? Discuss the various steps involved in conducting descriptive research study.

Q11. What types of errors arise in data collection? What are the sources of non-sampling errors?

❑❑❑

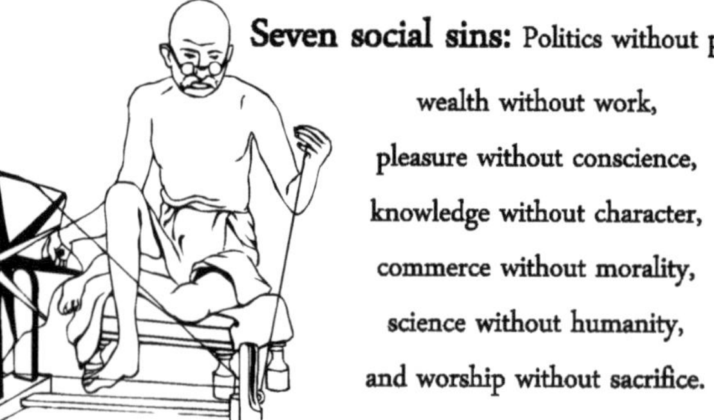

RESEARCH METHODS IN ECONOMICS: MEC-009

June, 2016

Note: Answer questions from each section as directed.

SECTION–I

Answer any two questions from this section.

Q1. What is the aim of science? Explain the characteristics of inductivitism as a method of science. What are its (inductivitism) limitations?

Ans. Refer to Chapter-1, Q.No.-1 and Q.No.-2

Q2. What do you mean by the term 'Scientific Explanation'? Explain how does Hypothetic-Deductive model of explanation defuses the conflict between the realists and instrumentalists.

Ans. Refer to Chapter-1, Q.No.-17

Q3. State the procedure to draw sample by the method of Simple Random Sampling With Replacement (SRSWR). How will you estimate the population mean and variance of sampling means with the sample drawn by SRSWR method?

Ans. Refer to Chapter-2, Q.No.-14

Q4. What kind of data will you need to assess the overall performance of Indian economy? Explain the various sources of such data.

Ans. Refer to Chapter-6, Q.No.-5

SECTION–II

Answer any five questions from this section.

Q5. Distinguish between research design and research methods. What type of research design would you suggest for experimental research?

Ans. A research method is a general framework guiding a research project. Different methods can be used to tackle different questions. Research design is a specific outline detailing how our chosen method will be applied to answer a particular research question.

Research Methods: Research methods are generalised and established ways of approaching research questions (e.g., qualitative vs. quantitative methods). Not all methods can be applied to all research questions, so the choice of method is limited by the area of research that you wish to explore.

Research Design: Research design involves determining how our chosen method will be applied to answer our research question. The design of our study can be thought of as a blueprint detailing what will be done and how this will be accomplished. Key aspects of research design include: research methodology; participant/sample collection and assignment (if different conditions are being explored); and data collection procedures and instruments.

Relationship: Choice of research methods and design should be thought of as a reciprocal process extending well into our study. For example, it may arise over the course of our study that there is a flaw in the design. Changing the design of the study may lead to the choice (or addition) of a different method which, in turn, may lead to subsequent changes in the design to accommodate the new method(s).

Q6. State the various forms of regression models. Which form of regression model would you like to suggest to analyse the growth rate of the economy? Give illustration in support of your answer.

Ans. Refer to Chapter-3, Q.No.-16

Q7. State the various positive measures of inequality. Explain the computation device for construction of Kohn's index.

Ans. Refer to Chapter-4, Q.No.-1

Q8. Distinguish between any three of the following:

(a) Methodological monism and methodological dualism.

Ans. Refer to June-2011, Q.No.-11(a)

(b) Parameter and statistic

Ans. Refer to Chapter-2, Q.No.-10 (b, c)

(c) Sampling and non-sampling error

Ans. Refer to Chapter-2, Q.No.-8

(d) Cross section data and time series data

Ans. Refer to Chapter-3, Q.No.-8

(e) Participatary Rural Appraisal (PRA) and Rapid Rural Appraisal (RRA)

Ans. Refer to Chapter-5, Q.No.-5

Q9. Identify the various assumptions of classical Linear Regression Model. What will be the consequence of violation of the assumption of homoscedasticity?

Ans. Refer to Chapter-3, Q.No.-12, 23

Q10. What do you mean by Deseasonalisation of a time series data? Explain the procedure to apply multiplicative model to extract seasonal elements.

Ans. Refer to Chapter-4, Q.No.-10

Q11. Distinguish between quantitative and qualitative data. Which tools and techniques are used to collect qualitative data?

Ans. Refer to Chapter-2, Q.No.-1 and Refer to Chapter-5, Q.No.-9

Q12. Briefly state the various steps involved in carrying out a research study.

Ans. Refer to Chapter-2, Q.No.-4

❑❑❑

Those who say religion has
nothing to do with politics
do not know what religion is.

RESEARCH METHODS IN ECONOMICS: MEC-009

December, 2016

Note: Answer questions from each section as directed.

SECTION–A

Answer any two questions from this section:

Q1. **Which are the methods of science? State the features of hypothesism. What are its limitations?**

Q2. **State the difference between laws and ordinary statement. Explain the characteristics and limitations of covering law model of scientific explanation.**

Q3. **What is meant by 'the sampling distribution of a statistic' and 'sampling variance of a statistic'? How does random sampling procedure help in correcting for the bias of an estimate? Illustrate with the help of an example.**

Q4. **What is the need to make estimates of National income and related macro aggregates? Why is the base year is changed from time to time? Which have been the base year so far for national income and related aggregates?**

SECTION–B

Answer any five questions from this section:

Q5. **What is meant by hypothesis? How does review of literature help to a researcher in formulation of a hypothesis?**

Q6. **What is multicollinearity? How can you tackle this problem?**

Q7. Distinguish between positive measures and relative measures of inequality. Explain the computation device of construction of gini index/coefficient as measurement of inequality.

Q8. State the various steps involved in hypothesis testing.

Q9. Distinguish between any three of the following:

(a) Quota sampling and Snowball sampling

(b) Control group and experiment group

(c) Induction and deduction

(d) PRA and RRA

(e) Descriptive and explanatory research

Q10. State the procedure for construction of consumer price index. What are the uses of such price indexes?

Q11. Briefly discuss the techniques of data analysis.

Q12. Identify the various stages involved in planning and organising the surveys.

❑❑❑

RESEARCH METHODS IN ECONOMICS: MEC-009

June, 2017

Note: Attempt questions from each section as per instructions given below.

SECTION–A

Attempt any two questions from this section.

Q1. "The relation between two successive paradigms is incommensurable". Examine Kuhn's viewpoint on it.

Q2. Which data-sources assess the social consequences of development? Is quality of life measurable? How?

Q3. What role sample size plays in getting desired level of precision in random sampling? Suggest measures for determining such a sample size.

Q4. Compare and Contrast the different consumer Price Indices available in India.

SECTION–B

Attempt any five questions from this section.

Q5. What is reverse regression technique? Where is it applied?

Q6. Enlist the different types of industrial statistics available in Annual Survey of Industries (ASI).

Q7. How is 'Emic perspective' the strength of RRA approached?

Q8. The average score of Virat Kohli in a One-day International (ODI) cricket tournament is 90 runs. To evaluate his current performance, his scores in World Cup 2015 matches are taken and the average is found as 75. Can you use hypothesistesting to find whether there is a significant difference in his ODI average? If so, how?

Q9. What are the deciding factors for inclusion and exclusion of explanatory variables in regression models?

Q10. What are the data-sources available if one wants to examine the levels (standards) of living in India.

Q11. What is the criteria for acceptability of theory or hypotheses according to Milton Friedman? Why is his methodological approach widely criticized?

Q12. Distinguish between any three of the following:

(a) Descriptive and diagnostic research

(b) Cross-sectional and pooled data

(c) Normative and positive measures of Inequality

(d) Social mapping and Resource mapping

(e) Cyclical and seasonal movements in time-series

RESEARCH METHODS IN ECONOMICS: MEC-009

December, 2017

Note: Attempt questions from each section as per instructions given below.

SECTION–A

Attempt any two questions from this section:

Q1. **"A testable theory is a falsiable theory". Logically explain the statement using philosophical perspectives.**

Q2. **What are the properties of ideal index numbers? Why do they not have a unit attached to them?**

Q3. **What is the distinction between quantitative and qualitative approach of research? What are the techniques of primary data collection under qualitative approach?**

Q4. **What are the indications of quality of employment? What are the data sources available for a researcher who wants to assess quality of employment?**

SECTION–B

Attempt any five questions from this section:

Q5. **What are the critical pre - requisites needed for application of RRA approach?**

Q6. **How can one test the precision and reliability of results in sampling theory?**

Q7. **Why Marxism is considered as a pseudo -scientific theory?**

Q8. **Explain the problem in classical regression model caused by polishing of data.**

Q9. **Explain health mapping as a technique of participatory mapping.**

Q10. Briefly explain how would you measure inequality using Lorenz curve. Also explain its relationship with Gini coefficient.

Q11. What is the philosophy of science? Give a historical review of the aims and methods of science.

Q12. Distinguish between any three of the following:

(a) Operationalism and Descriptivism

(b) National Census, Economic Census and Agricultural Census

(c) Purposive and Snowball Sampling

(d) Correlation and Autocorrelation

(e) Research Design and Research Method

RESEARCH METHODS IN ECONOMICS: MEC-009

June, 2018

Note: Attempt questions from each section as per instructions given below.

SECTION–A

Attempt any two questions from this section in about 700 words each:

Q1. 'Karl Popper attacked Marxism calling it a pseudo-scientific theory.' Do you agree? Give reasons in support of your answer.

Q2. Recently, air quality deterioration has taken place in major Indian cities. What are its reasons? What are the various sources of data on environment? List and highlight their importance.

Q3. 'RRA/PRA framework provides a strong basis for collection of reliable as well as in-depth databases.' Explain the above statement critically.

Q4. Distinguish between research design and research process. Explain the steps to be undertaken in a research process.

SECTION–B

Attempt any five questions from this section in about 400 words each:

Q5. What are the limitations of applying models of scientific explanation to social sciences?

Q6. What is the meaning of linearity in regression model? How would you transform a non-linear regression equation into a linear one?

Q7. What is stratified sampling? How is it different from cluster sampling?

Q8. What are the various sources of data that assess Quality of Life?

Q9. Distinguish between Wholesale and Consumer Price Index Numbers.

Q 10. Distinguish between random and non-random sampling. State the various methods of non-random sampling.

Q11. Distinguish between any two of the following:

(a) Induction and Deduction

(b) Experimental Hypothesis and Research Hypothesis

(c) Census and Sample Survey

(d) Primary and Secondary data

RESEARCH METHODS IN ECONOMICS: MEC-009

December, 2018

Note: Attempt questions from each section as per instructions given below.

SECTION–A

Attempt any two questions from this section in about 700 words each:

Q1. What are the various Governmental and Non-Governmental sources of data in the Indian statistical system? What is the relevance of metadata?

Q2. Why Lorenz curve is a positive measure of inequality? Explain its relationship with Gini coefficient.

Q3. Identify the major steps in compilation of qualitative data.

Q4. Popper and Kuhn differ fundamentally in their attitude towards transition from one theory to another theory in science. How?

SECTION–B

Attempt any five questions from this section in about 400 words each:

Q5. What are the various costs incurred during Census or Sample Surveys?

Q6. Distinguish between any two of the following:

(a) Linear and Reciprocal Regression Model

(b) Science and Pseudo-science

(c) Population and Economic Census

(d) Qualitative and Quantitative Research

Q7. How are theories the basic building blocks of scientific explanation?

Q8. How is Consumer Price Index useful in wage indexation?

Q9. What are the assumptions of Classical Linear Regression Model? What are the consequences of violation of normality assumption?

Q10. What is the meaning of 'Emic perspective'? Elucidate with a suitable example.

Q11. What is the basis for the choice between census or sample survey?

❑❑❑

RESEARCH METHODS IN ECONOMICS: MEC-009

June, 2019

Note: Attempt questions from each section as per instructions given below.

SECTION–A

Answer any two questions from this section. Word limit is 700 for each question.

Q1. What is the distinction between Quantitative and Qualitative Research? Which are the commonly used methods for conducting qualitative research? Explain any two in detail.

Q2. What are tenets of positivism? What were the grounds of criticism of positivist science which led to the development of post-positivist philosophy of science?

Q3. Distinguish between Systematic sampling and Cluster sampling. What points need to be kept in mind for choosing an appropriate sampling method in socio-economic studies?

Q4. Do you think that deterministic regression models are relevant in Social Sciences? Illustrate in the context of Macro economic modeling.

SECTION–B

Answer any five questions from this section word limit is 400 for each question:

Q5. What is distinction between general explanation and scientific explanation of a phenomenon in social sciences? Discuss the features of Hypothecative-deductive model.

Q6. Suppose you have been asked to conduct a primary survey on electricity consumption in a village. Which tools would you use for data-collection?

Q7. What is the relationship between Lorenz curve and Gini coefficient? How do they measure inequality?

Q8. How can one detect multicollinearity in a dataset? What are its consequences?

Q9. Distinguish between any two of the following:

(a) Seasonal and cyclical movements in time-series.

(b) Cross-sectional data and pooled data

(c) Methodological dualism and methodological monism.

(d) Sampling and non-sampling error.

Q10. Define non-random sampling and explain its any three methods with examples.

Q11. How can one evaluate the trustworthiness of processed qualitative data?

RESEARCH METHODS IN ECONOMICS: MEC-009

December, 2019

Note: Answer questions from each section as directed.

SECTION–A

Answer any two questions from this section. (word limit : 700 word):

Q1. What are different types of price index numbers? Explain how consumer price index (CPI) for agriculture labour and CPI for industrial workers are constructed.

Q2. Distinguish between Inductivism and Hypothesism. State the tenets of Popper's falsification approach.

Q3. Distinguish between explanatory and descriptive research. Discuss the various steps involved in making a research proposal.

Q4. What do you mean by scientific explanation? Discuss the features of Hypothetico-Deductive model. How does this model defuse the conflict between realists and instrumentalism?

SECTION–B

Answer any five questions from this section. (word limit : 400 words):

Q5. Explain the properties of ideal index numbers. Also discuss the various steps involved in constructing price index numbers.

Q6. How do you measure the growth rate of GDP of a country when there exists cyclic fluctuation in the economy?

Q7. What are the critical elements to be considered for presenting content analysis?

Q8. How does Karl Popper differ from Thomas Kuhn on the essence of science?

Q9. Explain the various steps involved in survey method of data collection. Do you think that census method is always better than sampling method in economic analysis?

Q10. Distinguish between any three of the following:

(a) Correlation and Regression

(b) R-square and Adjusted R-square

(c) Descriptive and Diagnostic research

(d) National Industrial Classification (NIC) and National Classification of Occupations (NCO)

Q11. Explain the kinds of saving and investment data available in India. How is capital formation is measured for Indian economy?

❑❑❑

RESEARCH METHODS IN ECONOMICS: MEC-009

June, 2020

Note: Attempt questions from each Section as per instructions.

Section–A

Attempt any two questions from this Section in about 700 words each.

Q1. What is the aim of Science as Cognitive Enterprise? Explain thc basic tenets of positivism.

Q2. What are the various methods of Random Sampling? State the operational procedure for selection of sample by Simple Random Sampling without Replacement (SRSWR). How will you judge whether the sample drawn through SRSWR is efficient?

Q3. Discuss the various approaches followed by Indian Statistical System in generating data on GDP and NDP.

Q4. What is Hetero-scedasticity? How can you detect it? What are its consequences?

Section–B

Attempt any five questions from this Section in about 400 words each.

Q5. What are the various constituents of Research Methodology? How does knowledge of research perspective help a researcher to undertake research study in Social Sciences?

Q6. State the various normative measures of inequality. Discuss the computational device of Sen's Index.

Q7. State the various components of time series. Discuss the various techniques of smoothing of time series data.

Q8. What is the distinction between quantitative research and qualitative research? Discuss the various strategies of qualitative research.

Q9. What do you understand by the term Rapid Rural Appraisal (RRA)? How does RRA approach is an improvement over sample survey approach for data collection?

Q10. State the various assumptions of Linear Classical Regression Model. How is the regression model non-deterministic in nature?

Q11. What is a scientific explanation? State the features of Hypothetic Deductive Model as a model of scientific explanation.

Q12. Explain any three of the following:

(i) Verification of a phenomenon

(ii) Paradigm

(iii) Sampling error

(iv) Goodness of fit

(v) Auto-correlation

RESEARCH METHODS IN ECONOMICS: MEC-009

February, 2021

Note: Attempt questions from each section as per instructions given.

SECTION–A

Answer any two questions from this section in about 700 words each.

Q1. **In what sense is science rational? Explain the basic differences between Popperian and Kuhnian Models of science.**

Q2. **Distinguish between Cluster and Multistage sampling. State the operational procedure to draw sample through cluster sampling. How will you judge whether cluster sampling is efficient ?**

Q3. **Which data set will you use to evaluate the growth and employment of the Indian economy? What are the sources of such data?**

Q4. **What is multi-collinearity? How will you detect it? What are the consequences of multi-collinearity?**

SECTION–B

Answer any five questions from this section in about 400 words each.

Q5. **How does review of literature help a researcher to undertake a research study?**

Q6. **Distinguish between positive and normative measures of inequality. Discuss the computation device for construction of Gini index.**

Q7. **Discuss the procedure involved in construction of consumer price index. What are the various applications of consumer price index?**

Q8. What do you mean by the term 'hypothesis' ? Is it necessary to formulate hypothesis in all types of research studies ? Give reasons.

Q9. Distinguish between quantitative data and qualitative data. Discuss the various methods for processing the qualitative data.

Q10. State the various functional forms of Regression model. When do you think the use of log linear regression model is most appropriate?

Q11. What is scientific explanation ? State the rules of logic.

Q12. Explain any three of the following:

(a) Epistemology

(b) Non-sampling error

(c) Falsification

(d) Goodness of fit

(e) Parameters

RESEARCH METHODS IN ECONOMICS: MEC-009

June, 2021

Note: Attempt questions from each section as per instructions given.

SECTION–A

Answer any two questions from this section in about 700 words each.

Q1. What do you mean by the term 'scientific explanation'? Explain the features of Deductive Nomological model as a model of scientific explanation.

Q2. What is the difference between theoretical research and applied research? Discuss the various steps involved in conducting research in social sciences.

Q3. What is Simple Random Sampling With Replacement (SRSWR)? State the operational procedure for selection of sample by SRSWR. How will you judge the precision of estimation?

Q4. State the features of classical normal regression model. What are the assumptions of this model?

SECTION–B

Answer any five questions from this section in about 400 words each.

Q5. Discuss the various methods of data collection for carrying out participatory research.

Q6. Is PRA/RRA approach superior to sampling survey approach? Explain.

Q7. Distinguish between positive and normative measures of inequality. State the procedure to measure inequality of income through Lorentz curve.

Q8. Distinguish between any two of the following:

(i) **Research methodology and Research Methods**

(ii) **Parameter and Statics**

(iii) **Stratified sampling and Cluster sampling**

(iv) **Regression and Correlation**

Q9. What do you understand by the term 'Hypothesis'? Is it necessary to formulate hypothesis in each research study? Give reasons.

Q10. State the various tools that are used for collection of qualitative data.

Q11. Explain the various uses of consumer price index.

Q12. State the various methods used in analysis of quantitative data.

RESEARCH METHODS IN ECONOMICS: MEC-009

December, 2021

Note: Attempt questions from each section as per instructions given.

SECTION–A

Answer any two questions from this section in about 700 words each.

Q1. What is scientific explanation? Explain the features of hypothetico-deductive model of scientific explanation.

Q2. Distinguish between Research methodology and Research methods. State the various steps involved in conducting research in Social Sciences.

Q3. State the operational procedure to draw the sample by systematic sampling. How will you judge whether the estimators of systematic sampling are unbaised?

Q4. What are the major sources of data on agriculture? How are such data useful for agricultural policy?

SECTION–B

Answer any five questions from this section in about words each.

Q5. In what way does review of literature help a researcher in carrying out research?

Q6. Distinguish between quantitative research and qualitative research. Which tools will you apply to analyse the qualitative data?

Q7. Distinguish between any two of the following:

(a) Group discussion and Focus group discussion

(b) Estimate and Estimator

(c) R2 and Adjusted R2

(d) Cross-section data and Time series data

Q8. What is Gini Ratio? State the computation device of Gini Ratio.

Q9. State the various forms of Regression Model. Give illustration.

Q10. State the various tools that are used for collection of quantitative data.

Q11. What is the important contribution of Hutchison in the area of logical empiricism?

Q12. How is PRA different from RRA? In what situation would you like to use RRA method in conducting research?

Gullybaba.com

Simply Scan QR Codes to Jump at Our Latest Products

HELP BOOKS

TYPED ASSIGNMENTS

HAND WRITTEN ASSIGNMENTS

READYMADE PROJECTS

CUSTOMIZED PROJECTS

COMBOS OF BOOKS/ ASSIGNMENTS

Note: The above QR Codes can be scanned and open through QR Code Scanner Application/App of your smart mobile Phone.

www.ingramcontent.com/pod-product-compliance
Ingram Content Group UK Ltd.
Pitfield, Milton Keynes, MK11 3LW, UK
UKHW021707190726
13853UKWH00001B/450